# THE HAMLYN LECTURES
## FORTY-FOURTH SERIES

# SPEECH & RESPECT

**AUSTRALIA**
The Law Book Company
Sydney

**CANADA AND U.S.A.**
The Carswell Company
Toronto, Ontario

**INDIA**
N.M. Tripathi (Private) Ltd.
Bombay
*and*
Eastern Law House (Private) Ltd.
Calcutta
M.P.P. House
Bangalore
Universal Book Traders
Delhi

**ISRAEL**
Steimatzky's Agency Ltd.
Tel Aviv

**PAKISTAN**
Pakistan Law House
Karachi

# SPEECH & RESPECT

by

**RICHARD ABEL**
*Professor of Law*
*University of California Los Angeles*

*Published under the auspices of*
THE HAMLYN TRUST

LONDON
STEVENS & SONS/SWEET & MAXWELL
1994

Published in 1994
by Stevens & Sons Ltd./Sweet & Maxwell Ltd.
South Quay Plaza, 183 Marsh Wall, London E14 9FT
Computerset by
York House Typographic Ltd.,
London W13 8NT

Printed by Thomson Litho Ltd.,
East Kilbride, Scotland

A CIP catalogue record for this book
is available from the British Library

ISBN   0 421 50210 X (H/b)
          0 421 50220 7 (P/b)

# Contents

# The Hamlyn Lectures

## The Hamlyn Lectures

# The Hamlyn Lectures

# The Hamlyn Trust

The Hamlyn Trust owes its existence to the will of the late Miss Emma Warburton Hamlyn of Torquay, who died in 1941 at the age of eighty. She came of an old and well-known Devon family. Her father, William Bussell Hamlyn, practised in Torquay as a solicitor and JP for many years, and it seems likely that Miss Hamlyn founded the trust in his memory. Emma Hamlyn was a woman of strong character, intelligent and cultured, well-versed in literature, music and art, and a lover of her country. She travelled extensively in Europe and Egypt, and apparently took considerable interest in the law and ethnology of the countries and cultures that she visited. An account of Miss Hamlyn by Dr. Chantal Stebbings of the University of Exeter may be found, under the title "The Hamlyn Legacy," in volume 42 of the published lectures.

Miss Hamlyn bequeathed the residue of her estate on trust in terms which it seems were her own. The wording was thought to be vague, and the will was taken to the Chancery Division of the High Court, which in November 1948 approved a Scheme for the administration of the trust. Paragraph 3 of the Scheme, which closely follows Miss Hamlyn's own wording, is as follows:

"The object of the charity is the furtherance by lectures or otherwise among the Common People of the United Kingdom of Great Britain and Northern Ireland of the knowledge of the Comparative Jurisprudence and Ethnology of the Chief European countries including the United Kingdom, and the circumstances of the growth of such jurisprudence to the Intent that the Common People of the United Kingdom may realise the privileges which in law and custom they enjoy in comparison with other European Peoples and realising and appreciating such privileges may recognise the responsibilities and obligations attaching to them."

*The Hamlyn Trust*

The Trustees are to include the Vice-Chancellor of the University of Exeter, representatives of the Universities of London, Leeds, Glasgow, Belfast and Wales and persons co-opted. At present there are eight Trustees:

From the outset it was decided that the Trust's objects could best be achieved by means of an annual course of public lectures of outstanding interest and quality by eminent Lecturers, and by their subsequent publication and distribution to a wider audience. Details of these Lectures are given on page vii. In recent years, however, the Trustees have expanded their activities by organising supplementary regional lecture tours and by setting up a "small grants" scheme to provide financial support for other activities designed to further public understanding of the law.

The forty-fourth series of lectures was delivered by Professor Abel at the University of Wales College of Cardiff in December 1992. The Trustees regret the delay in the publication of these Lectures, which arose in part as a result of Professor Abel's decision to include material not delivered in the original lectures and concern on the part of the Trustees and the publishers that some of this material might be regarded as objectionable or distasteful. In the event, it was decided to accede to Professor Abel's request that the additional material should be included in the published version of the Lectures on the basis that readers will judge for themselves the appropriateness of Professor Abel's decision, and, like the Trustees, become involved in a practical way with an issue which is central to The Lecturer's thesis.

**February 1994**                    **DESMOND GREER**
                                 *Chairman of the Trustees*

# Introduction

The goal of the Hamlyn Trust is to educate "the Common People of the United Kingdom" to "realise the privileges which in law and custom they enjoy in comparison with other European Peoples [so that they] may recognise the responsibilities and obligations attaching to them." Why did a Victorian/Edwardian single woman from a good West Country family feel the need to assert such superiority— to the Common People, whom she sought to instruct so that they, in turn, would feel superior to other European Peoples? With the condescension that each generation bestows on its predecessors we may look with amusement at the parochialism and ethnocentrism of Ms. Hamlyn's will, written before World War Two and expressive of attitudes formed more than a century ago. But such assertions of social superiority are no less pervasive today, if they take different forms. Status inequality and the challenges it provokes are the subject of my lectures. The Hamlyn Trust was inspired by a sense of paternalistic obligation. I explore the responsibilities of those privileged today by virtue of class, race, ethnicity, gender, religion, or sexual orientation.

I was very pleased that the Trustees chose Cardiff as the venue for the 1992 lectures, for several reasons. First, I probably owe my invitation to deliver these lectures to an invitation from Phil Thomas a decade earlier to participate in a conference on the Report of the Royal Commission on Legal Services (the Benson Commission). Although I had been teaching and writing about American lawyers, the 1600 page report introduced me to the legal profession in England and Wales and launched me on a comparative study of legal professions throughout the common law and civil law worlds. (The Report arrived during the 1979/80 winter—the rainiest in recent Los Angeles history; the constant drizzle not only inspired nostalgia for my days as a post-graduate student in London in the 1960s but also

1

created the necessary atmosphere for mastering the anachronistic minutiae of kite fees, court attire, and the conveyancing monopoly.) Second, for more than 20 years Cardiff has been a centre for socio-legal studies, not only in Britain but throughout the world. The *Journal of Law and Society* was founded there in 1973, just three years after the law school was established in the Faculty of Social Science, and quickly became one of the leading international journals in the field. Cardiff has hosted numerous conferences; its curriculum introduces undergraduates to sociology of law; and many faculty members engage in sociolegal research. Since my approach in these lectures is more sociological than legal, Cardiff offers a hospitable environment. Finally, it seems fitting that lectures about insiders and outsiders, dominant and subordinate cultures, should be delivered in Wales.

There is something anomalous about an American law professor addressing a British audience on the superiority of their laws and customs (which may be why I am only the second to be invited and the fifth from outside Britain). Because I naturally have drawn on the American experience and literature, I fear that many of my examples may appear arcane and exotic. Yet I believe there are common lessons to be learned. Status inequalities do not respect national boundaries; indeed, the massive increase in international migration has aggravated and complicated those inequalities. My first lecture deals at length with the conflict surrounding *The Satanic Verses*; and its other two topics—pornography and racial hatred—have provoked almost as much controversy in Britain as they have in the United States. I believe that the struggle for respect will continue to intensify in both countries. The United States often seems about a decade ahead of Britain in the construction of social problems (and California a decade ahead of the rest of the United States). When I moved to England in autumn 1965, after a summer as a civil rights lawyer in Mississippi, I was asked to speak about that experience to local Labour and Conservative Party meetings and at conferences. Those audiences always assured me that race was not a problem in Britain—an opinion I found hard to reconcile with the "no coloured" signs I constantly encountered in seeking a flat in London. Within a few years, not surprisingly, Britain heard Enoch Powell warn of "rivers of blood" and witnessed violent racial conflict, which has continued to escalate. At the same time, Britain is ahead of the United States in acknowledging the ways that speech reproduces status inequality and seeking to do something about them.

I have not re-written the lectures for this book (although I had to cut them slightly for oral delivery). Instead, I have appended extensive textual notes and references for those interested in greater detail, further examples, and the relevant literature.

I am grateful to those who read earlier drafts: my wife Emily Abel (chapters one to three), C. Edwin Baker and Steven Shiffrin (chapter two), Joel Handler and Lucie White (a shorter version), and my critical legal theory seminar (the entirety, or so they claim). All of them have reservations about both substance and format—as do I.

# 1. The Struggle for Respect

I am going to begin these lectures with three stories, which illustrate the drama, variety, and complexity of the struggle for respect through speech.

## *I. Pornography*

By the end of the 1960s the champions of free expression and sexual liberation had declared victory over a century of prudery and puritanism.[1] Notorious novels like *Ulysses* and *Lady Chatterley's Lover*, banned just decades earlier, no longer raised many eyebrows. Pornography proliferated in movies, books, and magazines and eagerly exploited the new media of videos, cable television, and telephones. This provoked a counterattack, not just from religion but also from the contemporaneous second wave of feminism. Gloria Steinem proclaimed: "A woman who has *Playboy* in the house is like a Jew who has *Mein Kampf* on the table."[2] Diana Russell condemned pornography as a backlash against feminism, "a male fantasy-solution that inspires nonfantasy acts of punishment for uppity females."[3] Susan Brownmiller maintained that "pornography, like rape, is a male invention, designed to dehumanize women, to reduce the female to an object of sexual access . . . ."[4] Judith Bat-Ada hyperbolised these diatribes.

> Sexual fascism means that . . . a few powerful men control our behavior, attitudes, fantasies, concepts of love and caring, integrity . . . to whom and how we make our genitalia available. . . .
> [the] triumvirate—Hugh Heffner, Bob Guccione, and Larry Flynt [publishers of *Playboy*, *Penthouse*, and *Hustler*] . . . are every bit as dangerous as Hitler, Mussolini, and Hirohito . . . . Just as the

4

Nazis built prisons around the Jews, and the white man put chains on the Black women and men, so pornographers have put women into equally constricting "genital service" structures. . . . All the special glitter that this male society produces for women—the makeup, the high-heeled shoes, the tight little dresses—single us out as women as effectively as did the yellow stars on the coats of the Jews in Nazi Germany.[5]

Yet feminists were deeply divided about pornography. Gayle Rubin denounced the inclusion of sado-masochistic images in the anti-porn documentary "Not a Love Story" as "on a moral par with . . . depictions of black men raping white women, or of drooling old Jews pawing young Aryan girls, to incite racist or anti-Semitic frenzy."[6] The 1982 Barnard conference on the "politics of sexuality" sought to examine the "link between sexual 'political correctness' and other forms of 'political correctness' both on the Left and the Right."[7] It was preceded by a "Speakout on Politically Incorrect Sex," organized by the Lesbian Sex Mafia, "self-identified 'S/M' lesbian feminists who argue that the moralism of the radical feminists stigmatizes sexual minorities such as butch/femme couples, sado-masochists, and man/boy lovers . . . ." In response, the Coalition for a Feminist Sexuality and against Sado-Masochism picketed the conference, protesting the exclusion of "feminists who have developed the feminist analysis of sexual violence, who have organized a mass movement against pornography, who have fought media images that legitimize sexual violence, who believe that sadomasochism is reactionary, patriarchal sexuality, and who have worked to end the sexual abuse of children."[8]

The renewed American legal battles over pornography were fought in this emotionally charged atmosphere. In 1977 Minneapolis neighbourhood groups had secured passage of an ordinance zoning out adult bookstores, which they believed lowered property values. Five years later the courts declared it unconstitutional on the application of the Alexander family, who dominated the local pornography industry and were represented by the Minnesota Civil Liberties Union. When the city sought to redraft the zoning law, Naomi Scheman, a feminist philosophy professor at the University of Minnesota, put councillors in touch with Catherine MacKinnon and Andrea Dworkin, who were co-teaching a course on pornography at the Law School. Never ones to mince words, Dworkin had identified "the eroticization of murder" as "the essence of pornography," and MacKinnon had asserted: "if you understand that pornography literally means what it says, you might conclude that sexuality has become the fascism of contemporary America and we are moving into the last days of Weimar."[9] Anticipating my second story, she called pornography a "Skokie-type injury" and condemned the ACLU and MCLU as "pornographers' mouthpieces," while Dworkin dismissed the First Amendment as "an instrument of the ruling class."

MacKinnon and Dworkin drafted an innovative ordinance, whose preamble declared that "pornography is central in creating and maintaining the civil inequality of the sexes." It prohibited the sexually explicit subordination of women, conferring rights to damages and an injunction on both women coerced into producing pornography and sexual assault victims who could show a causal nexus with a specific publication. Controversy about the ordinance was intense. Women poured ink over *Playboy* and *Penthouse* in the student union, threw magazines on the floor of the Rialto (adult) Bookstore, and disrupted the screening of a pornographic movie at the Rialto Theatre. Dworkin ridiculed the zoning approach: "I think you should say that you are going to permit the exploitation of live women, the sado-masochistic use of live women, the binding and torture of real women and then have the depictions of those women used in those ways sold in this city . . . ." The star witness was Linda Marchiano, who testified that she had been coerced into portraying Linda Lovelace in "Deep Throat" and was raped on screen. Other witnesses found the hearings cathartic, voicing abuses they had never disclosed. The audience was partisan and vociferous, "booing and hissing, moaning and crying." City councillor Barbara Carlson described the campaign for the ordinance as *"onslaught, onslaught, onslaught!* I mean literally, they were in everyone's office. A month and a half!"

The MCLU vigorously opposed the ordinance, which its director called a "constitutional mockery" and an "obscenity in itself." So did the library board. Catherine MacKinnon sought to discredit gay and lesbian criticism, asserting that "the gay male community perceives a stake in male supremacy, that is in some ways even greater than that of straight men." The city's Office of Civil Rights was uncomfortable with its enforcement role. And the president of the Minneapolis Urban League saw it as a "white folks issue," which would divert energy from the struggle for racial equality.

When the liberal mayor vetoed the ordinance, which had passed by one vote, Dworkin responded: "This city doesn't give a damn about women." "There's only one question before the City Council:

Are they helping the pornographers or helping women?'' During debate over an amended bill a woman with a history of mental illness, who had testified at the earlier hearings, set fire to herself at the pornographic Shinder's Read-More Bookstore, leaving a note declaring that "Sexism has shattered my life. Because of this I have chosen to take my life and to destroy the persons who have destroyed me.'' As she lay in hospital in a critical condition 24 women were arrested for disrupting the climactic council meeting, which passed the revised ordinance by the same vote, only to have it vetoed again. Dworkin blamed the defeat on the Council's links to the Mafia. In the backlash against the campaign, *Forum* (a *Penthouse* publication) listed the names of some of the women who had testified to sexual abuse, exposing them to further harassment. While the Pornography Resource Center, which had organised support for the ordinance, continued to make presentations to women, the Rialto Theatre and Bookstore across the street expanded its offerings to include nude dancing.[10]

The struggle shifted to Indianapolis, the largest Republican city in the nation, headquarters of the American Legion and birthplace of the John Birch Society, with a smaller feminist community than Minneapolis and weaker civil libertarians. City Councillor Beulah Coughenour, who led the crusade, had chaired the state's successful Stop ERA campaign and opposed abortion and marital rape laws. She was supported by Rev. Greg Dixon, a fundamentalist Baptist who had founded Citizens for a Clean Community, warning that "the river of smut that is flowing down our cities is . . . one of the greatest indications of a totally decadent society . . . . we have lost our moral moorings . . . [and become] hedonistic, humanistic, materialistic, nihilistic . . . .'' City Prosecutor Steven Goldsmith and Mayor William Hudnut, who had built their political careers on efforts to close adult bookstores, theaters, and massage parlors, ignored the city attorney's opinion that the Minneapolis ordinance was unconstitutional.

This time MacKinnon kept a low profile, managing to convince some ordinance backers that she, too, was conservative, and Dworkin never visited the city. Conservatives dominated the hearings, to the exclusion of feminists. Police officers claimed that rapists and sexual abusers often were arrested in possession of pornography, which the city prosecutor connected to a recent sensational murder. Edward Donnerstein, the leading social scientific investigator of pornography's effects, was questioned by MacKinnon so skillfully that some city councillors concluded, erroneously, that he asserted a

7

causal nexus to violence. Activists from the Baptist Temple and Citizens for Decency through Law packed the audience, booing and hissing the ineffectual opposition by the Indiana Civil Liberties Union, the Urban League president, and a feminist former city attorney.

The ordinance passed 24–5, although most proponents had not read it and some thought it unconstitutional. Black Democratic Councillor Rozelle Boyd then moved to limit city spending on legal defence to $200,000 but was defeated 19–7. As soon as the mayor signed the law the American Booksellers Association and the ACLU sought a federal injunction, supported by an amicus brief from the Feminist Anti-Censorship Taskforce, signed by Betty Friedan, Kate Millett, and Adrienne Rich, among other notables.[11] Judge Sarah Evans Barker, a Reagan appointee sworn in just a month before, granted the injunction. The Seventh Circuit affirmed in an opinion by Frank Easterbrook, another Reagan appointee, who criticised the ordinance as "thought control" for establishing "an 'approved' view of women, of how they may react to sexual encounters, of how the sexes may relate to each other." By the time the Supreme Court denied the appeal the city's legal expenses exceeded $300,000. Almost a decade after the Minneapolis ordinance was drafted, variants are still being debated in the Massachusetts legislature and the U.S. Congress. Women have written dozens of letters to the Senate Judiciary Committee urging their passage as an apology for the Clarence Thomas confirmation and the William Kennedy Smith rape acquittal.[12]

## II. Racial Hatred

My next story concerns racial hatred. In 1950 Joseph Beauharnais distributed leaflets for the White Circle League in the form of a petition to the Chicago city council and mayor

> to halt the further encroachment, harassment, and invasion of white people, their property, neighborhoods and persons, by the Negro . . . . If persuasion and the need to prevent the white race from becoming mongrelized by the negro will not unite us, then the aggressions . . . rapes, robberies, knives, guns and marijuana of the negro surely will.

He was convicted under the state group libel law, which the U.S.

8

Supreme Court upheld.[13] Twelve years later, the Chicago branch of the American Nazi Party, led by Malcolm Lambert, passed out flyers in front of a Chicago theatre showing a movie featuring Sammy Davis, Jr.

> Niggers! You Too Can Be a Jew . . . . It's Easy; It's Fun . . . Sammy-the-Kosher-Coon Shows You How . . . In Ten Easy Lessons . . . Be One of The Chosen People . . . Here's some of the Things You Learn: Jewish customs and traditions such as how to force your way into social groups . . . How to make millions cheating widows and orphans . . . How to Hate-Hitler and get believing he killed six million of us even though we are all over here living it up on the dumb Christians.

When 40–60 members of an angry crowd of 200 threatened to attack Lambert, who refused to leave, police arrested him. He was convicted of defamatory leafleting and criminal libel.[14]

In the early 1970s Frank Collin and the dozen members of his National Socialist Party of America applied to several North Shore suburbs for permission to demonstrate, after being rebuffed by the Chicago Park District. He saturated the region with tens of thousands of leaflets featuring a swastika with hands reaching out to choke a stereotyped Jew and the caption "We Are Coming!" A *Chicago Sun-Times* story quoted Collin at length.

> I hope they're terrified. I hope they're shocked. Because we're coming to get them again. I don't care if someone's mother or father or brother died in the gas chambers. The unfortunate thing is not that there were six million Jews who died. The unfortunate thing is that there were so many survivors.

When only Skokie replied, demanding a $350,000 bond, Collin targeted the village, unaware that nearly half the residents were Jewish and 800–1200 Holocaust survivors. (Collin's own father was not only Jewish but a Dachau survivor!) "Lieutenant" Roger Tedor explained the Party's motivation: "We had a picket in Berwyn and got into a brawl with the JDL. Later, we went to the same place on the pretext of picketing for free speech. We got a lot of publicity." After trying the same tactic in Skokie in April 1977 and being stopped by the police, they hurried to their headquarters to watch themselves on the evening news and pose in uniform for cameramen.

When the village passed an ordinance requiring a $350,000 bond for demonstrations and prohibiting racial hatred and military uniforms, the ACLU sued to enjoin enforcement. Its Public Relations Director said that "those who preach changes in constitutional law are the enemy, possessed of sinister motive and intent . . . ." He and his family received death threats. A Holocaust survivor called ACLU lawyer David Goldberger "A rotten person and an opportunist. . . . during the Nazi era . . . we had people like that. They were collaborators." Goldberger's own rabbi denounced him during services. Skokie Holocaust survivors, a close and somewhat isolated community, rejected the B'nai B'rith Anti-Defamation League policy of ignoring the Nazis. One explained: "The minute somebody comes and tries to attack my home, I have to defend myself." When Collin threatened to march without a permit, Jewish Defense League leader Meir Kahane told the press: "the streets of Skokie will run with Nazi blood." Collin was delighted with the response: "I used [the First Amendment] at Skokie. I planned the reaction of the Jews. They are hysterical." When a state appellate court permitted him to march but not display swastikas, he was defiant: "This is my party identification, that is my symbol, and we will not be parted from it." Finally allowed by the state supreme court to flaunt the swastika, Collin threatened to march on Hitler's birthday. More then a hundred organisations of Blacks, Latinos, and Ukrainians joined Jews in promising to mobilise 50,000 people for a counter-demonstration; the JDL, Jewish War Veterans, and Coalition Against Violence(!) threatened to attack the NSPA. Israeli Prime Minister Menachem Begin visited the village and gave Mayor Smith an expense-paid trip to Israel, where he was presented with the keys to Jerusalem.

Fearing the counterdemonstration might overwhelm his own and endanger him physically, Collin was persuaded by the U.S. Justice Department's Community Relations Service to march at the Federal Plaza courthouse in downtown Chicago. Over the shouts of more than 6000 anti-Nazis, few could hear Collin's cry that "the creatures should be gassed." Yet he claimed ultimate victory.

We faced the alternatives of either dying or coming up with something so dramatic that we could get it up in the world's headlines. In the courts I was a mouse in a maze, so this was an end-run . . . . Skokie was traumatic. We lost many members. Many older people left us because the Jews were on television and said they'd kill us. Even hard core people left us. There's a parallel to Hitler. He had many people until the *Putsch*. Then he found

10

himself with no movement. But when we started making publicity, we gained numbers all over the country.

The ACLU also suffered, losing a third of its income in Illinois and 15 per cent of its national membership.

The incident's aftermath exhibited several striking ironies. The village hired a public relations firm, which launched a "Skokie Spirit" campaign to erase its image as a stronghold of militant Jews—earning the council a charge of anti-Semitism. The NSPA informed the police that Collin was sexually molesting young boys, leading to his arrest and imprisonment. And surveys found that substantial majorities of Skokie residents and Illinois citizens disagreed with the courts that the Constitution protected Nazi speech. Skokie Holocaust survivors put it more vividly. One called Nazi speech "obscene," while another said: "It's impossible to think that the people who wrote the Constitution, that they would say that a murderer has the right to come and express his opinion and to say that we are going to murder a certain segment of people."[15]

## III. The Satanic Verses

Because readers will be familiar with the events of my third story, about *The Satanic Verses*, I will concentrate on the participants' language. Three months before its September 1988 publication, Dr. Zahid Hussain, the Peterborough City Council race relations officer, told Viking that he and the eight other referees read the book as history rather than fiction and feared it would cause great offence.[16] Penguin Group chairman Peter Mayer decided not to publish the book in India when his local adviser, journalist Khushwant Singh, warned that it would "cause a lot of trouble."[17] Interviewed by the Indian press, however, Salman Rushdie insisted that he had sought to "distance events from historical events" by changing the names of people and places. "My theme is fanaticism." "There are no subjects which are off limits and that includes God, includes prophets."[18]

Syed Shahabuddin, an ambitious Muslim MP in the Janata party, saw in these interviews an opportunity to embarrass the ruling Congress (I) Party, which was losing popularity and facing a general election within a year. Shahabuddin was already a leading actor in Muslim opposition to Hindu attempts to build a temple on the site of an ancient mosque in Ayodhya.[19] When the Finance Ministry banned the book, Shahabuddin wrote triumphantly to *The Times of India*, denouncing Rushdie as an "overrated Eurasian writer," the product of a "fatigued culture," spokesman for a West "which has not yet laid the ghost of the crusades to rest . . . ." He reserved his worst insults for the "Anglicised elite," the "pukka Sahibs," the "entire 'liberal establishment,'" while welcoming the slurs of Rushdie and his supporters: "Call us primitive, call us fundamentalists, call us superstititious barbarians." He refused to read the book: "I do not have to wade through a filthy drain to know what filth is."[20]

Rushdie responded in an open letter to Prime Minister Rajiv Gandhi, stressing that the book was fiction, not history, and invoking the support of Indian newspapers, publishers, and booksellers, international organisations opposed to censorship, and "such eminent writers" as Kingsley Amis, Harold Pinter, Stephen Spender, and Tom Stoppard.[21] He followed this with an article in *The Illustrated Weekly of India*, accusing Gandhi of playing communalist politics.

> Perhaps you feel that by banning my fourth novel you are taking a long-overdue revenge for the treatment of your mother in my second; but can you be sure that Indira Gandhi's reputation will endure better and longer than *Midnight's Children*? Are you certain that the cultural history of India will deal kindly with the enemies of *The Satanic Verses*? You own the present, Mr. Gandhi; but the centuries belong to art.[22]

Nevertheless, most countries with substantial Muslim populations followed India in banning the book.

British Muslims quickly took charge of the attack. In a book entitled *Be Careful with Muhammad!*, Shabbir Akhtar compared Rushdie's "calculated attempt to vilify and slander the Prophet of Islam" with the abortive 1970s plot by Jewish extremists to blow up Al-Aqsa mosque in Jerusalem. Rushdie was a "*literary* terrorist," who called the Prophet by the derogatory name Mahound, suggested that the Qu'ran was not divine revelation, applied the adjectives bum, scum, black monster and bastard to historical personalities, and had prostitutes take the names of Mohammed's twelve wives. "[A]ny Muslim who fails to be offended by Rushdie's book ceases, on account of that fact, to be a Muslim." Christianity had exposed its weakness in failing to respond to "continual blasphemies." "Any faith which compromises its internal temper of militant wrath is destined for the dustbin of history . . . . God does not guide a people who sell his signs for a paltry price." Raising the spectre of a "Western conspiracy" against Islam, he issued a much quoted warning: "the next time there are gas chambers in Europe, there is no doubt concerning who'll be inside."[23] Qureshi and Khan, who subtitled their own book on the controversy "Unmasking Western Attitudes," located it within a larger war.

[*The Satanic Verses*] inflamed the feelings of nearly 1 billion followers of Islam. . . . Attacking the Muslim community became legitimate and fashionable for anyone for a variety of reasons. Racists found a new cause in protesting against the protests of the Muslim minority; the secularists found their cause in hatred of all religion; others in anti-Islamism, if not anti-semitism, and the assimilationists against multi-culturalists.[24]

Tariq Modood dismissed the book as "no more a contribution to literary discourse than pissing upon the Bible is a theological argument."[25] Dr. Saki Badawi, liberal head of the Muslim College in Ealing, protested that Rushdie had hurt Muslims worse than if he had raped their daughters.[26] Ali Mazrui, an American professor of political science, reported that Pakistani friends told him: "It's as if Rushdie had composed a brilliant poem about the private parts of his parents, and then gone to the market place to recite that poem to the applause of strangers . . . and he's taking money for doing it." Mazrui himself proclaimed that " 'The Satanic Verses' could be one of the most divisive books in world politics since Hitler's 'Mein Kampf.' "[27] Hesham el Essawy, chairman of the Islamic Society for the Promotion of Religious Tolerance in the U.K., urged Penguin to withdraw the book; otherwise "we might as well knight muggers and give mass murderers the Nobel prize." M.H. Faruqi, editor of *Impact International*, described Rushdie as "a self-hating Indo-Anglian, totally alienated from his culture, who has also learnt that it is possible to make money by selling self-hate." Determined to "show them all," he had engaged in "a continuous striptease, from soft to hard and even harder porn."[28]

Muslim outrage elicited unprecedented ecumenical solidarity. The Archbishop of York asked why "the freedom of writers to write what they like" was superior to all other claims of "sacredness."[29] The Archbishop of Canterbury declared that "offence to the religious beliefs of the followers of Islam or any other faith is quite as wrong as is an offence to the religious beliefs of Christians."[30] The Chief Rabbi deprecated "not only the falsification of established historical records but [also] the offence caused to the religious convictions and

13

susceptibilities of countless citizens" and called for legislation prohibiting "socially intolerable conduct calculated or likely to incite revulsion or violence by holding up religious beliefs to scurrilous contempt."[31] The Vatican newspaper *L'Osservatore Romano* expressed respect for the "offended sensibilities and religious consciences [of millions of believers] . . . . [I]t is not the first time that, by invoking artistic motives or the principle of free expression, people have sought to justify the improper use of sacred texts . . . ."[32] Yet Islam was not monolithic. Fadia Faquir recounted the history of Islamic censorship, which she also had suffered.[33] And Southall Black Sisters joined the Southall women's section of the Labour Party in proclaiming: "We have struggled for many years in this country and across the world to express ourselves as we choose within and outside our communities. We will not be dictated to by fundamentalists."[34]

Rebuffed by both publisher and government, British Muslims resorted to direct action. When their first public meeting was ignored by the media they decided to burn the book in front of Bradford police headquarters. Sayyid Abdul Quddus of the Council of Mosques notified the press. More than a thousand Muslims participated, holding placards reading "Rushdie Eat Your Words" and "Rushdie Stinks." Liaqat Hussein of the Jamiaat Tabligh ul Islam expressed both jubilation and outrage: "All the newspapers commented. *Times, Daily Telegraph, Guardian, Yorkshire Post.* They compared us to Hitler!"[35] Rushdie broke a silence of more than four months to denounce the "contemporary Thought Police" and observe how life was imitating art.

"Battle lines are being drawn up in India today," one of my characters remarks. "Secular versus religious, the light versus the dark. Better you choose which side you are on." Now that the battle has spread to Britain, I can only hope it will not be lost by default. It is time for us to choose.

When Mohammed seized power in Mecca he executed two writers and two actresses for performing satirical texts.

Now there you have an image that I thought was worth exploring: at the very beginning of Islam you find a conflict between the sacred text and the profane text, between revealed literature and imagined literature. . . . It seems to me completely legitimate that there should be dissent from orthodoxy, not just about Islam, but about anything . . . . Doubt, it seems to me, is the central condition of a human being in the twentieth century.[36]

Now the initiative shifted a third time. Thousands of Pakistanis tried to storm the U.S. Information Center in Islamabad in February 1989, screaming "American dogs" and "God is great," and thousands more demonstrated in Karachi the next day. In controlling the crowds, police killed six and injured dozens. Not to be upstaged, Ayatollah Khomeini issued his notorious *fatwa*: "I call on all zealous Muslims to execute [Rushdie and his publishers] wherever they find them, so that no one will dare to insult the Islamic sanctions. Whoever is killed on this path will be regarded as a martyr, God willing." He denounced Rushie as an apostate, "an agent of corruption on earth," who had "declared war on Allah."[37] To encourage those insufficiently motivated by religious zeal, the director of the Fifth of Khordad Foundation put a price on Rushdie's head: $3 million for Iranian assassins, $1 million for foreigners.[38]

Having been led to expect a pardon, Rushdie and Viking immediately apologised. Instead, Iran banned all Viking publications, and President Ali Khameini joined the chorus of vilification: "As the enemy's attack on our frontiers brings us into action, the enemy's attack on our cultural frontiers should evoke a response from us at least to the same degree, if not more." Rushdie tried again: "I profoundly regret the distress that publication has occasioned to the sincere followers of Islam. Living as we do in a world of many faiths this experience has served to remind us that we must all be conscious of the sensibilities of others." But Khomeini was implacable: "Even if Salman Rushdie repents and becomes the most pious man of time, it is incumbent on every Muslim to employ everything he has got, his life and his wealth, to send him to hell."[39] To which Rushdie replied: "SV is a clash of faiths . . . or more precisely it's a clash of languages . . . . It's his word [Khomeini's] against mine."[40]

These threats produced the predictable reaction in Britain. *The Observer* editorialised: "neither Britain nor the author has anything to apologise for." The *Sunday Sport* hypocritically assumed a high moral tone and offered £1m to anyone bringing Khomeini to trial in England. Not to be outdone, Robert Maxwell promised $10m to anyone getting Khomeini to recite the ten commandments (although Maxwell's own knowledge was rather shaky). The *Independent* regretted that Britain had been "too tolerant for too long." The *Daily Mirror* put that into tabloidese, denouncing both the "Mad Mullah" and British Muslims who followed their imams "with sheeplike docility and wolf-like aggression." And *The Star* fulminated:

> Isn't the world getting sick of the ranting that pours from the disgusting foam-flecked lips of the Ayatollah Khomeini? Clearly the Muslim cleric is stark raving mad. . . . Surely the tragedy is that millions of his misguided and equally potty followers believe every word of hatred he hisses through those yellow stained teeth.[41]

Athough such language might be expected from the media, many intellectuals were equally intemperate. Joseph Brodsky expressed surprise that nobody had put a price on Khomeini's head, adding "mind you, it shouldn't be too big." Peter Jenkins maintained that "the offence done to our principles" by the burning of *The Satanic Verses* in Bradford was "at least as great as any offence caused to those who burned the book." He denounced the "obscurantist Muslim fundamentalism" and "medieval intolerance" of the "geriatric prophet in Qom." Anthony Burgess called the *fatwa* a *jihad*. "It is a declaration of war on citizens of a free country . . . . It has to be countered by an equally forthright, if less murderous, declaration of defiance." Christopher Hitchins applied Shelley's anathema of King George to Khomeini: "an old, mad, blind, despised and dying king," adding: "Is it not time, as a minimal gesture of solidarity, for all of us to don the Yellow Star . . . ?" Fay Weldon wallowed in religious chauvinism: "The Koran is food for no-thought. . . . You can build a decent society around the Bible . . . but the Koran? No." Conor Cruise O'Brien unconsciously inverted Shabbir Akhtar's call to arms: "A Westerner who claims to admire Muslim society, while still adhering to Western values, is either a hypocrite or an ignoramus or a bit of both." He reviled the Muslim family as "an abominable institution" and Muslim society as "repulsive" and "sick." Norman Mailer, always spoiling for a fight, sounded like a *New Statesman* competitor imitating Hemingway:

> [N]ow the Ayatollah Khomeini has offered us an opportunity to regain our frail religion which happens to be faith in the power of words and our willingness to suffer for them. He awakens us to the great rage we feel when our liberty to say what we wish, wise or foolish, kind or cruel, well-advised or ill-advised, is endangered. We discover that, yes, maybe we are willing to suffer for our idea. Maybe we are even willing, ultimately, to die for the idea that

serious literature, in a world of dwindling certainties and choked-up ecologies, is the absolute we must defend.[42]

British politicians also felt compelled to intervene. When Sayyid Abdul Quddus, secretary of the Council of Mosques, boasted that "members of our religion throughout the country have sworn to carry out the Ayatollah's wishes should the opportunity arise," Conservative MP Terry Dicks demanded his deportation (although Quddus was a citizen). Roy Jenkins regretted that the government had not "been more cautious about allowing . . . in the 1950s, substantial Muslim communities [to come] here." The Home Secretary told Birmingham Muslims: "no ethnic or religious minority is likely to thrive in this country if it seeks to isolate itself from the mainstream of British life," which a tabloid headline promptly translated into the command: "Behave like British, or don't live here." John Townsend, Conservative MP for Bridlington, concurred: "when Muslims say they cannot live in a country where Salman Rushdie is free to express his views, they should be told they have the answer in their own hands—go back from whence you came." Home Office Minister of State John Patten wrote an open letter reminding Muslim leaders of their obligation to live harmoniously in a multi-cultural Britain.[43]

Divisions deepened within and between countries. Imam Bukhari of a Delhi mosque and the Mufti of the Al Aqsa mosque in Jerusalem endorsed the *fatwa*. Ahmed Jebril of the Popular Front for the Liberation of Palestine-General Command offered to execute it. But Dr. Tantawi, the Cairo mufti and grand sheikh, condemned Khomeini, and Egyptian Interior Minister General Zaki Badr raised the ante by calling the Ayatollah a dog and a pig. When a Saudi Arabian Imam showed lenience toward Rushdie on Belgian television, he and his Tunisian aide were assassinated.[44]

The struggle within Britain was replayed on the Continent, if at lower intensity. The twelve European Community foreign ministers denounced the *fatwa* and imposed diplomatic sanctions on Iran; the United States, Sweden, Canada, Australia, Norway and Brazil promptly followed suit. Iran recalled all its diplomats from Europe. A thousand Muslims demonstrated in Paris, prompting SOS Racisme to organise an equally large counterdemonstration against fundamentalist extremism. Paris Mayor Jacques Chirac denounced those threatening Rushdie and his publishers: "If they are French they need to be pursued; if they are foreigners, they should be expelled." Neo-fascist politician Jean-Marie Le Pen welcomed this fuel for racist

17

fires: "What Khomeini has just done with revolting cynicism is exactly what I fear . . . the invasion of Europe by a Muslim immigration."[45]

Muslim actions and threats seriously impeded distribution of the book (while simultaneously increasing sales). The British Library put it on "restricted" locked shelves. Arsonists firebombed Collets Penguin bookshop on Charing Cross Road, persuading the chain to remove the book, and damaged a Dillon's store. The *fatwa* scared large American chains like Barnes & Noble, B. Dalton, and Waldenbooks and many independents into withdrawing the book, but most resumed selling it. After the bombing of a small newspaper that had defended Rushdie, Senator Daniel Moynihan denounced "intellectual terrorism" and sponsored a resolution: "Let it be understood in the parts of the world from whence such threats emanate: We are not intimidated and the resources of civilization against its enemies are not exhausted." Rushdie's French and German publishers dropped the book, citing threats, but announced that consortia would bring out translations. In Italy Muslims severely wounded his translator, burned a bookshop, and threatened to blow up the Ravenna monument to Dante, who had consigned Mohammed to the ninth pit of hell 700 years earlier. The Japanese translator was stabbed to death. A year after publication, when a paperback version normally would have been in press, a memo from the board of directors of Viking Penguin's parent corporation urged delay: "Some principles have to be fought to the death, but I am quite clear this isn't one of them." Six months later, however, Rushdie protested that failure to issue the paperback would mean that he and the publisher "in some sense have been defeated by the campaign against the book."[46]

Britain was profoundly polarised. The Bradford Council of Mosques, unscathed during the previous decade, was attacked four times, while its president was threatened and his home vandalised. Rushdie's name became a taunt, used by white children against Blacks and white sports fans against Bradford City supporters. Warders forced Muslim prisoners to listen to passages from *The Satanic Verses*. Walls in Muslim areas were defaced with graffiti reading: "Rushdie rules," "Kill a Muslim for Christmas," and even "Gas the Muslims."[47] These attacks helped to unify the fragmented Muslim community and inspire cultural pride, intensifying demands for halal food in schools and single-sex education.[48] On May 27, 30,000 Muslims marched from Hyde Park to Parliament Square carrying banners reading:

Freedom of speach, yes! Freedom to insult, no!
Penguin will pay for its crims!
Rousseau greatest champion of human liberty and equality deeply
inspired by the Prophet Muhammad
"Islam is the only suitable creed for Europe," George Bernard
Shaw
Dr John W. Baker: "Islam the greatest blessing for mankind"
Rushdie is a devil!
Rushdie is a son of Satan!
Kill the bastard!
Jihad on agnostics!

One poster displayed Rushdie on the gallows, his head sprouting
horns, wearing a Star of David, and attached to a pig's body —
imagery that could have come from the novel, except for the anti-
Semitism. Women Against Fundamentalism, who staged a counterdemonstration, were attacked by both Muslim men and white
racists.[49]

After almost two years in hiding Rushdie sought reconciliation
with the community of British Asians, especially Indian Muslims, by
undergoing a conversion, while reiterating his criticisms of the
sexism and homophobia of Islamic priests. He agreed:

1. To witness that there is no God but Allah and that Muhammad is
His last prophet.
2. To declare that I do not agree with any statement in my novel
*The Satanic Verses* uttered by any of the characters who insult the
Prophet Muhammad or who cast aspersions upon Islam or upon
the authenticity of the Holy Quran, or who reject the divinity of
Allah.
3. I undertake not to publish the paperback edition of *The Satanic
Verses* or to permit any further agreements for translation into
other languages, while any risk of further offence exists.
4. I will continue to work for a better understanding of Islam in the
world, as I have always attempted to do in the past.

He offered further justification in *The Times*: "*The Satanic Verses*
was never intended as an insult . . . it is a source of happiness to say
that I am now inside, and a part of, the community whose values
have always been closest to my heart." The six Islamic scholars who
accepted this apology agreed he had no evil intent, and the Cairo
Grand Shaikh formally forgave and blessed him. But this merely

heightened the hostility of Iran, which reiterated the *fatwa* in March 1991 and doubled the price on Rushdie's head.[50]

Both sides expressed frustration at the stalemate. The International Committee for the Defence of Salman Rushdie denounced the British government for capitulating to Iran. But when prominent intellectuals, artists, and media figures planned a 24-hour vigil in London, New York, and Los Angeles to commemorate the author's thousand days in hiding, the Foreign Office pressured Rushdie to cancel the rally for fear of delaying the return of western hostages. At the same time, Iqbal Sacranic, Joint Convenor of the U.K. Action Committee on Islamic Affairs, wrote to *The Guardian*.

What bewilders is that nothing is being done or said to stop the circulation of the book which continues to cause unspeakable distress and anguish to more than one billion Muslims all over the world. . . . [We] have consistently demanded its withdrawal and appropriate public apology and redress by the publishers.[51]

Rushdie now reversed his strategy. Appearing in public for the first time in nearly three years, at a Columbia University tribute to the First Amendment and retired Supreme Court Justice William Brennan, he compared his plight to drifting in a balloon incapable of carrying him to safety while gradually losing air.

[H]as it really been so long since religions persecuted people, burning them as heretics, drowning them as witches, that you can't recognize religious persecution when you see it? . . .
[In the] upside-down logic of the post-*fatwa* world . . . [a] novelist can be accused of having savaged or "mugged" a whole community, becoming its tormentor (instead of its . . . victim) and the scapegoat for . . . its discontents. . . .
I've been put through a degree course in worthlessness . . . . My first teachers were the mobs marching down distant boulevards, baying for my blood and finding, soon enough, their echoes on English streets. . . . as I watched the marchers, I felt them trampling on my heart. . . .
Sometimes I think that one day, Muslims . . . [will] agree, too, that the row over *The Satanic Verses* was at bottom an argument about who should have power over the grand narrative, the Story of Islam, and that that power must belong equally to everyone.
. . .
I faced my deepest grief, my . . . sorrow at having been torn away

from . . . the cultures and societies from which I'd always drawn my . . . inspiration . . . . I determined to make my peace with Islam, even at the cost of my pride. . . .
I had always argued that it was necessary to develop the nascent concept of the "secular Muslim," who, like the secular Jew, affirmed his membership of the culture while being separate from the theology. . . . But my fantasy of joining the fight for the modernization of Muslim thought . . . was stillborn. . . . I have never disowned *The Satanic Verses*, nor regretted writing it. . . . [Within days [after my meeting with the six Islamic scholars] all but one of them had broken their promises, and recommenced to vilify me and my work, as if we had not shaken hands. I felt (most probably I had been) a great fool. The suspension of the paperback began at once to look like a surrender. . . . *The Satanic Verses* must be freely available and easily affordable, if only because if it is not read and studied, then these years will have no meaning. . . . I have learned the hard way that when you permit anyone else's description of reality to supplant your own . . . then you might as well be dead. . . . I must cling with all my might to . . . my own soul . . . .
"Free speech is a non-starter," says one of my Islamic extremist opponents. No, sir, it is not. Free speech is the whole thing, the whole ball game. Free speech is life itself . . . .
You must decide what you think a writer is worth, what value you place on a maker of stories, and an arguer with the world.[52]

This launched another cycle of recriminations. A Muslim wrote to the *New York Times*:

Salman Rushdie's greatest flaw is his lack of shame. . . . Instead of repenting, Mr. Rushdie is "sorrowful;" instead of admitting guilt, he becomes the grand preacher of a new order in Islam. . . . Mr. Rushdie's preaching for a "carefree" Islam will further alienate him from the Islamic fold.

Paul Theroux, the cosmopolitan author and traveller, leapt to Rushdie's defense.

I have made a point of asking all the Muslims I meet their views on Mr. Rushdie and his book. . . . It ought to happen everywhere: first the question—*What about Rushdie?*—and if the answer is hostile, set them straight. . . . I have no doubt that eventually the message will get through, and he will be free.[53]

More than three years after the *fatwa* an anonymous consortium published an American paperback. Rushdie withdrew his acceptance of Islam. "After three years of having my life smashed about by religion, I don't feel like associating myself with it. I'm fighting for my life against it."[54] Contemporaneously Iranian leaders reiterated the death sentence, under the headline: "A Divine Command to Stone the Devil." Rushdie was rebuffed when he visited Washington to seek American support. White House Press Secretary Marlin Fitzwater declared: "There's no reason for any special relationship with Rushdie. I mean, he's an author. He's here. He's doing interviews and book tours and things authors do. . . . We have often said that we want better relations with Iran." Rushdie disavowed pecuniary motives: "The purpose of the paperback is to make a point about First Amendment rights . . . ." Shortly thereafter an Indian historian's call to lift the ban on *The Satanic Verses* led to student protests, which closed his university, the country's leading Muslim institution.[55]

# IV. Negotiating Respect

These stories about pornography, racial hatred, and *The Satanic Verses* share a common core. They concern values that inspire deep emotions: fury at the sexual objectification of women versus conviction that sex is irreducibly ambiguous; racism versus equality; the truth of Islam versus religious scepticism. Each confrontation implicates more fundamental controversies: group and individual, particular and universal, tradition and innovation, authority and freedom—antinomies that have haunted humankind for millenia. Each side views its values as absolute while vilifying its opponent's as an antithesis for which no synthesis is possible. This Manichaean struggle allows no compromise; anything less than total victory is ignominious defeat.

If values constitute the manifest content of these stories, however, respect is their subtext. Women are demanding respect from producers and consumers of pornography, who make them instruments of voyeuristic pleasure. Racial and religious minorities are asserting equality against racists and anti-Semites who defend their own superiority. Muslims are asserting equality with Christians, immigrants with natives, traditionalists with modernists, locals with cosmopolitans, while religious sceptics and creative artists challenge orthodox hegemony. Disembodied values are not colliding in vacuo. Every assertion of value is an act of symbolic politics, a competition for status. In championing values, speakers simultaneously claim moral superiority for their groups. This is most visible in the controversy provoked by *The Satanic Verses*. Muslims feel the honour of Islam is at stake, while westerners maintain the superiority of their intellectual, artistic, and political traditions. Shabbir Akhtar's warning to "Be Careful with Muhammad!" elicited Norman Mailer's "great rage" "when our liberty to say what we wish . . . is endangered." The eternal verities of religion encountered the "absolute" of "serious literature." Islam invoked its billion adherents and centuries of tradition while Rushdie paraded his support by "eminent" English writers and claimed that "the centuries belong to art." "[T]he row over *The Satanic Verses*," he said, "was at bottom an argument about who should have power over the grand narrative . . . ." Status is equally visible in the other controversies. NSPA leader Frank Collin sought to humiliate Jews: "I hope they're terrified. I hope they're shocked. Because we're coming to get them again." JDL leader Meir Kahane replied: "the streets of Skokie will run with Nazi blood." "I am not predicting violence—I am promising violence." Women demand passage of anti-pornography legislation to redress the humiliations of Clarence Thomas's confirmation and the William Kennedy Smith's acquittal.

That struggles over collective status should continue to preoccupy society violates the modernist credo, now a century old, which characterises history as an inexorable movement from status to contract, particularism to universalism, gemeinschaft to gesellschaft. Marx saw status as a feudal relic largely eradicated by the bourgeoisie and irrelevant to the proletariat— a theorisation that blinded generations of marxist scholars to the importance of race and gender. Instead of disappearing, however, status groupings embody an irrepressible nostalgia for community, an imperative to preserve, recreate and strengthen collective identity. Regional political and economic integration not only co-exists with a resurgent nationalism but actually accelerates the very international migration and communication that invigorates status competition.

Language (and other symbolic communication) is the principal medium of collective status competition.[56] Although wealth and power can confer status or derive from it, the three attributes are relatively independent. A dominant group whose wealth or power is declining often clings desperately to its residual tokens of respect, while a subordinate group frustrated in its aspirations to wealth or power may still assert its dignity. Because status, unlike wealth, is an indivisible good whose meaning is relational, competition is a zero-sum game. Even if a subordinate group asks only a minimum of respect, the dominant group rightly perceives this as challenging its superiority.[57]

Collective status competition pervades daily life. It motivates controversies over legislation ostensibly directed toward practical ends: homosexuality in the military, AIDS, abortion, animal rights, tobacco, gun control, crime and social disorder, welfare and immigration. The campaign against sexual harassment significantly redefines the relative status of men and women. Status is implicated whenever the state engages religion (as in the battle over Ayodhya in India). It resonates in the curriculum wars: multiculturalism in schools, the revision of the literary and historical canon in universities. Intrareligious conflicts over the ordination of women or the celebration of homosexual marriages affect status. Public events and exhibits define and modify status: the exclusion of gays and lesbians from the St. Patrick's Day parades in New York and Boston, or commemoration of the Columbus Quincentenary. The treatment of ancestral bones arouses collective passions—the recently discovered black graveyard from colonial New York or the display of Indian skeletons in museums—as does the appropriation of Indian names and mascots by sports teams. The media have become increasingly sensitive to such issues, as shown by the furor over the portrayal of gays and lesbians in the film "Basic Instinct"; so have public officials, as illustrated by the response to Bill Clinton's remark that Mario Cuomo acts like a Mafioso. The legal system receives intense scrutiny because of its visible power and explicit commitment to equality; the initial acquittal of the four Los Angeles police who beat Rodney King provoked the largest uprising in twentieth-century American history. Nations compete for status (often when they are declining along other parameters): Japan-bashing in the United States, for instance, or European Community conflicts over the languages of diplomacy. Aggressor nations like Germany and Japan must be particularly sensitive to their former victims, as shown by the uproar over Korean "comfort women" or the Emperor's visit to China, Germany's hospitality to Kurt Waldheim or its handling of neo-Nazi violence against foreigners.

Re-reading my three stories as status competition illuminates their many common features. Each borrows buzz words from the others.

Gloria Steinem likened *Mein Kampf* to *Playboy*, while Ali Mazrui compared it to *The Satanic Verses*. Feminists called pornographers sexual fascists, while Rushdie supporters saw memories of Nuremberg in the flames of the Bradford book burning. A feminist identified women with Jews, while a writer urged colleagues to ally with the Muslim apostate by donning yellow stars. Shabbir Akhtar warned that "the next time there are gas chambers in Europe, there is no doubt concerning who'll be inside them," while racists defaced Midlands walls with graffiti screaming "Gas the Muslims." After Holocaust survivors denounced American Nazis as obscene, Catherine MacKinnon reversed the metaphor by calling pornography a Skokie-type injury, while the Minnesota Civil Liberties Union condemned MacKinnon's ordinance as an obscenity. Muslims equated *The Satanic Verses* with strip-tease, raping one's daughter, pissing on the Bible, and describing a parent's genitals in public.

In each story, some actors portrayed ultimate values as mere instruments of status conflict. Nazi "Lieutenant" Roger Tedor admitted that their anti-Semitic demonstrations used "the pretext of picketing for free speech" by carrying placards reading "Free Speech for White America," while Frank Collin gloated: "I used [the First Amendment] at Skokie." Andrea Dworkin dismissed the First Amendment as "an instrument of the ruling class," and Catherine MacKinnon called civil libertarians the "pornographers' mouthpiece." Muslims ridiculed Rushdie's claims to "free" speech by pointing to his large advance for the book and the £100,000 that *The Independent on Sunday* allegedly paid for his article "In Good Faith." Some politicians cynically manipulated values and status aspirations: the Indianapolis mayor and city prosecutor in local American politics, Syed Shahabuddin in Indian communalist politics, and Ayatollah Khomeini in Muslim world politics.

Status competition is conducted through language whose ambiguity can vary. Neo-Nazi racial hatred is wholly evil, although it can be disguised as science, history, or politics. Like all literature, *The Satanic Verses* was capable of numerous interpretations. Even if read as an attack on Islam, it could invoke the license of liberalism to criticise ideas. The eternal arguments about human sexuality have grown more complex and intense over the last century.

Given the ambiguity of speech, context is vitally important in the attribution of meaning: who is addressing whom, before what audience, in light of what history. Decades of English racism, especially the experience of Muslim pupils in Midlands schools, heightened the anger of Bradford's Muslims at *The Satanic Verses*.

Jewish memories of the Holocaust, which a thousand Skokie residents had suffered first-hand, strongly contributed to the village's ban of the Nazi march. Women respond to pornography in light of their daily experience of sexual harassment and objectification. The speaker's identity may be critical: it was worse for a Jewish ACLU lawyer to represent the Nazis, a Muslim to criticise Islam, a lesbian to endorse sado-masochistic pornography. Style tends to overshadow content. Islam has suffered worse attacks than *The Satanic Verses*, but they were couched in less emotive language.[58] Art and erotica shade imperceptibly into pornography. The Nazis might have demonstrated without incident (but also without an audience) had they abandoned their uniforms and swastika. But of course provocation often is the purpose: Rushdie's use of historical figures, Khomeini's *fatwa*, Bradford's book burning, Nazi taunts of Jews, the Lesbian Sex Mafia's choice of a name. The speaker's motive is central but often opaque. Did Rushdie intend to liberate Islam from patriarchy and authoritarianism, ridicule Mohammed, titillate readers, win fame, sell books—or all of these? Do pornographers seek to explore sexual frontiers, objectify and degrade women, make money—or all three?

Rejecting the nursery rhyme's false reassurance that "names can never hurt me," critics of degrading speech hold it responsible for "sticks and stones" and "broken bones." Pornography is the theory, say feminists, rape the practice. Hate speech causes racist attacks. Violence clearly does follow some speech: police killed protesters in Pakistan, Muslims were assassinated in Belgium, Rushdie's Japanese translator was murdered and his Italian translator assaulted, English bookstores were bombed. But consequentialist arguments run the risk of empirical falsification and distract attention from the real harm—the reproduction of status inequalities by the very act of speaking.

Alternatively, speech victims conflate representation with reality, reduce art to mimesis, deny the very possibility of imagination. Muslims insisted on reading *The Satanic Verses* as history rather than fiction. MacKinnon asserted that "a woman had to be tied or cut or burned or gagged or whipped or chained" to produce pornographic films. Dworkin denounced Minneapolis for permitting "the binding and torture of real women." Skokie Holocaust suvivors equated neo-Nazis who applauded murder with actual Nazi murderers. Critics of *The Satanic Verses* called Rushdie a "literary terrorist," attributing to him every word, opinion, and action of his characters.

Status competition through speech tends to escalate and ramify.

Fearing that the Nazis were trying to attack their homes, Holocaust victims threatened to "tear these people up." A Minneapolis woman attempted suicide because "sexism has shattered my life." Muslims heard echoes of the Crusades in western applause for *The Satanic Verses*; westerners condemned the *fatwa* as a *jihad*. Each aggressor presented itself as victim. A billion Muslims claimed to be threatened by a single dissident under sentence of death, proving once again the paradoxical superiority of pen to sword. White heterosexual males who dominate the polity, economy, and culture decried the oppression of "politically correctness" whenever women, racial minorities, and homosexuals sought equality. Hyperbole flourished on every side. Both pornography and *The Satanic Verses* were equated to rape and murder. Rushdie's literary honours were maligned as "knight[ing] muggers" and "giv[ing] mass murderers the Nobel Prize." Muslims who called Rushdie a literary terrorist were denounced in turn for intellectual terrorism. British intellectuals and politicians drew false parallels between book burning in Bradford and Nuremberg. Insult provoked insult, and violence bred violence. If Rushdie called Mohammed "Mahound," Muslims responded by giving the author a devil's horns, a pig's body, and a Star of David. Nazis traded threats with the JDL. When Iran put a price on Rushdie's head, English newspapers offered three times as much for Khomeini's humiliation.

Status competition makes even stranger bedfellows than other forms of politics. Jewish leaders expressed sympathy for fundamentalist Muslims. Rushdie was championed by such improbable allies as the neo-fascist Jean-Marie Le Pen and the *Sunday Sport*, whose audience probably had never heard of the author and certainly had not read him. The campaign against pornography united born-again Christians with radical feminists, while civil rights leaders distanced themselves from both. White racists helped Muslim men assault Muslim feminists. Ukrainian-Americans, whose homeland had committed some of the worst nineteenth-century pogroms and condoned Nazi atrocities, supported the Jews against the NSPA. Inspired by principle or realpolitik, such alliances expanded the conflict: Israel applauded Skokie's resistance to the Nazis; the Islamic world confronted a West united against the *fatwa*. Neutrality became impossible. Just as AIDS activists declare that "Silence Is Death," so inaction became complicity. Holocaust survivors demanded: "How dare the government sanctify this thing by permitting [it] to take place on public property?" According to Dworkin, Minneapolis had only two choices: help women or pornographers.

27

Shabbir Akhtar declared that "any Muslim who fails to be offended by Rushdie's book ceases, on account of that fact, to be a Muslim." Conor Cruise O'Brien responded: "A Westerner who claims to admire Muslim society, while still adhering to Western values, is either a hypocrite or an ignoramus, or a bit of both." Principled civil libertarians in the ACLU were reviled as the hired guns of pornographers or Nazis. At the same time, each collectivity displayed major fissures: feminists over pornography, Muslims over the *fatwa*, Jews over civil liberties, British intellectuals and politicians over Rushdie.

Because status competition is a zero-sum game conducted through the medium of values, compromise is extremely difficult. Civil libertarians quickly become moralistic absolutists. The Executive Director of the Minnesota Civil Liberties Union declared: "Bookstores cannot be censored. That's all there is to it." The Chicago ACLU public relations director characterised those who sought to stop the Nazi march as "the enemy, possessed of sinister motive and intent" and declared that "the Village of Skokie shredded the First Amendment." François Mitterand declaimed: "All dogmatism which through violence undermines freedom of thought and the right to free expression is, in my view, absolute evil." Rushdie concluded that "free speech is life itself." On the other side, MacKinnon demanded zero tolerance for "the sexually explicit subordination of women," many Jews would deny Nazis any right to speak, and many Muslims would accept nothing less than suppression of *The Satanic Verses* and execution of its author.

Once offensive speech had impaired its victims' status, they demanded a remedy that would correct the inequality. Apology is just such a degradation ceremony. Rushdie offered an apology after the *fatwa*, acknowledging and regretting the hurt his words had caused, but Khomeini refused to forgive. Almost two years later Rushdie made another obeisance, embracing Islam, repudiating his characters' words, and postponing translations and a paperback. The rejection of this self-abasement, which crowned a "degree course in worthlessness," convinced Rushdie that "there is nothing I can do to break this impasse." Further apologies threatened annihilation: he "might as well be dead." To restore his self-respect and reputation, he denied that he had ever "disowned" *The Satanic Verses* or regretted writing it. Describing suspension of the paperback as a "surrender," he secured its publication within months. And he re-asserted his worth as a "writer," a "maker of stories," an "arguer with the world."

These narratives pose an intractable problem. Speech is essential to self-realisation, social life, politics, economic activity, art, and knowledge. But speech can also inflict serious harm. In particular, it can reproduce and exaggerate status inequalities. How should we deal with this tension? The remaining lectures consider three alternatives. The next explores the civil libertarian position, some of whose deficiencies have already emerged. Private action can constrain speech as seriously as the state: feminists picketing pornography, the JDL threatening the NSPA, the Bradford book burning and Khomeini's *fatwa*, Penguin's publication decisions. Tolerance can be self-destructive: both the ACLU and the First Amendment lost support in the wake of Skokie. My third lecture discusses the other obvious alternative of state regulation. Again, these stories have revealed a central drawback—efforts to suppress a message may merely amplify it: banning a movie enlarges its audience, the Nazis received much more publicity from Skokie's opposition than the pitiful band ever could have gotten from walking down the street—swastikas and all; and Muslim fundamentalists greatly increased Salman Rushdie's name recognition and sales (if not his readership). In the final lecture I suggest that we may avoid some of these pitfalls if communities encourage speech victims to seek apologies through informal processes.

## Notes

[1] For a sociological analysis of anti-pornography campaigns, see Zurcher & Kirkpatrick (1976).

[2] Quoted in Lederer (1980d).

[3] Russell & Lederer (1980: 28).

[4] "Against Our Will," quoted in Russell & Lederer (1980: 32).

[5] Quoted in Lederer (1980d: 127–28).

[6] Rubin (1984: 298).

[7] Alderfer (1982); Perry (1992).

[8] Ferguson (1984); 9(1) Feminist Studies 180–82 (Spring 1983); see also Linden et al. (1982); Gubar & Hoff (1989). For British debates, see Barrett (1982); Bower (1986); Chester & Dickey (1988); Assiter (1989); Marxism *Today* 22 (July 1990).

[9] Dworkin (1989); MacKinnon (1987: 15).

[10] This account is taken from Downs (1989: 61–89) and Brest & Vandenberg (1987).

[11] Hunter & Law (1987/88).

[12] Downs (1989: 85–139); Brest & Vandenberg (1987: 656–57); Duggan et al. (1985: 130); *New York Times* A15 (January 17, 1992); *New York Times Book Review* 1 (March 29, 1992). The Senate bill (S.1521) has

been nicknamed "the Bundy bill" after the serial killer who claimed to have been incited by pornography. Hearings on the Massachusetts bill repeated the earlier consequentialist claims. Pat Haas testified that her boyfriend forced her to act out what he had seen in porn flicks. "He did what was in the movies. If he had seen a snuff film, I wouldn't be here." *Time* 52 (March 30, 1992).

[13] *Beauharnais* v. *Illinois*, 353 U.S. 250 (1952).

[14] *Chicago* v. *Lambert*, 47 Ill. App. 2d 151 (1964). For a history of the pre-Skokie cases, see Arkes (1975).

[15] Downs (1985); Barnum (1982) (survey research).

[16] *Independent* (March 8, 1989), cited in Qureshi & Khan (1989: 30).

[17] Ruthven (1990: 85).

[18] *India Today* (September 15, 1988) and *Sunday* (September 18–24, 1988), quoted in Appignanesi & Maitland (1989: 38–41).

[19] Ruthven (1990: 85).

[20] *The Times of India* (October 13, 1988), quoted in Appignanesi & Maitland (1989: 45–59).

[21] Appignanesi & Maitland (1989: 42–44).

[22] Ruthven (1990: 90).

[23] Shabbir Akhtar, "The case for religious fundamentalism," *Guardian* (February 27, 1989), reproduced in Appignanesi & Maitland (1989: 238–41); Akhtar (1989: 1, 6, 11–12, 25, 35, 102); Qureshi & Khan (1990: 1).

[24] Qureshi & Khan (1990: i).

[25] Modood (1990: 154).

[26] Ruthven (1990: 29); Qureshi & Khan (1990: 10).

[27] Appignanesi & Maitland (1989: 220–28); Ruthven (1990: 29). Elsewhere Mazrui asserted: *"The Satanic Verses* is like a rotten pig placed at the door of *Dar es Islam*, the home of Islam." (1990: 36).

Rustom Bharucha declared that Rushdie "has made himself the enemy of his people." (1990: 62). Feroza Jussawalla (1989), who argued that Rushdie should be "accountable" for his distortions and misrepresentations, found his own critique censored before it could be published in India. Quotations from *The Satanic Verses* were replaced by page references—to a book that was itself banned!

[28] Ruthven (1990: 84, 86, 91–94, 96).

[29] *The Times* (March 1, 1989), in Akhtar (1989: 61).

[30] Qureshi & Khan (1990: 25).

[31] *The Times* (March 4, 1989), in Akhtar (1989: 122); Appignanesi & Maitland (1989: 215–16).

[32] Qureshi & Khan (1990: 26).

[33] *Times Literary Supplement* (June 1, 1989), in Appignanesi & Maitland (1989: 236–38).

[34] Appignanesi & Maitland (1989: 241–42). For a thoughtful, sympathetic discussion by two British Asian academics of the book and the response it provoked, see Marxism *Today* 24 (June 1989) (Bhikhu Parekh and Homi

Bhabha). For a study of the "cultural politics" of the response, focusing on the worlds of India and Islam, see Spivak (1989; 1990).

[35] Ruthven (1990: 103).

[36] Appignanesi & Maitland (1989: 27–29, 74–75).

[37] Akhtar (1989: 83); Qureshi & Khan (1990: 41). No one seems to have mentioned the book's devastating portrait of Khomeini as the Imam determined to end history, who sacrifices millions of his followers in the pursuit of power. Although he could not have read it, his advisers must have conveyed the gist. Rushdie (1988: 205–16, 234)

[38] Appignanesi & Maitland (1989: 25, 64–65, 92–95, 103); Akhtar (1989: 80, 93).

[39] Ruthven (1990: 113), Appignanesi & Maitland (1989: 4, 81, 84–85, 87, 106–07, 120, 122); Webster (1990: 52).

[40] *The Times of India* (January 27, 1989), quoted in Nair & Battacharya (1990: 21).

[41] Appignanesi & Maitland (1989: 123–24, 126–27); Ruthven (1990: 119–21).

[42] Appignanesi & Maitland (1989: 102, 127, 171, 174); Qureshi & Khan (1990: 39); Jenkins (1989); Webster (1990: 43).

[43] Appignanesi & Maitland (1989: 65, 101, 134, 140–41); Akhtar (1989: 26) Qureshi & Khan (1990: 5, 19); Ruthven (1990: 118).

[44] Appignanesi & Maitland (1989: 132, 142, 145, 154, 191–93); Ruthven (1990: 114–17).

Egyptian Nobel laureate Naguib Mahfouz initially supported Rushdie, accusing Khomeini of "intellectual terrorism." Three years later, however, he called the two of them "equally dangerous." An author "must be ready to pay the price for his outspokenness." Although he had not read *The Satanic Verses* because of bad eyesight, it had been explained to him; parts were unacceptable. Rushdie did not "have the right to insult anything, especially a prophet or anything considered holy." Mahfouz's own novel *The Children of Gebelawi* was still banned in Egypt for encouraging readers to repudiate Islam, but the author protested that critics had misunderstood the allegory! *New York Times* B3 (August 5, 1992).

[45] Appignanesi & Maitland (1989: 183–84, 186).

[46] Appignanesi & Maitland (1989: 143, 154–56, 159, 164–65, 180-81, 185–87); *Mother Jones* (April 1990); *Los Angeles Times* A16 (March 14, 1990).

[47] Ruthven (1990: 81); Webster (1990: 107–09, 132); Modood (1990: 143).

[48] Appignanesi & Maitland (1989: 128–29); Qureshi & Khan (1990: 12–13)

[49] Ruthven (1990: 1, 4–5); Rutherford (1990a: 25).

[50] *The Times* (December 28, 1990); 20(2) *Index on Censorship* 34 (February 1991); Rushdie (1991), reprinted in Rushdie (1992: 430).

[51] *Article 19 Bulletin* 12 (July 1991); *Independent on Sunday* 1 (November 3, 1991); *Guardian* 9 (November 7, 1991), 20 (November 14, 1991).

[52] *New York Times* A1, B8 (December 12, 1991), reprinted in Rushdie (1992: 430).

[53] *New York Times* 8 (December 28, 1991), A19 (February 13, 1992).

[54] *Los Angeles Times* A1 (March 25, 1992).

[55] *New York Times* B2 (January 29, 1992), B2 (February 20, 1992), B1 (February 14, 1992), 12 (March 14, 1992), A18 (March 26, 1992), A6 (March 1, 1992); *Los Angeles Times* A16 (March 26, 1992). In May 1992 a group of Iranian intellectuals and artists issued a public statement in defence of Rushdie. *New York Review of Books* 31 (May 14, 1992). When Rushdie expressed hope at the beginning of June about political changes in Iran the regime reiterated the $2 million reward for his death. *New York Times* A4 (June 18, 1992). In July Britain expelled three Iranians for death threats against Rushdie; one of them had gotten close enough to be spotted by Rushdie's guards. *New York Times* 1 (July 25, 1992).

[56] Murray Edelman laid the foundation of this approach (1964: 1971). For case studies, see, *e.g.* Gusfield (1963) (Prohibition); Dienes (1972) (birth control). Sennett & Cobb (1972) explored the status elements of class relations; Ehrenreich extended this analysis from workers to the middle class (1989). Goode (1978) generalised about "prestige." More recently, Hunter (1991) sought to explain all contemporary American conflict in these terms.

[57] On positional scaracity, see Hirsch (1976).

[58] Brennan (1989: 142).

# 2. The Poverty of Civil Libertarianism

In my first lecture I told stories about pornography, hate speech, and *The Satanic Verses*. Responses to such events oscillate between the poles of civil libertarianism and state regulation. In this lecture I will articulate the libertarian position and advance four criticisms: the costs of speech, the imperative of state regulation, the impossibility of state neutrality, and the illusion of private freedom.

## I. Civil Libertarian Theory

The most uncompromising civil libertarianism prohibits state inter-ference with private speech (which it views as inherently free) and mandates neutrality when the state speaks, directly or through others. A foundation of this position is scepticism about the possi-bility of resolving conflicts of value. Daily contact among the diverse cultures of the global village—not just through the media but increasingly as citizens of the same neighbourhood, workplace, and school—has reinforced ethical relativism. The accelerating pace of change during recent centuries vividly exemplifies the contingency of values. This perspective reflects not only experience but also the epistemological position that values cannot be proven. Belief expresses individual subjective preference; consensus is accidental and ephemeral. Empirical knowledge, by contrast, emerges from efforts at disproof, as the triumph of modern science dramatically demonstrates. For both reasons, political authority presupposes vigorous debate, which alone can generate consent and legitimacy. And because civil libertarianism holds the ontological view of humans as expressive and communicative, free speech also is essential to the full realisation of personhood.[1]

To support this position, civil libertarians can adduce endless examples of oppression in the name of absolute values. The history of religion is a narrative of parochial intolerance justified by appeals to the transcendent: the persecution of early Christians, the Crusades, the Inquisition, medieval religious wars, anti-Semitism, missionary zeal, communist attempts to extirpate religion, Muslim fundamentalism, Catholic orthodoxy, the religious right. Communist, fascist, and anti-communist repression in the present century are merely the latest manifestations of millenia of state efforts to silence dissent. Campaigns for cultural hegemony are a source of unrelieved embarrassment: patriarchy, racism, agitprop, Nazi fulminations against "degenerate art," and sexual repression running from the Puritans through Victorian prudery to Mary Whitehouse and Jesse Helms.

Yet civil libertarianism raises more questions than it answers. Is our ethical relativism really absolute? Haven't the horrors of recent centuries forged a consensus about the evils of slavery, colonialism, racism, anti-Semitism? Even patriarchy hides behind "family values," and homophobia barely dares to speak its name. Do the advantages of free speech always outweigh its costs—which we are learning from the previously silenced voices of women, people of colour, and homosexuals? Does the state refrain from regulation? Can it maintain neutrality? Is speech truly free in the absence of state intervention?

## II. The Costs of Speech

Most discussion of free speech emphasises the costs of prohibition— the subject of my third lecture. Recently, however, racial and religious minorities, women, and gays and lesbians have born witness to the pain inflicted by slurs, graffiti, threats, and stereotypes.[2] Let me begin with some examples.

In 1990 Russ and Laura Jones and their five children fled the drugs and crime of downtown St. Paul, Minnesota to become the only black family in Mounds Park, a working-class neighbourhood. Within two weeks their tyres were slashed. Soon thereafter they were awoken at midnight by a cross burning in their small fenced-in front garden. Mrs. Jones described her terror: "If you're black and you see a cross burning, you know it's a threat, and you imagine all the church bombings and lynchings and rapes that have gone before, not so long ago. A cross burning is a way of saying 'We're going to get you.'" Reported hate crimes had increased 21 per cent in

Minnesota over the previous year. Like cities in almost every American state, St. Paul had a hate crime ordinance, passed in 1982, to which it had recently added cross burning and swastikas and sexual bias. Arthur Miller 3d, an 18-year-old who lived across the street, pleaded guilty and served 30 days in jail. He testified in the trial of Robert A. Viktora, a 17-year-old high school dropout, that they and four friends were drinking that night and talking about getting into some "skinhead trouble" and "burning some niggers." Viktora appealed his conviction to the U.S. Supreme Court, supported by the ACLU and the conservative Center for Individual Rights, while amicus briefs were filed on behalf of the state by the NAACP, the Asian-American Legal Defense and Education Fund, and the liberal People for the American Way. In the course of oral argument Justice Scalia rejected the prosecutor's contention that speech and conduct motivated by racial bias aggravated the injury. "That's a political judgment." Some people might be more offended by a provocative speech about economics "or even philosophy." A protest against the placement of a home for the mentally ill would not violate the ordinance because "it's the wrong kind of bias. Why is that? It seems to me the rankest kind of subject-matter discrimination." Writing for four colleagues (and supported by the votes of four others, who concurred in the result), Scalia held that the ordinance unconstitutionally prohibited speech "solely on the basis of the subjects the speech addresses." The city could not "license one side of a debate to fight freestyle, while requiring the other to follow the Marquis of Queensbury Rules. . . . Selectivity of this sort creates the possibility that the city is seeking to handicap the expression of particular ideas." On hearing the decision, Mrs. Jones objected that her children, ranging in age from 2 to 11, were too young to deal with these injuries. "It makes me angry that they have to be aware of racism around them, that they notice it more and more."[3]

Attempts by American universities to protect subordinated groups from hurtful speech have been similarly frustrated. When white fraternity members staged an "ugly woman" contest in the student refectory by painting their faces black, donning fright wigs, and using pillows to exaggerate breasts and buttocks, George Mason University suspended them from social activities and sports for two years. Although the ACLU conceded that the contest was "inappropriate and offensive," it represented the fraternity because the penalty was "grossly inappropriate." The federal court agreed because the skit "contained more than a kernel of expression." At the University of Wisconsin the *UMW Post* and several students

35

challenged the hate speech code adopted in 1989 as part of a Design for Diversity and in response to several racist incidents, including a fraternity "slave auction." A federal court also invalidated this, declaring: "The problems of bigotry and discrimination sought to be addressed here are real and truly corrosive of the educational environment. But freedom of speech is almost absolute in our land."[4] After restricting the rule to face-to-face confrontations, the university repealed it following the Supreme Court's decision in the St. Paul case.[5]

Black popular music combines legitimate anger at racial oppression with misogyny, homophobia, and anti-Semitism. 2 Live Crew gained notoriety for its album "As Nasty As They Wanna Be," which contains a track called "The Buck." [See Appendix. Readers are warned they may find the lyrics extremely offensive.] 2 Live Crew were acquitted of obscenity in a trial at which Harvard English Professor Henry Louis Gates, Jr., himself African American, called the group brilliant artists who exploded racist stereotypes about black sexuality by presenting them in a comically extreme form.[6] An English court dismissed an obscenity charge against the LA rap group Niggaz With Attitude for its record "Efil4zaggin," which described oral sex and violence. Band member Eazy-E declared: "We are underground reporters." Geoffrey Robertson QC agreed: "It is often very bitterly sarcastic and rude and will appear to our ears rude and crude, but there it is, all part of the experience. It tells it like it is."[7]

The rap group Public Enemy appeared at its 1987 launch surrounded by bodyguards armed with fake Uzis. Its members praised Louis Farrakhan, the openly anti-Semitic leader of the Nation of Islam. Their song "Fight the Power" became the theme of Spike Lee's enormously successful movie "Do the Right Thing." In May 1989 "Minister of Information" Proffessor (*sic*) Griff (Richard Griffin) told an interviewer from the right-wing *Washington Times* that Jews were the cause of "the majority of the wickedness" in the world. The group fired him but soon thereafter issued "Welcome to the Terrordome," whose lyrics included: "Told a rab get off the rag," "Cruxifixion ain't no fiction/So-called chosen frozen/Apology made to who ever pleases/Still they got me like Jesus." That album, "Fear of Black Planet," which sold a million copies in its first week, also contained "Meet the G That Killed Me," with the homophobic lyrics: "Man to man/I don't know if they can/From what I know/The parts don't fit."[8]

The feminist argument that pornography reproduces the subordination of women receives striking support from the actresses who make it. Indian movie stars charge fees proportioned to how much skin they expose. As American actresses gain popularity they can, indeed must, refuse to perform nude. Michelle Pfeiffer, Kim Basinger, Geena Davis, Ellen Barkin, and Mariel Hemingway all rejected the lead in "Basic Instinct," largely because it required too much nudity and sexual simulation. When rising stars accept such parts they (or the studio) may insist on a "body double." Although Virginia Madsen had appeared nude in previous films, she demanded a double for the love scene with Don Johnson in "The Hot Spot," perhaps to assert her status aspirations. Julie Strain, double-in-waiting in "Thelma and Louise" for Geena Davis (who decided to do the motel sex scene herself), described the selection process.

> They brought a bunch of girls out to the director's trailer one by one, and we had to strip down and spin in a circle. If you had kept your underwear on, I'm sure he wouldn't have said anything. But it's just easier to show the whole thing, because if they're going to shoot a love scene they need to see there are no scars or marks.

Shelley Michele, who doubled Julia Roberts in "Pretty Woman" and was 33 seconds of Kim Basinger's arms and legs pulling on hosiery in zero gravity in "My Stepmother Is an Alien," also doubled for Catherine Oxenberg, daughter of Princess Elizabeth of Yugoslavia, in "Overexposed." "She's royalty," Michele explained. "It's not really moral for her to be doing nudity." Although union rules guarantee doubles up to $2000 a day, they naturally must remain anonymous.[9]

Advertising inflicts different kinds of costs. The tobacco industry's century-old disinformation campaign has been alarmingly successful. Although a panel of a hundred health experts rated smoking the single greatest hazard among 24 alternatives, 1200 randomly chosen adults rated it only tenth, below such risks as homes without smoke detectors.[10] Children are particularly suggestible. Glasgow 11–14-year-olds could recognise an average of five brands; 83 per cent could recall one cigarette ad and half remembered two. Those most aware of ads were more likely to become smokers; a quarter of fifth-formers already smoked. Camels' "Old Joe" campaign, which cost $100 million in 1990, expanded its market share from one per cent to 25–33 per cent of smokers under 18. Thirty per cent of three-year-olds could identify the cartoon character and connect him to the cigarette; 90 per cent of six-year-olds could do so—more than

37

recognised Mickey Mouse![11] Research also connects alcohol advertising to drinking and death. Urging a ban on advertisements suggesting that you can raise your athletic, social or professional status
by your choice of drink, the Washington State Medical Association
noted that 32 per cent of fatal car accidents among 16–20-year-olds
involved a driver whose blood alcohol exceeded 0.1 per cent. When
the ex-director of the New York State Division of Alcoholism and
Alcohol Abuse criticised Anheuser Busch for telling youth that its
beer was served at 87 per cent of "the parties your parents would
never attend," the company responded: "No one has ever been able
to establish a clear link between alcohol abuse and advertising." The
company undercut this disclaimer, however, by boasting to share-
holders that its market share had increased during a period when
beer consumption declined significantly.[12]

## III. The Imperative of State Regulation

Many governments own or control the media and use their pervasive
economic and political power to suppress dissent. Liberal democra-
cies declare their respect for freedom of speech but still regulate it in
myriad ways. Since respected judges, lawyers, and legal scholars,
have given an absolutist interpretation to the First Amendment's
cryptic declaration that "Congress shall make no law . . . abridging
the freedom of speech"|I will stress American examples in arguing
that state regulation is inescapable. The question is not *whether* to
regulate but *what* and *when*|

The civil libertarian position has to account for many disconcert-
ing exceptions. Although defamation is only supposed to punish
after the fact, Peter Matthiessen's book *In the Spirit of Crazy Horse*
was forced out of print when his publisher was sued by those he
accused of framing American Indian Movement leader Leonard
Peltier in the 1975 killing of two FBI agents.[13] Robert Maxwell was
notorious for suing anyone who mentioned him—even for drawing
parallels between his physiognomy or headgear and that of real or
fictitious criminals; his death terminated a hundred libel actions.
Unable to suppress a 1988 biography, he frightened many booksellers out of stocking it.[14] American courts have prohibited release
of the tapes of the Challenger disaster out of respect for the privacy of
the astronauts' families. States forbid the identification of rape
victims and juvenile accused, and judges close trials to press and
public.[15] Victims of hurtful words can sue for intentional infliction of

emotional distress. Courts and administrative agencies extensively regulate commercial speech under such rubrics as misrepresentation and professional advertising and solicitation.[16] They limit the promotion of dangerous products like alcohol and tobacco and require extensive disclosure about others.[17] California taxes tobacco sales to fund anti-smoking messages and education. After Secretary of Health Dr. Louis W. Sullivan, an African American, attacked R.J. Reynolds's "slick and sinister advertising campaign" for its new "Uptown" cigarette targeted at black smokers, the company withdrew the brand. He also denounced the Virginia Slims women's tennis tournament and other sports events for accepting "blood money" from tobacco manufacturers. Surgeon General Antonia Novello, a Latina, condemned industry efforts to increase tobacco sales in Latin America and declared: "In years past, R.J. Reynolds would have us walk a mile for a Camel. Today, it's time that we invite Old Joe Camel himself to take a hike."[18] Contract law endows speech with fateful consequences, while restrictive practices law prohibits the formation of certain contracts. The criminal law of conspiracy and attempt punishes language. And obscenity and pornography are proscribed, if their boundaries have shrunk. The Police Chief of Guilderland, New York, threatened local record stores with prosecution for selling 20 "obscene" tapes; although he retracted the warning, the casettes remained unavailable. Despite the unconstitutionality of hate speech ordinances, the New York City Metropolitan Transportation Authority abridged artistic freedom by removing a photographic exhibit from an underground station when the largely black ridership complained that it depicted Greek rather than African Americans.[19]

All governments invoke raison d'état to suppress speech. During the Persian Gulf War, 79 per cent of Americans approved of military censorship and 57 per cent thought it should be intensified. In response to the patriotic frenzy of those who waved the flag or wrapped themselves in it, newspapers reprinted a federal statute prohibiting use of the flag in wearing apparel, bedding or drapery or for advertising purposes, even though the Supreme Court had protected flag *burning*.[20] The California Department of Motor Vehicles recalled the vanity license plate "4 Jihad" until Kareem Jaffer, who owned the car, produced a birth certificate showing that his son's name was Jihad.[21] Desperate about the unfavourable opinion polls two weeks before the November 1992 election, President Bush condemned Governor Clinton for having demonstrated against the Vietnam War while a Rhodes scholar. "Maybe I'm old fashioned, but

to go to a foreign country and demonstrate against your own country when your sons and daughters are dying halfway around the world, I am sorry but I think that is wrong."[22]
Secrecy may be the British disease, but the United States also has a pretty bad case. The CIA is only now thinking about opening classified files more than 30 years old concerning the 1954 Guatemala coup, the 1961 Bay of Pigs invasion, and the 1963 Kennedy assassination.[23] Nations regulate speech by excluding or expelling speakers. For almost 40 years the McCarren Walter Immigration Act denied admission to such notables as Graham Greene and Gabriel Garcia Marquez. Even after repealing that ideological litmus test, the United States sought to deport Khader Hamide, a Palestinian who entered the country legally but incurred disfavour for distributing PLO literature. Britain deported Fred Leuchter, a self-proclaimed American "expert" on prison execution, who denies that the Nazis used cyanide in their gas chambers. The French government expelled Abdelmoumen Diouri after 17 years of legal residence for publishing *Who Owns Morocco?*, an expose of the personal fortune of King Hassan, France's close ally.[24]

Because blatant state regulation of speech often provokes resistance, which sometimes secures judicial protection, more subtle interference may actually be more intrusive. The freedom of government employees varies inversely with their visibility. Assistant Secretary for Health Dr. James O. Mason told the Seventh World Conference on Tobacco and Health that it was "unconscionable for the mighty transnational tobacco companies—and three of them are in the United States—to be peddling their poison abroad, particularly because their main targets are less-developed countries." Although he had cleared the speech with the White House and the Secretary of Health, he was forbidden to testify on the effects of American tobacco exports before the House Subcommittee on Health and the Environment. A Department of Health and Human Services spokesperson said that the opening of new cigarette markets was not a health issue but exclusively "a trade issue." It certainly was a trade issue—cigarettes earned a $4.2 billion surplus in 1989.[25] The Census Bureau fired Beth Osborne Daponte for estimating that 13,000 Iraqi civilians died in the Gulf war, more than twice the official figure. Although it charged her with insubordination, she had consulted three levels of bureaucracy and released the data only when the Bureau refused to do so. Under threat of litigation the Bureau reinstated her and retracted its calumny that the number was "a deliberate falsification."[26]

In its role as publisher, government also controls private speakers. *Taking Care of Your Child: A Parent's Guide to Medical Care*, which had sold a million copies, was distributed free to 275,000 federal employees but only after the deletion of six pages about contraception and adolescent sexuality, including such "controversial" passages as this:

> While a variety of techniques prevent pregnancy, the growing list and seriousness of sexual diseases serves as a reminder that other than abstinence only condoms used in combination with a spermicide can prevent infection. Your adolescent should discuss with his or her doctor the full range of contraceptive/disease prevention options.

Curt Smith, director of the Retirement and Insurance Group of the Office of Personnel Management, justified the cuts: "I wasn't going to allow a book like this to go to homes where some people would be offended. You know, these are issues that alarm people [like Catholics] very quickly. I felt silence would be best."[27]

During J. Edgar Hoover's long directorship, the F.B.I. often sought to limit the circulation and impact of critical books by discouraging bookstores from stocking them and planting unattributed derogatory reviews. Recently the Bureau sought to persuade judges to accept DNA "fingerprinting." When a British scientist testified as an expert witness for the defence, he was interrogated about his visa status, charged with fraudulent billing practices, and ordered to produce all his scientific papers—successfully deterring further courtroom appearances. A prosecutor warned a sceptical University of California professor to get a driver's license because the Oakland jail was not a good place to spend the night. After the prestigious journal *Science* accepted an article criticising DNA identification the editor forced the authors to soften their conclusions and took the highly unusual step of delaying publication until a rebuttal was prepared. While the manuscript was being considered, an official in the Department of Justice Criminal Division Strike Force asked the authors to withdraw it. One of their strongest critics received a $200,000 grant from the Justice Department to study DNA investigation and licensed his method to prosecutors. A government panel subsequently acknowledged concerns about the procedure.[28] Soon after the Gulf war Dr. Theodore A. Postol, professor of national security policy at MIT and former Pentagon science adviser, published a 52-page article in *International Security*, a Harvard peer-reviewed journal, asserting that the Patriot missile had been "almost a total failure." He was promptly investigated by Pentagon officials for revealing secret information. After refusing to meet with them Postol said he was told: "I could not speak about any part of my article in public without being in violation of my secrecy agreement." Although Raytheon, the missile manufacturer, had claimed 100 per cent success, the Army eventually conceded that Patriots had shot down only 70 per cent of Scuds in Saudi Arabia and 40 per cent in Israel.[29] Following the bitterly contested Clarence Thomas confirmation hearings, the special counsel of the Senate Rules Committee subpoenaed the telephone records of *Newsday*'s Timothy Phelps and National Public Radio's Nina Totenberg, suspected of leaking Anita Hill's accusations. Although the Senate withdrew the subpoenas under public pressure, the Reporters Committee for Freedom of the Press reported 100 similar threats in 1991.[30]

Governments retaliate against speech they view as lèse majesté. In his film "Grand Canyon," director Lawrence Kasden depicted the city of Inglewood as a high-crime area, commenting at its release:

[C]ities are supposed to be the hubs of civilization, not war zones. In Los Angeles, we had the fantasy that we could run to our neighborhoods and hide, but that illusion has been dispelled. One wrong turn plants you in enemy territory. There is no safe place any more, no sense of security. "Grand Canyon" is about the fact that we're all interconnected. If people on the bottom suffer, we all do. The world becomes an unlivable place.

In an open letter to Hollywood trade publications and the media the city expressed strong displeasure, threatening to ban all filming until the producers apologised and deleted all references to Inglewood, and to require future directors to agree not to disparage the community. The Inglewood Public Relations Director sought to soften the message: "We're not talking censorship. There's no book burning or movie burning going on. We're educating Hollywood about how movies affect people." Several years earlier New Jersey Supreme Court Chief Justice Robert N. Wilentz, offended by a scene in "The Bonfire of the Vanities" depicting riotous blacks chasing judges down hallways, had prohibited Warner Brothers from shooting it inside the Essex County courthouse. The federal courts rejected the county's challenge for lack of standing.[31]

Although schools may be constitutionally obligated to tolerate some contumely in student newspapers, they still regulate much of what pupils may say.[32] The Oakland, California school board unanimously banned clothing and jewellery denoting gang identification, expensive jogging suits, hats, clothing designating membership of non-school organisations, and t-shirt slogans using profanity, approving drug use or violence, or denigrating people because of race, ethnicity, religion, sex, or sexual preference. For otherwise inarticulate youth obsessed with consumption and immersed in their peer culture, dress may be the most important mode of self-expression. Government denies schools as a venue for meetings expressing unpopular viewpoints. A New York City school board withdrew permission to the "Lost-Found Nation of Islam" to host a speech entitled "Are Jews Hiding the Truth?" Minister Abu Koss disavowed anti-Semitism: "You mean to ask a question is inflammatory?" School board spokesperson James S. Flasto responded to that false naïveté with equal hypocrisy, claiming that the group had misrepresented the meeting as a "self-help" gathering: "They did not tell the truth. And that is grounds for denying a permit." But he also acknowledged the real reason: "We cannot have hate or propaganda of any kind emanating from our schools."[33]

Government wields its enormous economic leverage to discourage speech. The Supreme Court has upheld the gag law forbidding federal grantees from counselling women about abortion. Although the Bush Administration purported to relax this in March 1992 by allowing doctors to give "complete medical information," it knew that few patients see doctors, who still could not refer them to abortion clinics.[34] Government also enforces contracts in which private parties buy silence. Defendants often settle tort claims with payments binding plantiffs to secrecy. The risks associated with silicon gel breast implants, for instance, were documented in a 1984 lawsuit whose record was sealed. Hundreds of thousands of women suffered disastrous consequences for another eight years before the Food and Drug Administration took action. Heart valve implant recipients who sued the manufacturer were prevented from disclosing information about defects. Private employees, like their public counterparts, may be sworn to secrecy. Management in Arista and BMG record companies could not reveal that Robert Pilatus and Fab Morvan lip-synched "Girl You Know It's True" on the 1988 album that sold millions and won them a Grammy. Other contracts can constrain speech. Paul Yule's "Damned in the USA," a British television programme about American cultural censorship, was banned in USA for months because a fundamentalist minister claimed that his participation had been conditioned on a promise that it not be rebroadcast.[35] Even divorce can seal lips. As part of her $22 million settlement with Donald Trump, Ivana agreed never to talk about the marriage. When the New York courts upheld this clause, Donald's lawyer explained: "The judges are saying that this is not a freedom of speech case. Mrs. Trump, for a price, waived her right of free speech when she voluntarily accepted money in consideration for surrendering that right." Donald planned to sue Ivana for breaking this contract by publishing her novel *For Love Alone*, which features a Czechoslovak professional skier like Ivana married to an American tycoon like Donald, whose affair with a younger actress leads to a messy divorce.[36]

That the United States, with its strong First Amendment tradition, constrains speech in so many ways does not prove the inevitability of regulation. But it certainly discourages hope in attaining the civil libertarian vision.

## IV. The Impossibility of State Neutrality

Some civil libertarians argue that what the state may not do directly through regulation it should not do indirectly. When the state speaks or finances speech it must be strictly neutral, neither amplifying some voices nor silencing others. It is equally impossible to depoliticise this role, however. Government officials have little hesitation in discouraging or discrediting critics. During the Gulf War, British Foreign Secretary Douglas Hurd expressed "a good deal of concern" about reporting from Baghdad and voiced the "strong feeling in the country" that television favoured Iraq in describing the American bomb that killed 400 civilians in a shelter. House of Commons Leader John MacGregor said the government had made representations to the networks. American officials are no more reticent. When Business Roundtable chief executives discussed proposed civil rights legislation with minority groups, they were told to break off negotiations by White House Chief of Staff John Sununu and White House Counsel C. Boyden Gray. White House Press Secretary Marlin Fitzwater equivocated. This was just "part of the kind of backstage wrangling that goes along with legislation. Anybody can talk to anybody." But the government, of course, is not just anybody, and it was telling people not to talk.[37]

The government's burgeoning role in financing speech is equally partisan and even more controversial. Public schools and libraries constantly make decisions about using and lending books, under pressure from fiercely opinionated constituencies.[38] The Duval County, Florida schools banned or restricted 60 books, including *Snow White*, Shel Silverstein's humour, and Nikki Giovanni's poetry. The Traditional Values Coalition forced California to delete from science textbooks passages asserting: "There is no scientific dispute that evolution has occurred and continues to occur; this is why evolution is regarded as a scientific fact." "These sequences show that life has continually diversified through time, as older species have been replaced by newer ones." After the Sandinistas were voted out of power, the new American-backed Nicaraguan government planned to destroy four million schoolbooks donated by Norway because of their allegedly leftist views. Mexico's first revision of its history textbook in 20 years eliminated laudatory descriptions of Emiliano Zapata, Fidel Castro, and Salvador Allende while rehabilitating Porfirio Diaz, whose 30-year dictatorship seems to be a model for President Salinas de Gortari.[39]

The State inevitably favours some voices over others in the allocation of radio and television frequencies to private companies, programming by public stations, museum exhibits, celebrations and ceremonies, and of course the appointment of officials—most visibly judges. Legal aid schemes constrain lawyers' clients, substantive areas, and strategies. American legal services lawyers cannot represent tort victims, draft resisters, women seeking abortions, voter registration or desegregation campaigns, or the "voluntary" poor.[40] The charitable deduction in tax codes directs money to some speakers and away from others. The notorious Clause 28 of the Local Government Act 1988 prohibited local authorities from "promoting" homosexuality, publishing such promotion, or promoting "the teaching . . . of the acceptability of homosexuality as a pretended family relationship."[41]

As science has become heavily dependent on government support, politics increasingly shapes the research agenda. The National Institute of Child Health and Human Development withdrew approval of a study of sexual behaviour by Edward Laumann, dean of social science at the University of Chicago, because it would be "political suicide." The Senate transferred $10 million from the first comprehensive surveys of adolescent and adult sexual behaviour to the Adolescent Family Life Program, which sponsor Senator Jesse Helms (R-NC) described as "the only federally funded sex-education program that counsels our children to abstain from having sexual relations until they are married." He denounced as prurient the defunded study's questions about homosexual behaviour. Their real purpose was "not to stop the spread of AIDS . . . [but] to compile supposedly scientific and Government-sanctioned statistics supporting ultra-liberal arguments that homosexuality is normal behavior." The National Institutes of Health cancelled a conference on "Genetic Factors in Crime" after objections by the Congressional Black Caucus.[42]

Because artistic taste is strongly associated with status groups, government support is a hotly contested terrain. Shortly after its launch in the 1960s, the National Endowment for the Arts became embroiled in a three-week furor because it had funded an improvisation for Baltimore schoolchildren, which used the word "bullshit."[43] Two decades later, perhaps hoping that a lawyer would avoid such flaps, George Bush appointed John E. Frohnmayer to head the NEA. One of his first acts was to suspend a $10,000 grant to "Witnesses: Against Our Vanishing," a New York exhibition about AIDS, because the catalogue contained an essay by AIDS-victim David Wojnarowicz criticising Rep. William E. Dannemeyer (R-Calif) and Sen. Jesse Helms, among others. Frohnmayer's justification revealed the incoherence of any aspiration to neutrality.

> I think it's essential that we remove politics from grants and must do so if the endowment is to remain credible to the American people and to Congress. Obviously, there are lots of great works of art that are political. Picasso's Guernica and the plays of Bertholt Brecht are strongly political. But the question is, Should the endowment be funding art whose primary intent is political? . . . The catalogue to this show is a very angry protest against the specific events and individuals involved over the last eight months in the most recent arts legislation in Congress [which prohibited the Endowment from funding "materials considered obscene, including sadomasochism, homoeroticism, the sexual exploitation of children, or individuals engaged in sex acts"]. It's very inflammatory.

Helms, who had sponsored the restrictive legislation, "was much more pleased by this than he was by the N.E.A.'s reaction under the former acting chairman to the Mapplethorpe exhibition." Dannemeyer, who contended that homosexuality was curable acquired behaviour, commended Frohnmayer "for doing what I think Congress told him to do." Within three years, however, Bush fired Frohnmayer, fearing that Republican presidential candidate Patrick

Buchanan was gaining too much political advantage by criticising the NEA. Frohnmayer's valedictory compared this "Frankenstein monster's" "shameless" attacks to the Nazi exhibit of "Entartete Kunst" (Degenerate Art): "A sign on the wall of that show said: 'Your tax money goes to support this filth.' That could come from the Congressional Record, my friends."[44]

Politics infects other government-supported expression.[45] Lynne Cheney, the conservative chair of the National Endowment for the Humanities, overruled several grant recommendations at each quarterly meeting of her national advisory council. To avoid this embarrassment, President Bush sought to pack the council with conservatives, such as University of Pennsylvania history professor Alan C. Kors, who compared his institution to Beijing University and urged fellow members of the conservative National Association of Scholars to transform universities into "the monasteries of the Dark Ages, preserving what is worth preserving amid the barbaric ravages in the countrysides and towns of academe."[46] Several senators sought to block funding for the Corporation for Public Broadcasting. Conrad Burns (R-Mont) was angry at "The Range Wars" for criticising grazing on public lands: "my constituency, which is a lot of cattlemen and sheepmen, absolutely went through the roof." John McCain (R-Az) attacked "Maria's Story" for "glorifying the life of a F.M.L.N. guerrilla in El Salvador." Jesse Helms lambasted "Tongues Untied" for portraying "homosexual men dancing around naked" and "blatantly promot[ing] homosexuality as an acceptable life style." Minority leader Robert Dole (R-Kan) summarised their fury: "I have never been more turned off and more fed up with the increasing lack of balance and unrelenting liberal cheerleading I see and hear on the public airwaves."[47]

Neutrality is unattainable. Indeed, no one wants it. All speakers, whether employed or supported by government, are expressing their partisan positions. Balance is a chimera; every mixture of views favours some over others.

## V. The Illusion of Private Freedom

Civil libertarians oppose state regulation and partisanship because they see it as the primary source of constraint. Once that is removed, private expression will again become a realm of authentic freedom. The implicit image of free speech is the colonial New England town meeting or Hyde Park's speakers' corner. In these mythic or marginal environments everyone has equal opportunity to speak, and each voice carries equal weight with the attentive unbiased audience. This section questions those assumptions, arguing that state action constructs the value of speech, state withdrawal exposes speech to powerful market forces, and private action is the greatest constraint on speech.

A. The State Valorises Speech

The "marketplace of ideas" in which Oliver Wendell Holmes urged that a proposition's truth be tested is no more free than any other "free market."[48] Politics constructs all markets; the state defines every right to property, including intellectual property. In an era of mass consumption, such rights can be incredibly valuable. During a recent two-year period, the pop group New Kids earned $115 million from their music. In 1992 Madonna signed a seven-year deal with Time Warner worth $60 million, similar to the one Michael Jackson had concluded with Sony a year earlier; Barbra Streisand had to make do with $40 million. Time Warner was not giving anything away; during the previous decade Madonna had generated gross revenues of $1.2 billion. Prince sought to top both rivals by valuing his contract with Warner Bros. Records at $100 million. But all this was petty cash to the software industry, where Apple Computer Inc. is suing Microsoft Corp. for $5.5 billion, alleging copyright infringement.[49]

Because habituation leads us to see property as a natural attribute rather than a political artefact, some marginal examples may usefully highlight its contingency. McDonald's Dutch subsidiary settled a $2.7 million claim by Paul Bocuse for an advertisement picturing the chef preparing chicken, on which was superimposed a bubble showing him thinking "Big Mac."[50] McDonald's is no less possessive of its carefully cultivated image. Claiming to have created a "McLanguage" by naming more than 75 products, it has sued La Capoterie for selling McCondoms, using a stylised yellow M as the logo.[51] Several American universities have commenced legal action against entrepreneurs selling notes taken without the lecturer's permission.[52] In order to promote its paper nappies and soap powder, Proctor & Gamble leased the panda logo from the World Wide Fund for Nature for £300,000 and the image of a mother cradling an infant from The National Childbirth Trust for £250,000.[53]

The state defines the rights of creative and performing artists. When Jeff Koons sculpted a "String of Puppies" to parody Art

Rogers's famous kitsch postcard of a couple with eight German shepherds, the judge found copyright infringement, angrily dismissing Koons's boast that "it was only a postcard photo and I gave it spirituality, animation and took it to another vocabulary."[54] Art Buchwald's successful suit against Eddie Murphy and Paramount Pictures for stealing the concept for "Coming to America" was only the latest in a series of Hollywood tiffs stretching back at least to Orson Welles's "Citizen Kane."[55] Courts are beginning to protect more subtle forms of creativity. Six years after the Beatles won a $10 million judgment against Beatlemania Inc. for a stage show and movie featuring four impersonators, Bette Midler won $400,000 against Young & Rubicam for hiring her former backup singer to imitate her style in a television commercial for Lincoln-Mercury cars.[56] Because rap music incorporates sound-bytes from other recordings, copyright owners have begun to sue for infringement.[57] Discovery as well as creation can confer rights: the full text of the Dead Sea Scrolls was withheld from the public for 45 years.[58] British libraries pay authors each time their books are borrowed; California artists earn royalties whenever their work is resold. Some cinéastes argued that directors should be able to veto "colourisation" of their black-and-white films. Technological advances constantly compel the state to redefine property rights: photography, lithography, computer software, genetically engineered plants and animals, records, analog and now digital casettes, compact disks, and video recorders.[59] State action can deny speakers the right to market their words. The "Son of Sam" law (named after a New York mass murderer), which prohibits criminals from selling their stories, has been applied to such famous convicts as Jean Harris (who murdered Dr. Herman Tarnower, author of the Scarsdale diet), Sidney Biddle Barrows (the "Mayflower Madam"), and Jack Henry Adam (the recidivist murderer and Norman Mailer protégé). After the law was invalidated in a case brought by Henry Hill, a mafioso who earned $96,000 for the story Nicholas Pileggi turned into "Wiseguy," New York Governor Mario Cuomo backed an amended version he hoped would withstand constitutional scrutiny.[60]

My purpose is not to criticise these rules but merely to demonstrate that the state inevitably encourages and discourages expression by conferring or withholding property rights.

## B. Has the Fall of Communism "Freed" Speech?

If the state is inherently oppressive and civil society the domain of freedom, as liberal theory posits, the demise of communism should have liberated speech in the former eastern bloc. In fact, however, the transition toward capitalism is replacing "Big Brother" with market forces whose burden may be less visible but remains onerous. *Pravda*, which boasted that it had been closed fourteen times— nine by the Czar, four by the Provisional Government, and most recently in August 1991 for supporting the coup—suspended publication in March 1992 because circulation had fallen 99 per cent from 1987, newsprint prices had increased twenty-fold, and annual subscription fees defrayed the costs of only the first 20 issues. *Izvestia* survived by carrying more advertising, renting or selling its extensive real estate, and launching *We-My*, a Russian-English paper published jointly with the virulently anti-communist Hearst Corporation.[61] The 10,000 members of the Soviet Writers Union, who had lived well under communism, now scrape by on state pensions of 600 rubles a month and risible royalties of 400 rubles per 24 pages. Although private publishers pay more, they want only detective stories, science fiction, and sex manuals. Even under Gorbachev's glasnost the pornography market had grown to an estimated 15 billion rubles by early 1991 (before the ruble collapsed). The writers' group *Aprel* complained: "The market threatens to become the grave of culture. Privatization of culture is above all privatization of the soul." The most unlikely authors suddenly earned big bucks. Col. Anatoly P. Privalov, vice-chairman of the Foreign Intelligence Veterans Association and former KGB operative in Turkey and Algeria, was negotiating with Hollywood to spill his members' secrets.[62]

C. The Ambiguous Value of Commodified Speech
If laissez-faire capitalism maximised freedom, then speech that bore the largest price tag would command most respect. Instead we find deep ambivalence toward commodified speech.[63] The claim to truth can be fatally compromised by the acceptance of money. Laypeople everywhere distrust and despise lawyers as hired guns, mouthpieces for sale to the highest bidder.[64] Governments require lobbyists to register and elected officials to declare their interests. Eyebrows were raised when 47 MPs with investments in brewing persuaded Lord Young, the Trade Secretary, to reverse his approval of the Monopolies Commission recommendation that breweries sell their pubs. That year the Brewers' Society contributed nearly £250,000 to the Conservative Party. Large donations from business sources can embarrass political parties, as the Tories discovered during the run-up to the last general election when newspapers

disclosed contributions of £2.5 million from a Greek shipping magnate, £100,000 from a Hong Kong entrepreneur interested in developing the new airport, £1m from a golf partner of Sir Denis Thatcher, and £1.5m from the founder of financially troubled Polly Peck.[65] In California, slate mailers that guide voters in casting their long complicated ballots sell their endorsements, earning Voter Guide $3.6 million in 1990. The Republican Vote by Mail Project accepted $20,000 to support the Democratic candidate for Attorney General, who blithely brushed off criticism: "It's known as a free press."[66] Of course, it was just the opposite.

Because science enjoys a far higher reputation for candour than does politics, the taint of money is even more damaging. The Princeton Dental Resource Center (no relation to the university) distributes a free newsletter to hundreds of dentists without mentioning that 90 percent of its costs are paid by a $1 million annual subsidy from M&M/Mars. The candy manufacturer was not named, said the editors, for fear of discouraging other donors. A recent issue cited scientific evidence that chocolate is as good for teeth as apples, concluding: "So the next time you snack on your favorite chocolate bar or bowl of peanuts, remember—if enjoyed in moderation they can be good-tasting and might even inhibit cavities." UCLA researcher Dr. Lawrence Wolinsky complained that the article grossly misrepresented his findings. Even Dr. Shelby Kashket, whose research was supported by Mars, objected when the editors interpreted him as suggesting that "sticky" snacks like chocolate and caramel dissolve out of the mouth faster than starchy foods like crackers and crisps.[67] The Tobacco Institute may have significantly tarnished scientists' claims to impartiality by paying them to keep denying any link between cigarettes and illness.[68] Lawyers delight in discrediting expert witnesses by asking how much they are paid and how often they testify for the opposing side. Those of us who consult reviews in choosing movies will be dismayed to learn that the reviewer may have rewritten the screenplay, advised the studio on marketing, have his own "treatment" sitting on the desk of the producer whose movie is under review, or produce a favourable blurb in order to be quoted in an advertisement, like the following rave a studio solicited for "Joseph Andrews": "Painted as a china figurine, glazed as a cherry donut, Ann-Margret as the aptly named Lady Booby adds a new dimension to an overcrowded gallery of well-etched portraits."[69] Payment does not free speech; it turns speakers into whores.[70]

D. The Unfree Market

If Milton Friedman is right that there is no free lunch, there can be no free speech either. As societies are massified and audiences expand, the cost of speech inevitably increases and intermediaries proliferate between speaker and audience, each with distinctive incentives and powers to shape what is said and heard.

Book publishers decide which manuscripts to accept; form contracts dictate terms to all but best-selling authors; editors "suggest" changes; and marketing departments decide price, distribution, and promotion.[71] Sometimes publishers go further. When Penguin issued a translation of *Massacre* by Sine, a well-known French cartoonist, English booksellers complained about its irreverence to Allen Lane, who had recently resigned as Penguin's director. That night he drove to the Harmondsworth warehouse with four accomplices, filled a trailer with the remaining stock, and burnt it. The next day Penguin reported the book out of print.[72] The Japanese publisher Hayakawa withdrew a translation of *The Engima of Japanese Power* because the Dutch author had written that the Burakumin Liberation League "has developed a method of self-assertion through 'denunciation' sessions with people and organizations it decides are guilty of discrimination."[73] Anticipating feminist criticism, Simon & Schuster cancelled publication of Bret Easton Ellis's *American Psycho* a month before it was to appear. When Random House brought out the book, the Los Angeles branch of the National Organization of Women urged a boycott, describing it as "a how-to novel on the torture and dismemberment of women" and offering a telephone reading of a passage about a woman raped and tortured with an automatic nailgun.[74]

Although booksellers' preoccupation with maximising profit has intensified as massive chains have displaced independents, ideology also affects decisions about inventory and display.[75] The London bookstore Gays the Word refused to carry the Marquis de Sade's *Juliette* or Bret Ellis's *American Psycho*. Some feminist bookstores bar men from displays of lesbian erotica. Many mainstream bookstores reverse these biases, excluding gay and lesbian literature. Waterstone's, Britain's second largest chain, also declined to stock Jeremy Pascall's *God: The Ultimate Autobiography*.[76] Prizes and reviews catapult a handful of books to instant fame while consigning most to obscurity. The Caldecott Medal (for American children's literature) virtually assures 100,000 sales in the first year and strong backlist performance. The National Book Award, the Pulitzer Prize, and the Booker Prize increase sales two or threefold. Some prizes

*The Illusion of Private Freedom*

simply amplify market forces. In 1991 the American Booksellers created a Book of the Year award for the volume they most enjoyed selling. The first "Abby" went to *The Education of Little Tree*, the purported memoir of an Indian orphan, which remained a best-seller even after its author was unmasked as a white racist.[77]

The production and dissemination of scholarship is supposed to be insulated from commercial or ideological considerations. After more than 20 years of writing for leading scientific journals Forrest M. Mims 3d applied to write the "Amateur Scientist" column of *Scientific American*, submitting good trial columns and impressive proposals for future projects. At the interview, however, Mims revealed that he was a creationist and opposed abortion. Armand Schwab, who soon thereafter retired as managing editor, attributed Mims's rejection to the fear that "*Scientific American* might inadvertently put an imprimatur on 'creation science,'" jeopardising the journal's credibility with biologists. Associate editor Tim Appenzeller conceded that Mims would have been hired had his religious beliefs not emerged. Mims was understandably aggrieved: "I have never, ever written about creationism . . . I'm willing to dialogue. But I'm not going to deny my faith. . . . I even told them I could be their token Christian, but they didn't smile at that."[78] After three years as general editor of the Dead Sea Scrolls, Harvard Divinity School Professor John Strugnell was removed "for ill health" when the Israeli newspaper *Haaretz* quoted him as saying that Judaism was "originally racist" and "not a higher religion." Israel was "founded on a lie, or at least on a premise that cannot be sustained." Judaism was "a horrible religion. It's a Christian heresy . . . . You are a phenomenon that we haven't managed to convert—and we should have managed."[79] Money buys scholars the means and time to research and write (and sometimes subsidises publication). In 1991 the conservative John M. Olin Foundation gave $12 million to support law and economics, the American Enterprise Institute, right-wing authors like Dinesh D'Souza, Harold Bloom, Linda Chavez, and Carol Iannone, and ex-politicians like William J. Bennett.[80]

A fundamental argument against state regulation of speech is the indispensability of an informed electorate to a democratic polity. But the market guarantees neither quantity nor quality in news reporting. Between 1975 and 1986 American network newscasts devoted 37 per cent less time to domestic policy issues and 50 per cent more to human interest stories. Most stations cut their news budgets 20–25 per cent between 1988 and 1990. The networks allocated only four hours to the four-day 1992 Democratic National Convention. Some stations even refuse political advertisements. KFI-AM, the fifth largest radio station in Southern California, has done so because the FCC requires broadcasters to charge their lowest rate. All-news station KNX-AM, the third largest in the region, has rejected commercials for state legislators and judges, who cannot otherwise reach their local constituencies.[81]

Although the American media, unlike the British, simulates neutrality, greed quickly strips away this mask. The Gulf war coincided with the ratings sweeps, whose audience estimates determine future advertising revenue. After viewers wrote and telephoned KABC-TV in Los Angeles to denounce its coverage of anti-war protests the station adopted a policy of ignoring the demonstrations. Universities use their subsidy of student newspapers to control tone and content.[82] The media decide how much attention to devote to candidates.[83] Just as *Pravda* compared market forces to Czarist repression, so Jerry Brown Americanised the metaphor when his 1992 campaign for the Democratic presidential nomination foundered: "We actually have a media and a party hierarchy that wants to shut down democratic debate. It reminds me of the Bolsheviks in Russia . . . . [They] would like to have one name on the ballot."

Even if the media impartially reported news and accepted political advertising, electoral competition would reflect differences in market power. Just as lawyers' clients get as much justice as they can afford, so politicians get only that much publicity. Unable to pay network prices, Jerry Brown had to make do with $200 an hour public-access cable television. Another outsider, Ross Perot, could threaten to spend "whatever it takes" to win—although his business instincts convinced him to turn off the spigot in July at $10 million.[84] Three weeks before the November 1990 election Congressional incumbents had outspent challengers $214.8 million to $60 million and had twenty times as much left for the campaign's crucial last days. 96 per cent of House incumbents were re-elected (having outspent challengers 9:1) as were all incumbent Senators but one (having outspent challengers 3:1). California initiative battles displayed similar disparities that year: industry spent nearly five times as much as public interest groups. The liquor lobby alone threw $28 million into a battle against a tax that would finance health research and education. Two years earlier the insurance industry had lavished $75 million on resisting premium reductions.[85]

As audiences for mass entertainment grow, entrepreneurial efforts to anticipate and shape consumer preferences increasingly override creative independence. Film studios decide which treatments to turn into screenplays, who will write, direct, and act, and how much to spend on production and promotion. The lessons of commercial failure are illustrated by "Radio Flyer," a 1992 flop costing $40–45 million. A despondent executive kvetched:

> Even if this film worked, how do you get an audience? If you tell an audience it's about child abuse, they won't come. So you tell them it's about childhood. So an audience shows up and sees the movie, and they say, "Hey, wait a minute. This is not what we paid seven bucks for. A kid is being beat." They walk out. They feel betrayed. They hate you!

It is not surprising that Hollywood, which invests an average of $38 million per film, tests audience reaction before releasing at least 75 per cent of the top 200 movies each year. According to the Columbia Pictures marketing president: "It's the same thing you do with a product. You sample it: Is it too sweet? Is it too hot?" Ron Howard, who directed the highly successful films "Parenthood" and "Cocoon," starts with a 3–4 hour rough cut and chops it in half on the basis of audience reaction to as many as 16 test screenings. The ending of "Fatal Attraction"—perhaps the most profitable movie ever made—was changed after negative test screenings.[86]

Non-economic considerations also shape film content. Tristar and Columbia Pictures were collaborating on "Hell Camp," a movie about sumo wrestlers, which Milos Forman had agreed to direct. After Sony bought Columbia it cancelled the project, claiming it could not get the Sumo Association to cooperate. When Matsushita bought Universal Pictures it had the studio substantially rewrite the script for "Mr. Baseball," about a boorish American joining a Japanese team, to make it more sympathetic to Japan.[87] The industry collectively shapes content through its rating system. Fearing that a ban on children under 17 would exclude "Basic Instinct" from some theatres, the producers wanted to cut the objectionable scenes. Director Paul Verhoeven and actor Michael Douglas resisted, convinced that the sex and violence would attract publicity and thus viewers. The studio won, although Verhoeven maintained he had only "replaced things from different angles, made it a little more elliptical, a bit less direct." At the same time, he dismissed protests by gays and lesbians about the bisexual murder suspect, who seduces women and men, keeps ice picks around the house, and writes books about fictional murders resembling the movie's events.[88]

55

Advertising strongly influences all media that sell it.[89] American tobacco companies spent $585 million on advertising in 1990, mostly in magazines and newspapers (because they are barred from television). American magazines were 40 per cent more likely to publish news articles about the dangers of smoking if they refused cigarette ads; women's magazines were twice as likely; indeed, six women's magazines that took tobacco money published no feature articles about smoking and health between 1982 and 1986.[90] *Financial World*, a journal with half a million subscribers, hired UC Berkeley Professor Graef S. Crystal in 1991 to write a column on executive remuneration. When advertising pages dropped 30 per cent in the next four months it quickly fired him. Editor Geoffrey N. Smith explained:

> I have tremendous respect for [Crystal] as an academician, He's the foremost authority in that field, but you know it's just pretty incendiary stuff. . . . [I]f you're a C.E.O. and it's your picture featured in that column . . . you don't always like it. Some of them have spoken to their lawyers. It's just been quite controversial.

Crystal noted that he had written a similar column for *Fortune* magazine until forced to retract his criticism that executives at Time Warner Inc, *Fortune's* parent, were overpaid. He concluded bitterly: "I can't find a niche in any American magazine that has advertising . . . ."[91]

Because television requires large audiences to generate the advertising revenue necessary to defray its high production costs, networks are wary of offending viewers. Each maintains a standards division, whose 60 employees examine every script and video.[92] After "L.A. Law" introduced a lesbian character who kissed another woman the producers quickly transformed her into a less threatening bisexual. A "Quantum Leap" script about a gay teenage naval cadet who committed suicide after being beaten by student vigilantes was rewritten to make the character older and have him saved from the beating and suicide. Even so, sponsor withdrawals cost the network $150,000. ABC earlier had lost $1.5 million when advertisers backed away from a "thirtysomething" episode showing two gay men in bed, and NBC had suffered pullouts from its movie about the Supreme Court's abortion decision. Although Dan Quayle has sought political capital by maligning the eponymous hero of "Murphy Brown" for choosing to have a baby alone, executive producer Diane English saw that as the less controversial decision. Had

Murphy had an abortion "it would have been lights out." A Saatchi & Saatchi executive was unashamed about advertiser influence: "When we use TV, we're not using it to support First Amendment rights or artistic freedoms, we're using it because it's a good business decision for our client . . . ."[93]

Advertiser anxiety can affect the marketability (and thus the commercial speech) of celebrities. After Earvin "Magic" Johnson disclosed he had AIDS, Pepsi, Nestlé, Spalding, and Kentucky Fried Chicken shunned him like the plague. A spokesperson for Target Stores squirmed: "It's a real predicament; because of his situation are we obliged to work with him forever?" (an unfortunate phrasing given his dramatically shortened life expectancy). Pepsi equivocated: "As a major advertiser, we need to rethink how to position Magic in a way that's right for him and right for us." A New York expert on celebrity advertising was more candid: "I don't think [Magic] has a future in advertising new products. Advertisers don't want to be associated with negatives. And this is a very solemn negative. He might die." Nine months later, however, when Johnson signed a $14.6 million contract with the Lakers for 1994/95—the largest single season deal in team sports—Pepsi revived its "We Believe in Magic" campaign, and athletic shoe manufacturers plotted to lure him away from Converse. The publisher of *Sporting Goods Intelligence* opined: "Reebok is the best bet. They're into all that stuff like social responsibility and Amnesty International. They could really get behind this AIDS thing and run with it."[94]

Some audiences confront speakers without waiting for intermediaries to interpret their views. We have seen feminists denounce pornography, Jews and anti-racists oppose neo-Nazis, and Muslims seek to silence Rushdie. The Province of St. Joseph of the Capuchin Order in Milwaukee bought stock in media and tobacco companies in order to attack cigarette advertising at shareholder meetings. It forced Philip Morris to extend the mandatory American warnings to cigarettes sold abroad. Gannett, which owns the largest American billboard company and earned 15 per cent of its annual $1.5 billion revenues from tobacco, insisted that cigarettes were "integral to the success of outdoor advertising companies" and that "the company is acting in a socially responsible manner . . . ."[95] Angered by a Cuban-American television commentator who blamed Puerto Rican poverty on the "thousands of single mothers, very young, who try to escape . . . through welfare or through new partners who then leave, and leave behind other children to worsen the problem," Puerto Rican groups in New Jersey persuaded advertisers to boycott

the station, which quickly terminated the talk-show.[96] Furious that
*The Miami Herald* was "soft" on Castro, the Cuban American
National Foundation attacked it in bus and billboard ads and
Spanish-language radio spots. The paper's executives received contemporaneous death threats, the newspaper suffered a bomb scare
and veiled boycott warnings, and vending boxes were vandalised
with paint, glue, and faeces.[97] Hostile audiences can even put
words in a recalcitrant speaker's mouth. When every house on his
Culver City (Los Angeles) block sported yellow ribbons to support
American troops in the Persian Gulf, Steve Raikin defiantly displayed
a peace sign. In the nights that followed two ribbons were tied on his
tree, one was painted on, and his car was spattered with yellow
paint. When he called the police, they asked why he did not simply
conform.[98]

I am neither endorsing nor condoning the myriad ways in which
private actions regulate speech but merely seeking to demonstrate
that such interference is pervasive and profound. Audiences
influence what speakers say, speakers limit what audiences hear,
and intermediaries do both in pursuit of their own ends. A civil
libertarian utopia without state regulation would be a world of
constraint, not freedom. Each instance of private power must be
evaluated by criteria that are substantive, not formal.[99]

## VI. The Burden of Choice

By obsessing about the power of state officials to constrain speech,
civil libertarian theory paralyses them. By disregarding the power of
private actors, civil libertarian theory fails to hold them accountable.
This vision of state abstention and neutrality joined to private
irresponsibility is fatally impoverished.[1] Just as public actors cannot
avoid regulation and partisanship, so private actors cannot avoid
power. Both must shoulder the burden of choice.

### Notes

[1] Holmes (1897; 1918); Popper (1969); Meiklejohn (1948; 1965); Emerson
(1970); Unger (1975); Schauer (1982); Ingber (1984); Baker (1989; n.d.);
Garry (1990); Smolla (1992). For an English debate, including the absolutist position, see Commission for Racial Equality (1988). For a comparison
of approaches in Canada and the United States, see Borovoy et al. (1988/
89). For a comprehensive world-wide survey, see Coliver (1992).

[2] Matsuda (1989); Bell (1987); Lawrence (1990); Delgado (1982); Williams (1991). Simon Lee acknowledges this inspiration in his recent book (1990).

[3] *In re the Welfare of R.A.V.*, 464 N.W.2d 507 (Minn. 1991), rev'd sub nom. *R.A.V.* v. *St. Paul*, 120 L.Ed. 2d 305 (1992); *New York Times* s.1 p.1 (December 1, 1991), B19 (December 5, 1991), A1, A10 (June 23, 1992). The Fairfax County (Virginia) School Board defied the Court by adding sexual orientation to its decade-old prohibition of hate speech in schools based on gender, race and ethnicity. The executive director of the National School Boards Association declared: "I don't think a judge in his right mind would find this unconstitutional. It is to prevent people from hurting others emotionally, and that is it." *New York Times* A7 (July 27, 1992).

[4] *Iota Xi Chapter of Sigma Chi Fraternity* v. *George Mason University* (E.D. Va. 91–785-A); *The UMW Post, Inc. et al.* v. *Board of Regents of the University of Wisconsin System* (E.D. Wis. 90-C-328); *New York Times* A12 (August 29, 1991); *Chronicle of Higher Education* A1 (October 23, 1991).

[5] *New York Times* A10 (September 14, 1992).

[6] A jury acquitted them for their live performance; a federal appeals court reversed the conviction based on the recording, finding it not without serious artistic value. A record store was appealing a $1000 fine for selling the album. *Los Angeles Times* A28 (May 8, 1992).

Although UCLA Law Professor Kimberle Crenshaw (1991), also African American, criticised the racism of a legal system that tolerated similar language by whites like television "humourist" Andrew Dice Clay, she condemned the lyrics as misogynist. Whether the song was intended, or heard by some, as humourous, it remained profoundly sexist.

[7] *Guardian* 2 (November 8, 1991).

[8] *New York Times* s.2 p.25 (April 22, 1990), 6 (January 11, 1992). In "Black Korea," rapper Ice Cube sang: "Oriental one-penny countin' mother-fuckers. . ./So pay respect to the black fist/Or we'll burn down your stores right to a crisp." This was his response to a March 1991 incident in which Soon Ja Du shot to death Latasha Harlins, a 15-year-old black girl she accused of stealing a $1.79 bottle of orange juice. In "Death Certificate" Ice Cube "commanded" N.W.A. (with which he had previously sung) to kill their Jewish manager: "Get rid of that devil, real simple/Put a bullet in his temple/'Cause you can't be a nigger for life crew/With a white Jew tellin' you what to do." Csathy (1992).

The furor over "Cop Killer" (described in chapter three) has sensitised record companies, several of which have established informal "lyric review committees." Two days after rapper Ice-T withdrew that record, Tommy Boy Records (owned by Time Warner, which produced "Cop Killer") ended their contract with rappers Almighty RSO after police organisations criticised the group's "One in the Chamber," and Time

59

Warner reexamined plans to release new albums by Ice-T, Juvenile Committee, and Apache. At the same time, MCA Music Entertainment Group withdrew FU2's "No Head, No Backstage Pass," about a sexual assault on a young female fan. Two months earlier women employees had refused to work on the project. A month after that men joined the revolt when marketing executives would only agree to delete the corporate name from the record. MCA Records president Richard Palmese allowed the men to withdraw as well but refused to pull the record, deferring to MCA Records Black Music president Ernie Singleton, who said: "I can see why women are upset. I wouldn't play this single for my wife or my kids, but I firmly believe in our Constitution and I think a black artist has a First Amendment right to express his own experience." The women persisted, sending the lyrics anonymously to chairman Lew Wasserman and president Sidney Sheinberg. They included:

. . .I'll drink champagne, she'll drink Ripple
Scream when I put the safety pins through her nipples
I know it sounds harsh, but the bitch is gonna love it
Hurt me, hurt me, push it harder, shove it. . . .

Sheinberg immediately had the record pulled. It was later issued by JDK Records, whose president said: "The lyric was written tongue in cheek. Yeah, it's a little risque. Yeah, it's a little controversial. Because hey, we realize that in this business, controversy sells. But it wasn't meant to offend anyone the least bit." *Los Angeles Times* F1 (August 20, 1992).

Although David Geffen has issued the homophobic, racist misogynist Andrew Dice Clay, he declined Getto Boys' "Mind of a Lunatic." "I've always felt that in issues of language, sex, etc. that everything is O.K. But when it got down to murder it was too much for me." *New York Times* s.2 p.20 (September 6, 1992).

[9] *Independent* 13 (November 8, 1991); *New York Times* s.2 p.13 (January 19, 1992), s.2 p.17 (March 15, 1992). Pornographic performance generally disqualifies an actor or model from other work. Stoller (1991). Even *Playboy* had its standards. "They were very picky about what flesh they exposed. They would never take any women who had already been in a porn movie—especially a hard-core porn movie." Lederer (1980c: 65).

Fashion models have expressed fury when they are photographed topless backstage and the pictures published. Roshumba,who modelled for Calvin Klein, Michael Kors, and Donna Karan, complained: "The minute we start changing, the photographers immediately run over. We hate it, all of us. They are disgusting." *New York Times* B4 (May 4, 1992).

[10] *Los Angeles Times* A27 (January 30, 1992).

[11] *Guardian* 9 (November 7, 1991); *New York Times* A12 (February 21, 1990), D22 (December 11, 1991), D1 (December 12, 1991), A5 (March 13, 1992). Camel's market share climbed 0.4 per cent in May 1992 to 4.5 per cent at a time when almost all other full-price brands were losing ground to discount cigarettes. The company was expanding its Camel

Cash programme by offering a new catalogue of "gifts." *New York Times* C16 (July 29, 1992). A Harvard literature professor offered a persuasive reading of Joe Camel as a phallic symbol. *New York Times* A21 (March 20, 1992) (op ed). Advertising can mislead doctors as well as children. A review by 150 doctors and clinical pharmacists of 109 full-page pharmaceutical advertisements in ten leading medical journals in 1990 found that 44 per cent contained information that could induce doctors to prescribe durgs inappropriately. The acting director of the Food and Drug Administration's Division of Drug Marketing, Advertising and Communications found that about half violated FDA guidelines and 57 per cent had little or no educational value. Drug companies spent $351 million on advertising in medical journals in 1991. Wilkes (1992); *New York Times* A1 (June 1, 1992); *Los Angeles Times* A3 (July 31, 1992) (re-analysis by Public Citizen Health Research Group).

[12] *New York Times* 7 (December 31, 1990).

[13] Matthiessen (1983). The book was reissued nine years later with an afterword describing the litigation. Matthiessen (1991).

[14] *Guardian* 23 (November 7, 1991); *New York Times Book Review* 10 (April 12, 1992). See generally Gillmor (1992).

[15] So far the Supreme Court has struck down state laws protecting the privacy of rape victims. *The Florida Star* v. *B.J.F.*, 491 U.S. 524 (1989).

[16] The distinction between commercial and non-commercial speech, central to contemporary First Amendment jurisprudence, is hopelessly vague. "Informercials" are now invading television—half-hour long talk shows featuring celebrities like Cher, Dione Warwick, and Ali MacGraw pushing products like Aquasentials, Psychic Friends Network, and Beauty Breakthroughs and generating $750 million in sales in 1991. Informercials were made possible when the Reagan Administration abolished the limit of 12 commercial minutes per hour, which the FCC had established in the 1950s. The business now has its own Informercial Marketing Association (to avoid federal regulation) and an annual ceremony to bestow PLAY awards (Program-Length Advertisment of the Year). *New York Times* B2 (October 5, 1992). The American Society of Magazine Editors has adopted guidelines urging the industry to distinguish clearly between advertising and editorial content, expanding those issued in 1982 to govern "advertorials" (special advertising sections). *New York Times* C17 (October 20, 1992).

[17] Federal courts have upheld laws prohibiting begging in subways and transportation terminals. A court recently invalidated New York's ban on street beggers, but the case is on appeal. *New York Times* A14 (October 2, 1992).

Even non-commercial enterprises can be compelled to speak. Under the 1972 Drug Abatement Act a court ordered a man found with less than an ounce of marijuana to post a sign that his house was under court order and could not be used for the sale of illegal drugs. *Los Angeles Times* A3 (July 24, 1992).

[18] *New York Times* A1 (January 19, 1990), A1 (January 20, 1990), s.1 p.4 (February 18, 1990), s.1 p.11 (March 18, 1990), A1 (March 10, 1992); *Los Angeles Times* A23 (February 24, 1990), A4 (March 13, 1992). In Boston and San Francisco, public transportation bans ads for tobacco and liquor; New York just banned tobacco ads. *New York Times* 16 (June 27, 1992). The Minnesota Department of Public Health has launched a $321,000 campaign to discourage women from smoking. A television commercial shows two male ad executives admiring a billboard depicting a young leotard-clad woman smoking. When one exclaims "Women will love it," the billboard model comes alive and stubs out her cigarette on his head. A radio spot has a female voice thank cigarette makers for "your portrayal of us as shallow and superficial. . .for making our hair smell like an ashtray. . .for staining our teeth and increasing our dry-cleaning bills. . .for the 52,000 cases of lung cancer you cause in women each year. We only hope we can return the favor some day." *New York Times* s.1 p.7 (September 6, 1992).

The U.S. Treasury Department persuaded Black Death vodka (targeted at young rock fans) to change its name to Black Hat, and Crazy Horse malt liquor to alter its label so that it did not resemble malt whiskey. In the summer of 1991 Heileman's introduced Power Master malt, targeted at black men, but quickly withdrew it because of objections that the name emphasised its high alcohol content (5.9 per cent). A year later it introduced Colt 45 Premium in a can with the same design and an alcohol content between 5.9 per cent and Colt 45's 4.5 per cent (regular beers are 3.5 per cent). When Dr. Novello condemned all three, the maker of Crazy Horse replied: "A free society requires freedom of choice in many areas, not the least of which is the consumer's right to select products they find attractive or distasteful. They vote with their pocketbooks." *New York Times* C1 (May 12, 1992); *Los Angeles Times* A16 (May 20, 1992).

[19] *New York Times* A32 (December 13, 1991), B2 (December 16, 1991), B3 (December 19, 1991), A16 (January 17, 1992), s.4 p.4 (January 19, 1992), A4 (February 14, 1992), C1 (February 18, 1992), A11 (April 16, 1992). Prosecutors in Nebraska have won convictions against record stores for selling 2 Live Crew's "As Nasty as They Wanna Be" to minors. *Los Angeles Times* F1 (April 23, 1992). Washington State bars sales to minors of records that a judge finds appeal to prurient interests and offend community standards. *New York Times* 7 (June 13, 1992).

Nassau County (Long Island) has banned sales of trading cards depicting "heinous crimes and criminals" to those under 17. The publisher of the "True Crime" series—110 cards of law officers, gangsters, serial killers, and mass murderers—said she sold 8 million in the first week ($1.25 for a package of 12). "They are the biggest selling cards we have ever had. Every state where there has been an attempt to ban them, people have begun calling and asking to open up accounts." *New York Times* B16 (June 16, 1992).

[20] *Texas v. Johnson*, 109 S.Ct. 2533 (1989). On superpatriotism, see Abel (1991). The first Bush ad in the 1992 campaign had to be withdrawn because it used the presidential seal in violation of federal law. *Los Angeles Times* A16 (August 11, 1992). After Rep. Cass Ballenger (R-NC) accused Bill Clinton of lying about the draft and involvement in protests agains the Vietnam war, the Speaker of the House of Representatives extended to presidential and vice-presidential candidates the rule of courtesy that forbids "derogatory, demeaning or insulting" references to the President, Vice President, or Members of Congress. *New York Times* s.1 p.18 (September 27, 1992).

[21] *Los Angeles Times* A11 (January 31, 1991), A9 (February 15, 1991), A3 (February 20, 1991). The California Department of Motor Vehicles screens vanity plate applications for offensive language, but multilingual punsters sometimes fool them.

[22] *New York Times* A1 (October 9, 1992). Criticised for this dramatic contraction of the First Amendment, Bush lashed back: "You let the liberal elite do their number today, trying to call me Joe McCarthy. I'm standing with American principle. It is wrong to demonstrate against your country when your country's at war." *Los Angeles Times* A1 (October 10, 1992).

[23] *Los Angeles Times* A1 (February 22, 1992). A University of California history professor has just won a protracted battle to obtain the 69-page FBI file on John Lennon, which Nixon ordered begun in 1971 in an effort to get him deported. *Los Angeles Times* A3 (June 23, 1992).

[24] *Mail on Sunday* 3 (November 17, 1991); *New York Times* A7 (November 27, 1990), s.1 p.34 (December 8, 1991), s.1 p.9 (March 22, 1992); *New York Times Book Review* 1 (March 29, 1992). Although South Africa has no shortage of native hate mongers, even it expels foreigners, like the English revisionist David Irving. *Weekly Mail* 15 (June 12, 1992). Israel threatened to apply its ban on talking to the PLO to the Palestinian representatives to the current Mid-East peace conference! *Los Angeles Times* A4 (June 20, 1992).

[25] *New York Times* A12 (January 26, 1990), A1 (May 18, 1990). When the Government cannot silence the speaker it withholds information. After Rep. Henry Gonzalez (D-Tex) began investigating the CIA, all executive branches stopped providing him with any information, on instructions from Attorney General William P. Barr. *Los Angeles Times* A23 (August 1, 1992).

[26] *New York Times* 5 (March 7, 1992), 1 (March 28, 1992), A14 (April 13, 1992).

In 1992 the Census Bureau's Assistant Director for Communications (a political appointee) was put on the pre-publication list for all reports. "I don't edit reports," he said "I do ask a lot of questions about press releases." In April a department director told subordinates they could not "give out simple numbers, such as the number of housing units in the U.S." without clearing this with the public information office. Although the Bureau's Director denied this was official policy, she circulated an old Commerce Department memorandum making it more difficult for reporters to gain access to experts. In the run up to the 1992 American election the Census Bureau delayed for months issuing a report showing that the proportion of full-time workers earning less than $12,195 (in constant dollars) declined in the 1960s, remained constant in the 1970s, and then grew from 12.1 per cent to 18 per cent during the 1980s. The head of the Division of Housing and Household Statistics caled this "unusual—indeed, unprecedented." When the report finally appeared, the press release downplayed its significance. *New York Times* A7 (May 12, 1992), 6 (May 23, 1992).

Two lawyers at the Resolution Trust Corporation (charged with selling insolvent savings and loan associations) were demoted when they criticised the RTC for failing to recover money. *New York Times* C1 (August 13, 1992).

FBI agent Jon Lipsky has been forbidden to tell a Congressional committee why no individuals were prosecuted and so few crimes charged for the mammoth environmental pollution at Rockwell International's Rocky Flats nuclear weapons plant in Colorado. *New York Times* s.1 p.15 (September 27, 1992).

27 *New York Times* A6 (April 11, 1992). In July 1991 the Army Times Publishing Co., which produces *Army Times*, *Navy Times* and *Air Force Times* with a combined circulation of more than 200,000, refused an advertisement praising gay soldiers in the Gulf War, insisting there had been none! *New York Times* A15 (August 20, 1992).

28 Robbins (1992); *New York Times* A20 (December 20, 1991), A1 (April 14, 1992), A1 (April 15, 1992).

As Franklin Roosevelt ran for an unprecedented fourth term in 1944 his doctor declared that he was "in splendid shape." When his feeble appearance prompted rumours of high blood pressure his press secretary got the FBI to investigate the doctor suspected of telling the truth. The story was killed and Roosevelt re-elected. He died after three months in office. *New York Times* A19 (April 23, 1992).

Blacklisted by the FBI for refusing to testify before the House Committee on Un-American Activities, Howard Fast was unable to find a publisher for his books. He wrote 20 under pseudonyms, several of which became best sellers and were made into movies. *New York Times* B2 (September 23, 1992).

In 1988 the FBI public affairs officer wrote Priority, the Los Angeles company that produced NWA's album "Straight Outta Compton," to complain that the song "Fuck Tha Police" encouraged violence against law enforcement personnel. *Los Angeles Times* A7 (May 2, 1992).

29 *New York Times* A8 (January 9, 1992), A10 (March 19, 1992), A9 (April 8,

1992). On government manipulation of news during the war, see MacArthur (1992); Miller (1992).

This must have semed like déjà vu to Postol, who had been an expert witness for *The Progressive* magazine in 1979, when the government was trying to stop it from printing an article demonstrating that the untrained laypérson could assemble virtually all the information about how to make a hydrogen bomb. Postol testified that the article "contains no information or ideas that are not already common knowledge among scientists, including those who do not have access to classified information." Hans Bethe, one of the many scientists supporting the government, himself had been prevented from publishing an article on thermonuclear weapons in *Scientific American* in 1950. Although the Atomic Energy Commission conceded that the article contained no secret information, it forced the magazine to capitulate and then supervised the destruction of the entire print run (not yet distributed) and the melting down of the type. Smolla (1992: 266–67).

Four days before the 1988 election federal prisioner Brett Kimberlin scheduled a press conference to disclose that he had sold marijuana to Dan Quayle. The next day he was put in solitary confinement. He was removed the following night when Nina Totenberg threatened to report the incident on National Public Radio, and a telephone news conference was re-scheduled for the day before the election. But moments before it was to begin he was returned to solitary until after the election. He is the only inmate ever known to have been placed in solitary by order of the Bureau of Prisons Director. A report of the Senate's Governmental Affairs Subcommittee confirmed this account; the Inspector General is investigating. *New York Times* s.1 p.15 (May 3, 1992), A23 (June 25, 1992), 1 (October 3, 1992); *Los Angeles Times* A17 (October 3, 1992); Singer (1992).

[30] *New York Times* A1 (February 14, 1992), A9 (March 18, 1992); *Los Angeles Times* A16 (March 17, 1992), A23 (March 26, 1992).

[31] *Los Angeles Times* B1 (February 14, 1992); *New York Times* 34 (January 1, 1992). The Secretary of State for Washington State, running for re-election, sought to prevent the producers of "Body of Evidence" from filming in the State Capitol Building: "the plot is that the character played by Madonna seduces a man to death. . . .the movie is filled with sex and violence. Why should we condone or cater to anything of this kind?" *Los Angeles Times* F1 (April 23, 1992).

[32] Compare *Bright* v. *Los Angeles Unified School District*, 18 Cal.3d 450 (1977) (protecting student speech under state consitution) with *Hazelwood School District* v. *Kuhlmeier*, 484 U.S. 260 (1988) (rejecting protection under federal constitution).

The Orange County (California) High School for the Arts covered up a painting at an exhibition because it portrayed two nude women embracing, with an explanatory statement by the artist, a Catholic senior: "I don't want to go to hell because of loving another woman." After protests

The Poverty of Civil Libertarianism

from gay and lesbian groups both were replaced. *Los Angeles Times* A3 (May 22, 1992), A28 (May 23, 1992).

[33] *New York Times* B2 (December 16, 1991), B3 (December 19, 1991), A13 (January 22, 1992).

[34] *New York Times* A17 (December 9, 1991); *Los Angeles Times* A1 (March 21, 1992).

After a campaign of criticism in which the *Metropolitan News-Enterprise* called Los Angeles Superior Court Presiding Judge Ricardo A. Torres a "despotic twit," a "petty and spiteful autocrat," and "the Queeg of Hill Street," Torres ordered his subordinates to limit county-paid subscriptions to one legal newspaper. 332 of them dropped the *MNE*, whose circulation had been only 2000. The publisher then wrote a mock memo from Torres to all Superior Court judges condemning the *MNE* for demeaning the "august status" of a judicial officer and declaring that "possession of that publication. . .shall not be tolerated." Three *MNE* employees were found distributing the memo in the courthouse and forcibly brought before the judge, who allegedly held them in contempt and refused to let them see a lawyer. Later that day there was a further hearing in which Torres disqualified himself in the contempt proceeding and offered to drop it if the paper apologised. The paper and the three employees are now suing Torres for $285,000 for false imprisonment and violation of civil rights. *Los Angeles Times* B3 (October 3, 1992).

[35] A federal court finally lifted the injunction, but Rev. Wildman still is seeking contract damages. *New York Times* A12 (September 10, 1992), A14 (September 23, 1992).

After Edward J. Rollins quit as Ross Perot's campaign manager and ridiculed the candidate, Perot required deputy manager Charlie Leonard to sign a contract agreeing to "refrain from making any disparaging remarks or negative comments, either publicly or privately, directly or indirectly, regarding Ross Perot" and then fired him. *New York Times* A19 (October 2, 1992).

[36] Trump (1992); *New York Times* A14 (February 18, 1992), 10 (March 21, 1992), 13 (April 18, 1992), A12 (September 10, 1992); *Los Angeles Times* F1 (November 16, 1990), F1 (January 2, 191).

[37] *New York Times* s.1 p.12 (April 14, 1991), s.1 p.15 (November 24, 1991), A8 (March 10, 1992); *Los Angeles Times* A15 (April 17, 1991), A7 (February 16, 1992).

[38] Ravitch (1974); Arons (1983); Kirp (1991); DelFattore (1992). For Canadian examples see 9(1–2) *Fuse* 7–8 (Summer 1985).

When the New York City School Board adopted a first-grade curriculum urging teachers to "include references to lesbians/gay people" "as real people to be respected and appreciated," a district in Queens voted unanimously to resist because it undercut their moral code. *New York Times* B3 (April 24, 1992). The Chancellor of the New York City school system, Mayor, and Borough Presidents of Manhattan and the Bronx denounced the decision by the city-wide board to recall a video and

pamphlet about AIDS because neither sufficiently emphasised abstinence. *New York Times* B1 (May 28, 1992), B3 (May 29, 1992). The
curriculum was revised to emphasise sexual abstinence, delete references
to contraceptive creams and anal intercourse, and omit information on
cleaning needles. *New York Times* B12 (June 24, 1992). 40 out of 200
AIDS education groups refused to stress abstinence, supported by the
Mayor and City Health Commissioner. *New York Times* A16 (August 28,
1992).

When the California health curriculum for public schools acknowledged the existence of "families headed by grandparents, siblings,
relatives, friends, foster parents and parents of the same sex" the Western
Center for Law and Religious Freedom objected to "treat[ing] the traditional family as the equal of these other kinds of families." the Traditional
Values Coalition decried "attempts to advocate and promote homosexuality as an acceptable and healthy life-style. . . .this is recruitment par
excellence. It is saying, hey, guys, same sex is viable, same sex is
meaningful." The State Board of Education referred the issue back to the
Curriculum Commission. *Los Angeles Times* A3 (July 28, 1992).

[39] *New York Times* A1 (November 10, 1989), s.1 p.11 (October 14, 1990),
s.1 p.10 (March 22, 1992), A3 (September 21, 1992) (Mexico); *Los
Angeles Times* H3 (September 22, 1992) (Mexico). Jean Mayer, a leading
Mexican historian, protested that his chapter was rewritten without his
consent to praise Salinas's achievements. His co-author Hector Aguilar
Camin, who as one of two principal editors presumably did the rewriting,
dismissed the dispute as "a trivial issue." Camin's foundation received a
government grant to write the book.

[40] Abel (1985a).

[41] *Marxism Today* 2 (February 1988), 22 (June 1988); Kaufmann & Lincoln
(1991).

Oregon voted in November 1992 on a state consitutional amendment
prohibiting the use of public money to "promote, encourage, or facili-
tate" homosexual behaviour and requiring state and local government to
"assist in setting a standard for Oregon's youth that recognizes homosexuality, pedophilia, sadism and masochism as abnormal, wrong, unnatural,
and perverse and that these behaviors are to be discouraged and
avoided." *New York Times* s.1 p.1 (August 16, 1992).

[42] *Chronicle of Higher Education* A1 (October 2, 1991); 11(6) *COSSA
Washington Update* 1 (April 6, 1992), *New York Times* 1 (September 5,
1992), B5 (September 5, 1992), B5 (September 15, 1992) (NIH conference). Sen. Robert Byrd (D-W.Va.) criticised NSF funding for 31 studies,
including sexual agression in fish in Nicaragua and the personal identity
of law school professors. President Bush has continued to veto support
for research using fetal tissue, and Congress has been unable to override.
11(10) *COSSA Washington Update* 1–2 (June 1, 1992).

[43] *Chronicle of Higher Education* A12 (March 11, 1992). For a history of
these controversies, see Mulcahy & Swaim (1982); Pindell (1990).

⁴⁴ *New York Times* B3 (November 10, 1989), B1 (March 24, 1992). The description of Helms's response is a quotation from his official spokesperson. See generally Bolton (1992).

Frohnmayer's successor, Anne-Imelda Radice, promptly vetoed two grants recommended by her 26-member advisory panel (one unanimously, one 11-1–1). The first, "My Wishes," contained one penis among more than 100 tiny photographs of faces, lips, and hair. The second, "Genital Wallpaper," was not "sexually explicit." Radice denied she had received instructions from the White House: "it wouldn't be necessary because those people know me and my work." *Los Angeles Times* F1 (May 4, 1992); *New York Times* B1 (May 13, 1992). The seven members of the sculpture panel responded by suspending consideration of applications. *New York Times* 12 (May 16, 1992). When a federal judge struck down the prohibition against funding "obscene" material, Rep. Ralph Regula (R-Ohio), who had drafted it, was confident that "under the rubric of artistic excellence [Radice] will continue to apply that subjective judgment call." *New York Times* A1 (June 10, 1992). She planned to by-pass her obstreparous advisory panel in allocating $750,000 in fellowships. *New York Times* 13 (August 1, 1992).

⁴⁵ *Problems of Communism*, launched by the United States Information Agency in 1952, claimed complete independence from the government. But in its early years the USIA refused to allow any mention of Marx, Engels, Lenin, or Stalin! It ceased publication after 40 years when there were no more problems with communism. *New York Times* s.1 p.26 (May 31, 1992).

The USIA withdrew a $35,000 grant to an exhibit on "La Reconquista: A Post-Columbian New World" by the Centro Cultural de la Raza at the Istanbul Biennial, whose theme was the "Production of Cultural Difference." The USIA and the U.S. Embassy in Turkey objected to an essay criticising the "violent history of conquest and domination." *Los Angeles Times* F1 (September 19, 1992).

⁴⁶ *Chronicle of Higher Education* A21 (February 19, 1992), A25 (April 8, 1992); *New York Times* B1 (February 24, 1992).

⁴⁷ *Los Angeles Times* F1 (February 21, 1992), F1 (February 28, 1992); *New York Times* A8 (March 4, 1992), A8 (March 5, 1992).

When the Public Broadcasting System hired British filmmakers to produce "The Lost Language of Cranes" it required them to make a different American version in which the nude men wore boxer shorts. When "Masterpiece Theatre" screened the BBC's "Portrait of a Marriage," it cut 34 minutes, including girlhood scenes in which Violet Trefusis, dressed as a man, climbed into bed with a fully-clothed Vita Sackville-West. In introducing the American version, Alistair Cooke characterised the lesbian relationship as a dangerous interlude threatening Vita's marriage with Harold Nicholson, rather than as the grand passion of her life. Jac Venza, PBS director of performance programmes, explained: "there are two things program managers have a hard time with: language and nudity. If I left it in, it would not be able to be seen in cities where I most want it to be seen." *Los Angeles Times* F1 (June 24, 1992).

[48] *Abrams* v. *United States,* 250 U.S. 616, 630 (1919).

[49] *Independent* 1 (September 16, 1991) (New Kids); *New York Times* B1 (April 20, 1991) (Madonna), C3 (March 20, 1992) (Apple); *Los Angeles Times* F1 (September 5, 1992) (Prince); *Los Angeles Times* F1 (May 11, 1992) (Streisand). Aerosmith got $35 million for four albums with Columbia, Motley Crue $35 million for five with Elecktra, and the Rolling Stones $42 million for three with Virgin. *Los Angeles Times* F1 (September 5, 1992). Television talk shows generate extraordinary profits. Although they cost only $10–20 million a year to produce, Oprah Winfrey grossed $157 million in 1991, Phil Donahue $90 million, and Sally Jessy Raphael $60 million. *New York Times* C1 (June 22, 1992). Even authors command staggering sums. Barbara Taylor Bradford signed a contract with HarperCollins for more than $20 million for three novels; she retained foreign language and film rights. *New York Times* B3 (May 6, 1992).

[50] *New York Times* C1 (February 18, 1992).

[51] *Los Angeles Times* D1 (March 15, 1992). With the collapse of communism the Moscow branch of the Smirnov family has sued Pierre Smirnov Company of Hartford, Connecticut, claiming that the émigré from whom it derived the name (and secret recipe) in 1939 was a gambler who had ceded his share to his brothers in 1905. The American firm had sales of $550 million in 117 countries in 1991. The 150 million Russians, however, drink 100 million bottles of vodka a day! *Los Angeles Times* A5 (August 14, 1992).

[52] *Chronicle of Higher Education* A35 (April 8, 1992). Editor and author Gordon Lish has sued *Harper's* magazine for publishing a marketing letter he sent to prospective students in his writing seminar. Courts have protected J.D. Salinger's letters and Gerald Ford's unpublished biography. *New York Times* B1 (September 22, 1992).

[53] *International Guardian* 3, 9 (September 14, 1991).

[54] *New York Times* B10 (April 3, 1992). The Supreme Court dismised Koons's appeal without comment. *New York Times* A9 (October 14, 1992).

[55] *New York Times* s.2 p.1 (March 15, 1992). RKO paid a Hearst biographer $15,000 to settle the claim after the trial ended in a hung jury.

Edgar Rice Burroughs Inc. has sued *Vogue* over a 14-page fashion feature called "Tarzan, Meet Jane," in the April 1992 issue. The company alleged that the sexually suggestive poses "are inconsistent with the good, wholesome and attractive images of Tarzan and Jane, which have been cultivated. . .over the course of 70 years." They claimed proprietary rights not just in the names but also in any "character in a loincloth with a knife in a jungle setting." A decade earlier they won a court order that the 1981 movie "Tarzan the Apeman" be edited to eliminate sex scenes with Bo Derek. *New York Times* B1 (April 28, 1992).

[56] *Los Angeles Times* F1 (March 24, 1992). Twenty years earlier Nancy Sinatra lost a lawsuit against Goodyear for dressing up a blonde in a miniskirt and go go boots in a commercial for a tyre called the Boot. Since the Midler victory Tom Waits won $2.5 million against Frito Lay and its advertising agency for imitating his voice in a jingle for Doritos. Infinity settled with Chris Isaak for using a guitar riff almost identical to his hit song "Wicked Game." *New York Times* s.2 p.23 (July 5, 1992). Did "Honeymoon in Vegas" pay the King's estate for permission to film the finale in which the Jumping Elvises sky-dive into the city?

[57] *New York Times* B1 (April 21, 1922).

[58] *New York Times* s.1 p.12 (April 19, 1992). Litigation is pending between the editor of the two-volume, 1750-plate "Facsimile Edition of the Dead Sea Scrolls" and the Israeli editor who claims a copyright on the 2000-year old manuscript. *Los Angeles Times* B4 (October 3, 1992).

[59] *New York Times* s.2 p.26 (April 12, 1992). The North American software industry estimated that $2.4 billion was illegally copied in 1990, compared to sales of $5.7 billion. Codes that prevented copying were eliminated because they interefered with loading programmes on hard disks. *New York Times* A1 (July 27, 1992).

In 1991 the National Institutes of Health sought patents on thousands of gene fragments, even though their functions were unknown. The Office of Patents and Trade Marks rejected the application, and the Department of Health and Human Services was considering resubmitting. Now both its General Counsel and numerous scientists (including Nobel laureate James Watson) have advised against this for fear of slowing the human genome project. *New York Times* A16 (October 8, 1992).

[60] *New York Times* A1 (December 11, 1991) (making it easier for victims to sue criminals for their profits). When KLM Productions paid high school student Amy Fisher $60,000 for the story of her shooting of Mary Jo Buttafuoco, with whose 39-year-old husband Amy claimed to have a year-long affair, Ms Buttafuoco sought to seize the money before Ms. Fisher could use it for bail. *New York Times* A16 (August 7, 1992). A New Jersey judge has imposed a lien on any money paid for the story of the convicted kidnap-killer of the Exxon International president. *New York Times* A13 (October 7, 1992).

The market naturally resists such regulation. Networks base 35–40 per cent of the movies they produce on real events, paying informants as much as $125,000. NBC's senior vice president for movies received seven pitches in a single day for the Amy Fisher story. "One agency called and simply said they were offering the L.A. riots. I said, what exactly are you representing?" HBO Pictures bought the story of a Texas mother who hired a hit man to kill her daughter's rival on the high school cheerleading team; an executive said "we're going to do it as a dark comedy." *New York Times* C1 (June 15, 1992).

Richard Nixon is still suing the government for payment for some of the

42 million documents and 4000 hours of tapes seized when he was forced to resign in 1974. *New York Times* A9 (September 15, 1992).

[61] *Los Angeles Times* A4 (February 22, 1992); *New York Times* 1 (March 14, 1992), A4 (April 7, 1992). In August a Greek capitalist bought the paper, which resumed publishing three times a week. *Los Angeles Times* A6 (August 12, 1992). Other previously subsidised journals saw subscriptions fall as prices soared: *Novy Mir* dropped from 2.5 million to 250,000, *Znamya* from 1 million to 250,000, *Druzhba Narodov* from 1.2 million to 90,000. Remnick (1992). The cost of newsprint rose from a heavily subsidised 300 rubles per ton to 29,000 in July 1992. When *Komsomolskaya Pravda* sought resubscriptions at a more realistic price, only a few hundred thousand of its 13 million former readers signed up. Gambrell (1992). Noting that it had published *Doctor Zhivago*, *The Gulag Archipelago*, and *1984*, *Novy Mir* appealed to the West to contribute $190,000 a year because its costs were twice its subscription income. *New York Review of Books* 61 (October 22, 1992).

Moscow sought to rent Red Square to advertisers for the spring festival that has replaced May Day, asking $1 million for bilboards on three sides and two dirigibles stationed above. Even this new-found passion for profit had its limits: nothing was to deface St. Basil's Cathedral or Lenin's tomb. *New York Times* A7 (April 24, 1992). But there were no takers.

[62] *New York Times* s.1 p.6 (March 22, 1992); *Los Angeles Times* A11 (April 13, 1991), F1 (March 26, 1992). For $3180 Russia is now offering photographs of strategic American sites taken from a spy satellite with a resolution of less than 2 meters. *New York Times* s.1 p.8 (October 4, 1992).

In Poland, railway station bookstores sell horoscopes, parapsychology and soft-porn like *Fanny Hill* and *Emmanuelle*; translations of Canadian Harlequin romances sell 1.5 million copies a month. Among novels, the sequel to *Gone With The Wind* topped the best-seller list, followed by Judith Krantz and Jackie Collins. The first translation of *Mein Kampf* sold out 20,000 copies days after a court refused to block publication; copies were quickly resold for three times the cover price. *New York Times Book Review* 14 (July 12, 1992).

Democratic capitalism may have similar consequences in the third world. The opposition press in Zimbabwe has introduced a "Page 3 Girl," one of whom recently posed topless in black transparent pantyhose, a string of beads, and a headscarf, with a caption saying "she is a traditionalist and would like other girls to feel the same way." Harare feminist groups were furious. *Weekly Mail* 15 (April 24, 1992).

[63] Whittle Communications distributes Channel One to 7.1 million students in 11,000 government schools in 45 states (and to private schools in three others). It provides the video equipment free on condition that schools require students to watch the daily 12-minute news programme. Whittle earns $630,000 a day for four 30-second commercials. The California Superintendent of Education, California Congress of Parents, Teachers

*The Poverty of Civil Libertarianism*

and Students, and two teachers sued to prevent its distribution in the state. One of the latter said: "I didn't become a teacher to sell Nikes, Colgate toothpaste and Pringles." *New York Times* A8 (June 4, 1992). An evaluation found that students retained detailed memories of the commercial but knew no more about current events than the control group.

The U.S. Department of Health and Human Services has investigated payments by doctors to hospitals for patient referrals. One group of radiologists had to pay half their gross receipts; another paid 25 per cent of their profits over $120,000. One hospital required pathologists to buy its billing services; another terminated radiologists who refused to pay $181,000 for "marketing." *New York Times* A1 (September 28, 1992).

[64] Wasserstrom (1975); Simon (1978); Luban (1984; 1988); Abel (1989a; 1989b); Curran (1977); Mindes & Acock (1982).

[65] *Guardian* 6 (September 27, 1991), 1 (September 19, 1991), 4 (September 29, 1991), 2 (October 7, 1991); *Observer* 9 (September 29, 1991).

In October 1990 the Congressional Human Rights Caucus held hearings on the Iraqi invasion of Kuwait. The star witness was a Kuwaiti girl, who described Iraqi soldiers removing 15 premature infants from incubators at Al-Adan Hospital and leaving them to die on the floor. Representatives Tom Lantos (D-Calif.) and John Edward Porter (R-Ill.) concealed the facts that she was the daughter of the Kuwaiti ambassador to the United States and her participation had been organised by a public relations firm representing the Kuwaiti government. *New York Times* A15 (January 6, 1991).

[66] *Los Angeles Times* A1 (November 3, 1990).

When the socialist Upton Sinclair won the 1934 Democratic nomination for Governor of California, MGM head Louis B. Mayer withheld a day's pay from each of his employees and committed it to supporting the Republican incumbent Frank Merriam. Dirctor Irving Thalberg formed a special unit at the studio to produce three shorts entitled "California Election News," which omitted the MGM logo in order to appear noncommercial. The first interviewed "average citizens": respectably-dressed actors impersonating Merriam supporters and derelicts representing Sinclair backers. The second indulged in shameless red-baiting. And the third depicted bums moving into California and camping in a hobo jungle in anticipation of the good times they expected under Sinclair. Merriam came from behind to win. When criticised, Thalberg asserted: 'Nothing is unfair in politics." *New York Times* s.2 p.15 (April 19, 1992); Mitchell (1992).

[67] *New York Times* A1 (April 15, 1992). Some people still are scandalised when academics are exposed as government spies. Diamond (1992).

[68] *New York Times* C1 (December 6, 1993) A14 (3. 15.94).

[69] *New York Times* B4 (March 9, 1992), B1 (March 11, 1992). The 1950s "payola" scandal revealed that companies paid disk jockeys to play their records.

Stars and studios control publicity in other ways. Some insist on choosing which writer will conduct the interview. Tom Cruise's public relations agent required journalists invited to a press junket for "Far and Away" to agree in writing to publish interviews only in connection with the initial theatrical release and not sell them to tabloids. Even without explicit constraints, the need for access limits candour. The editor of *Premiere* conceded: "It's easy to be blackballed in that world as a writer. It's very hard to shake a reputation as a killer if you've done one tough piece." After the journal published a strong article about "Aliens 3," 20th Century Fox pulled its ads for the movie. Warner Brothers barred the *Los Angeles Magazine* critic from future screenings after he wrote a critical piece about "Batman Returns." Paramount withdrew all ads indefinitely from *Variety* following a critical review of "Patriot Games." Its vice-president for communications said: "the trade [papers] are there to assess the commercial viability of a film and give exhibitors and industry people an enlightened interpretation of what the film can do. It's not like a review for The New York Times. . .that would be assessing the merits of the film." *Variety's* small circulation (well under 20,000) made it highly dependent on advertising. Its editor apologised and promised that the reviewer (who had almost 20 years experience) would never again be assigned a Paramount film and might be fired. He warned the reviewer that he objected "when [your] political opinions. . .(a) color the review emotionally, and (b) negatively critique the work done by artisans such as the composer, cinematographer, etc. . . these views are not subject for intellectual discourse; they are policy." *New York Times* D1 (June 1, 1992), B3 (June 10, 1992). A group of Indian film stars retaliated against six movie gossip magazines by refusing them any further interviews. *New York Times* s.1 p.5 (September 6, 1992).

When the editor of *Automobile* attacked General Motors at the annual Automotive Press Association dinner for closing 21 plants and eliminating 74,000 jobs, calling GM management "piano players in the whorehouse," the carmaker withdrew Oldsmobile and Buick ads for three months. The editor said that GM's 50–60 pages of advertisements a year (out of 900) could make the difference between profit and loss. The GM vice president for marketing and public affairs responded that "all G.M. vehicle divisions make their own decisions about how to spend advertising dollars." Toyota pulled its ads from *Road and Track* when it failed to make the 1991 "10 Best List." GM did the same when *Car and Driver* photographed an Opel Kadett in a junkyard and called it "the worst car in the world." *New York Times* C9 (June 26, 1992).

[70] Kennedy (1971). "A good lawyer is like a good prostitute . . . If the price is right, you warm up your client." Tybor (1978: 18), quoted in Galanter (1983: 159).

[71] Before Duckworth published D.H. Lawrence's *Sons and Lovers*, Edward Garnett cut 10 per cent of the text without consulting the author, partly because it was sexually too explicit. The complete version is being published by Cambridge University Press. *New York Times* B3 (May 6, 1992).

*The Poverty of Civil Libertarianism*

Although book publishing is generally less market-driven than other media, there are exceptions. When Ross Perot announced his candidacy, four biographies rapidly climbed to the top of the best-seller list, and several others were scheduled for release. When he withdrew, the books disappeared. Tony Chiu's *Ross Perot: In His Own Words* was the most successful: 19 days from concept to bookstore, a first printing of 300,000, sales of 500,000. The publisher gloated: "We didn't pay a lot of money up front and we got out there when the time was right. Listen, it's the occupational hazard of doing instant books. They have a shorter shelf life than lettuce." *New York Times* B5 (July 22, 1992).

[72] Webster (1990: 26–27).

[73] *New York Times* s.1 p.4 (October 14, 1990). Frank Upham has told me that his highly acclaimed book (1987) will not be translated into Japanese because it also discusses the Burakumin.

[74] *New York Times* B2 (December 6, 1990).

[75] HarperCollins organised a book signing at Rizzoli's bookstore in New York's World Financial Center for Bryan Burrough's (1992) expose of the American Express smear campaign against banker Edmond Safra. The event flopped because Amexco, which is headquartered in the same building, pressured Rizzoli not to publicise it. An Amexco spokesperson denied this but complained that Rizzoli had not been "neighborly." Safra earlier had won a judgement ordering Amexco to apologise publicly and pay $8 million to Safra and charities he selected. Harry Freeman, a former Amexco executive, is now suing Burrough and Dow Jones for $50 million, claiming that Burrough recklessly distorted the truth in a *Wall Street Journal* article that secured him a $1 million advance for the book. *New York Times* C8 (May 4, 1992); *Los Angeles Times* D1 (May 11, 1992).

[76] Edwards (1991); Webster (1990: 26–27); GLC Gay Working Party (1985: 13–14, 23).

Earvin "Magic" Johnson wrote *What You Can Do to Avoid AIDS*, donating all profits from the $3.99 book to his AIDS foundation. Nearly 500,000 copies were in print, and it was being translated into 12 languages. The American Medical Association declared: "Everbody—especially teenagers and parents—needs to read this book. This book could help save lives." But Wal-Mart's 1747 stores refused to stock it because "we found some of the material inappropriate." "The language was not in keeping with what our customers tell us they would want to read." Kmart also concluded that the book "doesn't fit the family orientation of a Kmart shopper," although it displayed Jackie Colins's *Hollywood Wives* and a *Cosmopolitan* issue on the etiquette of oral sex. *New York Times* A15 (August 3, 1992) (op ed).

[77] *New York Times* C8 (March 16, 1992). Less than two weeks after the 1992 Tony awards (for best play) the League of American Theatres and Producers dismissed 9 of the 12 panel members, claiming it wanted more working professionals and fewer academics. Panel members, who had

honoured two plays that had closed by the time of the award, said they had been afraid of displeasing the League. *New York Times* 12 (June 13, 1992).

[78] *New York Times* A14 (October 24, 1990).

[79] *New York Times* A1 (December 12, 1990).
Harvard law professor Randlall Kennedy invited Indiana University law professor Craig Bradley to contribute to a symposium on Clarence Thomas in Kennedy's *Reconstruction* magazine, whose goal is to foster "robust, wide-open debate." After telling Bradley that the article had been accepted, Kennedy rejected it "because of your references to the infamous Coke can [on which Thomas claimed to have found a pubic hair at the EEOC] and the matter involving pornography [testimony by a black woman law school classmate that Thomas had described x-rated films to her several times]." Kennedy explained: "I press for candor, but I also press for a certain degree of intellectual discipline. I thought there was a hint of smarminess in his piece. . . ." *New York Times* B12 (September 11, 1992).

[80] *Chronicle of Higher Education* A31 (January 22, 1992). Donors to universities can earmark funds for particular subjects and even choose the occupants of endowed chairs. Lee M. Bass (Yale '79 and member of a billionaire family) gave Yale $20 million for a new elective course of studies in Western Civilisation, "a field that for more than a decade has been under attack while many colleges and universities increased their emphasis on the study of people and cultures outside the Western tradition." Although Yale already offered a survey and three specialised courses on the subject, Stephen H Balch, president of the conservative National Association of Scholars, applauded the gift as "a very important gesture and message being sent to the rest of the academic community about what has been neglected for a long time and now should be addressed." *New York Times* A10 (April 18, 1991).

[81] *New York Times* A15 (November 5, 1990); *Los Angeles Times* A3 (March 16, 1992), A14 (April 21, 1992). In response to a finding by the Center for Media and Public Affairs that the average soundbite in the 1988 election was only 7.3 seconds CBS adopted a policy of not reporting as news any candidate statement less than 30 seconds long! *New York Times* A8 (July 3, 1992).
Stations are not required to accept issue-oriented ads. The CBS affiliate in Buffalo (WIVB) rejected a National Abortion Rights Action League ad showing the Statue of Liberty and flag as a narrator read a plea to make "abortion less necessary" by encouraging sex education and birth control. A WIVB spokesman explained: "Even if Operation Rescue had not been in town, I'd question the ad. It's a sensitive issue, and we elected not to get involved." Stations differ in the degree of documentation they require for factual statements. During the 1990 North Carolina senatorial race between Republican incumbent Jesse Helms and black pro-choice challenger Harvy Gantt, the state Republican party warned stations

planning to broadcast NARAL spots that they would be closely moni-
tored. *New York Times* A12 (June 11, 1992).

[82] *Los Angeles Times* A11 (February 26, 1991); *Chronicle of Higher Education* A35 (March 4, 1992).
Church-affiliated universities are even more intrusive. Georgetown
University, a Jesuit institution, withdrew the $150/year subsidy and
meeting space allocated to G.U. Choice for violating an agreement not to
participate in "advocacy or action on behalf of abortion." The group is
forbidden to demonstrate or distribute information on campus. *New York
Times* 9 (April 25, 1992).

[83] Entman (1989).

[84] *New York Times* A13 (March 26, 1992).
If poverty silences, those with resources may be compelled to speak. At
an April 1992 fund-raiser for President Bush, donors were invited to buy
tables for 10 for $15–20,000. One table got you a member of the House
of Representatives; a second got you a Senator; $92,000 got you a photo
opportunity with the President; and top contributors got to sit at his table.
(Michael Kojima, who bought a seat at the President's table for $500,000,
was simultaneously being sought by former wives and business associates
for large unpaid debts; he has since been jailed and forced to pay
$120,000.) James R. Elliott, president of Cherry Payment Systems of
Illinois, was under investigation by the FDIC and had already served a
prison term for bank fraud. He denied telling subordinates that their
contributions might secure him a Presidential pardon. But a letter from his
regional marketing director to Midwest offices described the dinner as
    a great opportunity. . .to rub elbows with the most powerful people in
    this country. . .
So what I suggest is that you do some soul searching and decide
whether you're going to go the distance. What I need is a phone call
from those of you that plan to participate in this event. There are other
perks that will go along with this. . . . If you're asking yourself, can I
afford to make this trip, then ask yourself, if you can afford not too! [sic]
We will truely [sic] see what kind of cloth your [sic] cut from when I
hear from those of you that plan to participate.
The company said the letter was unauthorised and its sender had been
reprimanded. It also insisted that an employee was dismissed for not
meeting sales performance targets rather than for refusing to contribute.
The dinner raised $9 million. *New York Times* A20 (April 24, 1992); *Los
Angeles Times* A1 (May 8, 1992), B1 October 16, 1992).

[85] *Los Angeles Times* A26 (November 3, 1990), A25 (November 8, 1990);
*New York Times* A15 (November 5, 1990).

[86] *New York Times* B1 (March 9, 1992), s.2 p.11 (April 19, 1992). Art
Linson, producer of such commercial successes as "Singles," "Melvin
and Howard," "Car Wash," and "Fast Times at Ridgemont High," hates
the review process.
    You're doomed the minute you start cutting your film because 100 kids

say they liked this but didn't like that. I can't tell you how many movies would have been ruined by preview cards because the natural impulse of an audience is to want a happy ending, to reach for what's familiar, not to be challenged. You really have to lead an audience, not follow them.
*New York Times* B1 (September 28, 1992).

[87] *New York Times* B1 (February 5, 1992). When the film appeared, the American had been chastened and civilised by falling in love with his Japanese coach's daughter. One reviewer observed:
[T]he finished version shows no signs of ever having been a hard-hitting satire. . . .The ending certainly smacks of compromise, since this is not a film willing to think seriously about Japanese attitudes toward an interracial romance. . . .Some of the film's crass American characters. . .are allowed to become caricatures. And there is a trace of hostility in the way one of Jack's teammates refers to him as "white trash." The film also makes room for the occasional lecture, as when Jack complains about what he calls "the Japanese way—shut up and take it." In response, he is told, "Sometimes acceptance and co-operation are strengths also."
*New York Timex* B6 (October 2, 1992); see also *Los Angeles Times* F12 (October 2, 1992).

[88] *New York Times* B1 (January 30, 1992), s.2 p.17 (March 15, 1992). An NC–17 rating may discourage movie chains from showing the film, media from accepting advertising for it, and video stores from stocking it.

Stephen Chao's meteoric rise to the presidency of Fox Television Stations was followed by his equally precipitate fall. At a panel on "The Threat to Democratic Capitalism Posed by Modern Culture" he discussed the constant pressures on television, illustrating his talk by having a male model strip before an audience that included NEH chair Lynne Cheney (and her husband, Defense Secretary Dick Cheney). Rupert Murdoch fired Chao on the spot, commenting "It was a tragedy to see a great career self-destruct." Chao explained: "I was questioning the conventions which govern TV in America, which are confused and hypocritical—such things as the difference between nakedness and lewdness or the predominance of violence in fictional programming." Murdoch needed no lessons in hypocrisy. Chao had played a major role in developing such hits as "America's Most Wanted," "Cops," and "Studs." The last, Fox's main money-maker, features three young women in tiny mini-skirts and two hunks engaging in half an hour of suggestive conversation whose prize is a "dream date." The programe cost $50,000 a week to produce while earning Fox $20 million in 1991/92 and an anticipated $60 million in 1992/93. *Los Angeles Times* D1 (June 22, 1992), A1 (June 23, 1992); *New York Times* C6 (June 29, 1992).

[89] Bagdikian (1987); Baker (1992). The November Company, a firm of advertising executives handling the Bush-Quayle campaign, told networks its decision about where to buy commercial time would be

influenced by the "good taste" and "moral values" of their regular programmes. *New York Times* C2 (July 14, 1992).

[90] *Los Angeles Times* A27 (January 30, 1992); Warner et al. (1992).

[91] *New York Times* C1 (February 25, 1992). Some executive compensation consulting firms refuse to talk to reporters. Business Roundtable members who are clients of Towers Perrin persuaded the firm to stop helping the *Wall Street Journal* prepare its annual executive pay survey. Half a dozen angry clients phoned Michael J. Halloran of Wyatt Company after he helped *Fortune* with its 1991 pay survey, which included stock options for the first time. Another firm assured clients that it had refused to cooperate with *Fortune*. *New York Times* C1 (August 25, 1992).

[92] They also examine advertisements for taste, fairness, and documentation. The vice president for comercial standards at ABC said that only 125–150 of the 46,000 commercials are challenged each year; about half are modified or withdrawn. A "What is Sexy" commercial for Jovan Musk exposed an inch of skin around a woman's navel, which the network inisted be covered. Jovan tried to circumvent such prudery by showing a man and woman undressing while an actor portraying the network censor explained what was acceptable. Censors would not allow Vitabath bath oil to show a woman in a bathtub using her toe to plug an annoyingly dripping faucet, which they felt was too suggestive of intercourse. Companies also seek civil damages when competitors malign them. *New York Times* s.3 p.10 (September 27, 1992). *The New Yorker* cancelled a two-page Benneton ad worth $73,000—a photo of an albino Zulu woman apparently being shunned by others—because it was inconsistent with the feature story about Malcolm X. Previous *New Yorker* editors had sometimes objected to ads. *New York Times* C13 (October 2, 1992).

[93] *New York Times* C15 (November 14, 1989), s.2 p.1 (December 8, 1991), 13 (February 1, 1992); *Los Angeles Times* F1 (January 17, 1992). Advertisers pulled $500,000 out of a "Law and Order" episode about the bombing of an abortion clinic and $350,000 from one about the assisted suicide of an AIDS victim. In the first half of 1990/91 it had more pullouts than any other network show, but the next year was nominated for six Emmys and won the National Board of Review's DW Griffith Award and the ABA's Silver Gavel award. Now shows can be cancelled after three episodes. "Quantum Leap" offered advertisers a plot synopsis beforehand and their money back if they were uncomfortable with it. *Los Angeles Times* F1 (September 1, 1992).

In 1973, when CBS reran an episode about the first abortion by a leading television character (Beatrice Arthur as Maude), not a single national sponsor bought ad time, and 39 affiliates refused the show. Meredith Berlin, editor-at-large of *Soap Opera Digest*, said: "Writers will fall all over themselves to avoid an abortion. Miscarriage is a convenient out. So is falling down stairs or off a horse. Or a hysterical pregnancy." Ashley Abbott, the good girl in "The Young and the Reckless," had perhaps the last abortion on a soap; she was punished by suffering a breakdown and being sent to an insane asylum. Linda Bloodworth-Thomason, creator of "Designing Women," feared that "abortion is coming to such a head that we may have to do it. But it's tough when you're doing a comedy and people see that favorite character week after week and remember what happened to her." *New York Times* s.2 p.1 (May 31, 1992).

[94] *Los Angeles Times* D1 (December 28, 1991), C1 (October 2, 1992); *New York Times* C13 (October 2, 1992).

[95] *New York Times* C6 (April 6, 1992).

[96] *New York Times* 1 (December 21, 1990).

The Media Image Coalition of Minorities and Women (including the American Jewish Congress, Los Angeles Black Media Coalition, Nosotros Inc., LA GLAAD, and the Association of Asian Pacific American Artists) urged advertisers to boycott "Driving Miss Daisy," a 1992/93 CBS television series spawned by the successful play and movie. The Coalition objected to the stereotypfication of Hoke Colburn, who spoke in southern Black dialect. *Los Angeles Times* F1 (August 18, 1992). Robert Guillaume, who played the African American chauffeur in all three media, said: "It's one of the few times I've been able to watch my work without ducking or putting my hands over my eyes." But the Coalition spokesperson derided the series as "a situation comedy about a situation that isn't funny, just like the Holocaust is not inherently funny." When a women friend called FDR a nigger lover in the pilot, Miss Daisy ordered her out the house but Hoke said nothing. "Hoke is powerless to react or respond. He hides his anger and holds it back." Guillaume replied: "if you're a 65-year-old man in that time and you are called a nigger, is it historically true that he could have said 'I'm out of here?' We know that is not something that happened a lot." *Los Angeles Times* F1 (August 20, 1992).

Some viewers are more equal than others. When Catholics were outraged that singer Sinéad O'Connor tore up the Pope's picture on NBC's "Saturday Night Live," shouting "Fight the real enemy," the manager of the Notre Dame student union implicitly threatened to pull Notre Dame football games off the network. NBC vice president Curtis Block quickly declared: "It goes without saying the NBC does not condone something like that. . . . I was offended, the executive producer. . . . likewise was offended and surprised." *Los Angeles Times* F1 (October 6, 1992).

[97] *New York Times* A8 (March 19, 1992), A12 (August 19, 1992) (Americas Watch "Dangerous Dialogue" report on repression of dissent by Miami Cuban-American community). The Cuban American National Foundation threatened to sue the Public Broadcasting System for its documentary "Campaign for Cuba," which accurately stated that the Foundation had accepted $780,000 from the National Endownment for Democracy and contributed over $500,000 to the Free Cuba PAC Inc. *New York Times* A9 (October 13, 1992).

In South Africa, the ANC launched a boycott of the *Eastern Province*

*The Poverty of Civil Libertarianism*

*Herald* and *Evening Post* by burning old copies. ANC spokesman Phila Nkayi said the papers were waging "malicious" attacks on the organisation. "The media is at liberty to criticise the ANC-led alliance, but we could not take the vilification and bossy stance that appears to have been adopted. . . ." Editor Derek Smith said the *Herald* would "not become an ANC paper" or be dictated to. But on the first full day of the boycott the newspapers' management approached the ANC for talks, and the South African Union of Journalists branch also sought to negotiate. *Weekly Mail* 4 (July 31, 1992).

A week after the opening of "Minbo no Onna" (Woman Mob Fighter), a film about yakuza (gangsters), director Juzo Itami was attacked by three men in front of his house, who slashed him in the face, neck and hand. *New York Times* A1 (June 15, 1992). One reporter for the *Asahi* newspaper was murdered in 1987 and another seriously wounded. The Tokyo Broadcasting System received 140,000 protests after it criticised the Unification Church. The office of a magazine that criticised Kofuku no Kagaku (Institute for Research in Human Happiness) was attacked. *Los Angeles Times* H2 (October 13, 1992).

[98] *Los Angeles Times* J1 (March 14, 1991).

At the 1992 Republican National Convention the leader of the Virginia delegation organised a group of hecklers to follow NPR reporter Nina Totenberg around the floor, interrupting her interviews by yelling "Nina, Nina. Have you had an affair?" This was retaliation for *another* woman reporter who had asked Bush about an affair. When Democratic Party Chairman Ron Brown and other officials tried to hold a news conference inside a Houston restaurant, 100 members of the Republican Youth Coalition disrupted it. The co-chairwoman of the Republican National Committee congratulated them: "I want to tell you all that you have really done wonderfully. You have really kept us in the news this week. I saw you take on the other side's rally the other day and that was great." The field director of the College Republican National Committee explained: "If the Dems are going to come to the Republic National Committee [sic] and try to steal media attention, they should expect a little confrontation." *New York Times* A12 (August 21, 1992).

[99] Jansen (1991).

[1] *Cf.* Wolff (1968).

80

# 3. The Excesses of State Regulation

If civil libertarianism can neither avoid politics nor maximise freedom, the conventional alternative of state regulation inevitably invites authoritarian excess. The history of laws against blasphemy, defamation, pornography, obscenity, and hate speech hardly inspires enthusiasm or encourages emulation. Law dichotomises reality, rupturing continua and magnifying the importance of arbitrary boundaries. Its pigeonholes strip events of the context and history that give them meaning. Law cannot deal with the irreducible ambiguity of symbolic expression. Art accentuates ambiguity; indeed, unambiguous literature, drama, dance, painting, or sculpture is not art but agit-prop. Yet the qualities that justify art's immunity from state intrusion are extraordinarily elusive. Law has great difficulty attending to the speaker's identity and motive, audience perception, and the capricious cultural environment—all of which can transform the harm and moral quality of speech. The liberal state can exercise power only through formal law, but formality inflicts heavy costs on partipants and the state, slows the response, and fosters procedural fetishism. The severity of state sanctions can be justified only by consequentialist reasoning—speech is punished not for what it is but for the actions it provokes. Consequentialism is empirically problematic, however, whether pornography is blamed for rape or hate speech for racial attacks. And if consequences are the rationale for state regulation, why focus on aberrant extremes rather than the manifold harms of daily life? Legal regulation of speech often encourages evasion; even when effective it constructs deviance, valorises evil, attracts attention, and confers martyrdom. I will address these arguments in turn.

## I. The Unhappy History of Regulation

⌐The British government's response to hate speech is deeply discouraging. Although Britain has a long history of prejudice against Catholics (especially Irish), Jews, and now people of colour, state remedies were infrequent and ineffective prior to the 1965 Race Relations Act.[1] Imperial Fascist League leader Arnold Leese, who applauded the rise of Hitler and insinuated that British Jews were responsible for unsolved child murders, was acquitted of seditious libel but convicted of public mischief. Yet he was not prosecuted for repeating the statements after his release from prison. In 1947 James Caunt wrote in a paper he edited:

> [T]here is very little about which to rejoice greatly except the pleasant fact that only a handful of Jews bespoil the population of the Borough! . . . If British Jewry is suffering today from the righteous wrath of British citizens, then they have only themselves to blame for their passive inactivity. Violence may be the only way to bring them to the sense of their responsibility to the country in which they live.

A jury took just 13 minutes to acquit him of seditious libel. Yet National Socialist Movement leader Colin Jordan was convicted under the 1936 Public Order Act for declaring at a Trafalgar Square meeting: "Hitler was right . . . our real enemies, the people we should have fought, were not Hitler and the National Socialists of Germany but world Jewry and its associates in this country."

Opening debate of what became the 1965 Act, the (Labour) Home Secretary, Frank Soskice, revealed his government's ambivalence toward regulating hate speech—sounding very much like German Social Democrats equivocating about asylum today.

> [C]riticism should be allowed, however jaundiced and one-sided it may be. . . . Nobody can be prevented from arguing, for example, that particular groups should be returned to their country of origin because their presence in this country causes an excessive strain on our social services. What is prohibited . . . is the intentional fomentation of hatred of that group . . . because of the origin of its members[,] by public abuse, however camouflaged as motivated by a sincere intention[,] dishonestly simulated, to promote discussion of the public interest.[2]

After its passage, Soskice cautioned that the Act was "designed to deal with the more dangerous, persistent and insidious forms of propaganda campaigns . . . which, over a period of time, engender the hate which begets violence." Fascists immediately exploited a loophole by establishing the Viking Book Club "for the study of literature dealing with the Jewish Question and other racial problems which it is not permissible to sell to the general public . . . ."

The first prosecution was directed at a 17-year-old white labourer who stuck a Greater Britain Movement leaflet entitled "Blacks not wanted here" on the door of MP Sid Bidwell and threw another through his window, wrapped in a beer bottle—neither of which, the court held, was "publication or distribution." A jury convicted Colin Jordan, rejecting his claim that a pamphlet about "The Coloured Invasion" was only trying to inform the public about a grave national problem. But there were almost as many successful prosecutions of black power advocates, while sophisticated racists evaded punishment.[3] During debate over the Commonwealth Immigrants Act 1968, which denied entry to East African Asians holding UK passports, the Racial Preservation Society journal *Southern News* denounced the "dangers of race mixing," speculated about genetic differences, and urged repatriation as a "humane solution." It celebrated its acquittal by reprinting a "Souvenir Edition" defiantly captioned "The Paper the Government Tried to Suppress."

One of the most troubling trials involved British National Party chairman John Kingsley Read, who harangued 300 people:

Fellow racialists, fellow Britons, and fellow Whites, I have been told I cannot refer to coloured immigrants. So you can forgive me if I refer to niggers, wogs and coons. [Commenting on the murder of Gurdip Singh Chagger, he added:] Last week in Southall, one nigger stabbed another nigger. Very unfortunate. One down and a million to go.

The first jury hung after two hours. On retrial, Read insisted his epithets were a "jocular aside" and the numbers referred to immigration, not murder. Instructing the jury, Judge McKinon mentioned that his own public school nickname had been "nigger" and told a story about another old boy, a Maharajah, who had greeted him by that endearment years later during a chance encounter in Picadilly. The law, he said,

does not contemplate reasoned argument directed to stemming

83

the flow of immigration, or even advocating the repatriation of people who have come here from abroad . . . . It is claimed that jobs will be lost, that, goodness knows, we have a million and a half or more unemployed already and that all the immigrants are going to do is to occupy the jobs that are needed by our local population. These are matters upon which people are entitled to hold and to declare strong views expressed in moderate terms . . . . Were [the words "One down and a million to go"] threatening? abusive? insulting? It is said that he insulted the dead. There is no charge known to the law of insulting the dead . . . . [I]s there anything that is pointed to that indicates that he was urging action activated by hatred? . . . He is obviously a man who has had the guts to come forward in the past and stand up in public for the things that he believes in.

The obedient jury acquitted in ten minutes. Discharging Read, McKinon added: "You have been rightly acquitted but in these days and in these times it would be well if you were careful to use moderate language. By all means propagate the views you may have but try to avoid involving the sort of action which has been taken against you. I wish you well."

Summing up the first decade under the Act, the Home Office conceded that racists had learned to evade it; propaganda "tends to be less blatantly bigoted, to disclaim any intention of stirring up racial hatred, and to purport to make contribution to public education and debate."[4] The government responded by amending the law to obviate the requirement of intent. The next prosecution should have been an easy victory even under the old law. Two British Movement members had ranted in the Warwick marketplace about "wogs, coons, niggers, black bastards." "It was shocking that white nurses should have to shave the lice ridden hair of these people." "[A] nurse wiping froth off a coon's mouth and, as a result, dying of rabies. That is what these black bastards are doing to us." The defence chose the novel tactic of arguing that these views were so extreme that "what was stirred up more than anything was sympathy for the coloured people . . . ." An all-white jury acquitted under the Act, though it convicted one speaker of words likely to cause a breach of the peace. Suspending a six-month sentence, the judge cautioned: "You have got to learn to curb what you say. It is not a question of preventing people from expressing their proper opinions but there is a way in which it can be properly expressed."[5]

Although juries convicted 15 of the 21 tried during the first four years of the amended law, penalties remained small fines and short prison terms, usually suspended. Attorney General Samuel Silkin QC, whose consent was required, declined to prosecute when "enforcement will lead inevitably to law breaking on a scale out of all proportion to that which is being penalised or to consequences so unfair or so harmful as heavily to outweigh the harm done by the breach itself."[6] He struck the balance against prosecution when the British Resistance Movement published a leaflet entitled "Jews Bomb Themselves," mocking the 1980 terrorist bombing of a Paris synagogue: "It is an old trick of the Jews to blow up their own synagogue, machine gun their school buildings and desecrate their cemeteries and daub them with swastikas . . . ." Nor was he moved when a National Front member published a book of photographs with captions like: "Asian thugs," "Black Savages," "Ape-Rape— the wrong one is behind bars," "I'm a death camp survivor. I was nearly exterminated 5, no six million times, in my life." If the victims of hate speech were its only audience the Attorney General would not act, even when the language clearly met the statutory require- ments: "The Jew is an arch parasite . . . . Blacks, that only a few months ago were Banana eating savages."

When the CRE urged that the law forbid "words which, having regard to all circumstances, expose any racial group in Great Britain to hatred, ridicule or contempt," the Home Affairs Committee demurred, fearing that "an increase in the rate of successful prosecu- tions . . . might create the impression among the public that the sensibilities of ethnic minorities were being protected in a manner not extended to other groups in society."[7] The contemporaneous Government Green Paper on Public Order agreed that punishing opinions "would be totally inconsistent with a democratic society in which—provided the manner of expression, and the circumstances, do not provoke unacceptable consequences—political proposals, however odious and undesirable, can be freely advocated."[8]

This dismal record illustrates many of the problems inherent in state regulation of speech. It focused on extremes, implicitly con- doning the myriad ways in which mundane discourse reproduces status inequality. Style was more important than content to both legislators and judges. Legal formalism equated black resistance with white racism. The law misconstrued the relevance of the audience by exculpating hatred directed at its targets or sympathetic listeners. The ambiguity of speech facilitated evasion—some of the most outrageous abuse was dismissed as self-defeating.[9] The boun- dary between legitimate political debate and proscribed vituperation

85

was arbitrary. Although motive is central, difficulties of proof led the government to dispense with intent. Juries shared the government's belief that penalties were excessive. Prosecution further disseminated hate speech, generated sympathy for the accused and resentment against their victims, and left racists unrepentent.

## *II. Dichotomising Continua, Denying Ambiguity*

The formal legal system dichotomises reality into what it expressly condemns and what its tolerance implicitly approves. It does this in part because criminal and civil sanctions are so harsh and legal procedures so onerous that only clear moral judgments can justify them. Tort liability, for instance, turns on whether or not the defendant caused the plaintiff's injury, although science describes causation in terms of continuously varying probabilities of populations of events. Causal actors have a duty to refrain from inflicting particular emotional injuries—being forced to witness the death of a spouse but not the death of a lover or being told of a spouse's death—although the actual damage varies continuously. Law's arbitrary rupture of the continuities of experience becomes even more troubling when the behaviour being regulated is speech. Just as liberal abstention sends the unfortunate message that the state condones the harms of speech, so criminalisation punishes behaviour that is unobjectionable or even praiseworthy while exonerating greater evils. Enforcement of American pornography laws illustrates both pitfalls. The federal government entrapped an elderly Nebraska farmer into buying a single copy of *Boys Who Love Boys*, convicting him of a felony and costing him a job as a school bus driver and the friendship of neighbours. At least four of the nearly 150 men convicted in this sting operation committed suicide.[10] By contrast, New York State, with a population of nearly 20 million, made only 23 felony *arrests* during a recent six-year period. Two of the even rarer convictions involved a Rochester man who gave neighbourhood children photographs of himself having sex with a dog.[11]

Every attempt to dichotomise speech is fundamentally flawed.[12] Gloria Steinem, who once equated *Playboy* with *Mein Kampf*, sought to evoke the shade of Oliver Wendell Holmes by insisting on the "clear and present difference" between pornography and erotica.

Look at any photo or film of people making love; really making love. The images may be diverse, but there is usually a sensuality and touch and warmth, an acceptance of bodies and nerve endings. There is always a spontaneous sense of people who are there because they want to be, out of shared pleasure. Now look at any depiction of sex in which there is clear force, or an unequal power that spells coercion. It may be very blatant, with weapons of torture or bondage, wounds and bruises, some clear humiliation, or an adult's sexual power being used over a child. It may be much more subtle: a physical attitude of conquerer and victim, the use of race or class to imply the same thing, perhaps a very unequal nudity, with one person exposed and vulnerable while the other is clothed. In either case, there is no sense of equal choice or equal power.[13]

How would she categorise Bernini's sculpture of "Apollo and Daphne," or Shakespeare's "The Taming of the Shrew," or Manet's "Déjeuner sur l'herbe"? Her definition would condemn any art, literature, dance or drama realistically portraying our pervasive sexualised inequality. Catherine MacKinnon would prohibit expression depicting the sexually explicit subordination of women. Like most such proposals, however, this disregards both author intent and audience response. Would it not proscribe works in which the creator deliberately evokes moral condemnation, such as Bizet's "Carmen," Tolstoi's "Anna Karenina," Hardy's "Tess of the d'Urbervilles," or Bergman's "The Virgin Spring"? The British Advertising Standards Authority makes equally arbitrary judgments in purporting to distinguish the erotic from the sexually explicit. It censured Goodmans Industries for posters promoting car audio systems by posing amorous couples in the front seats of cars with the caption "Britain's second favourite in-car entertainment." But when the public complained about a *Sun* newspaper poster showing a woman on a beach looking at a man in swimming trunks and saying "Is that a *Sun* tucked up your shorts, or are you just pleased to see me?" the Authority dismissed this as "representative of the editorial content of *The Sun*."[14]

Mari Matsuda would punish a speaker who directs a persecutorial, hateful and degrading message of racial inferiority against a historically oppressed group.[15] But she then carves out loopholes that virtually give away the game. The exception for scientific arguments would condone the racism of H.J. Eysenck, A.R. Jensen, Richard Herrnstein, and William B. Shockley.[16] Her tolerance of satire could protect Andrew Dice Clay.[17] Her exemption of museums might permit a neo-Nazi display of Hitler memorabilia.[18] As we will see below, Holocaust revisionists and black anti-Semites have sought refuge in the "neutral reportage" she would immunise. And the literary realism she would protect did not satisfy black critics of William Styron's *The Confessions of Nat Turner* or feminists incensed by Bret Easton Ellis's *American Psycho*.

Speakers often don the raiment of Art when threatened by state regulation. A publisher justified disseminating the Marquis de Sade's *Juliette* by claiming that "his works are considered by many academics and students of history, literature and philosophy to address serious issues of personal liberty and freedom of expression."[19] That not only is tautological—every defiance of state regulation raises "serious issues of . . . freedom of expression"—but also offers carte blanche to dress pornography in the trappings of art by hiring reputable scriptwriters and directors, adding plot and character, attending to "production values," and seeking historical verisimilitude.[20]

In any case, aesthetic judgements do not close the enquiry. Some artists assault their audience in an effort to demonstrate originality, attract attention, and intensify response. The novelist and critic John Gardner nicely captured this impulse.

> The man who blows up grand pianos is howled at from every side, "Fraud! Not art!" but what counts is that the crowd is there to howl, though it may not be there next time. Something happens to them as they watch the instrument blown up—some will even admit it. They experience a shock of terrible metaphor—"Grand pianos are in my way, the whole tradition is in my way, and *you* are in my way: I can say nothing, do nothing, affirm nothing because of the piano's intolerable high-tone creamy plinking, which you fools adore; I will therefore destroy them, I will destroy you all![21]

Our century has had no shortage of those who aim to shock, from Dada through performance art. In 1971 a British court found the "Oz" School Kids Issue obscene because it showed a naked Rupert Bear having sex with a gigantic Gypsy Granny.[22] At the Newcastle festival twenty years later Karen Finley invited viewers to drink red wine and spit on the American and British flags. Annie Sprinkle, former prostitute and porn queen, performed "Sluts and Goddesses" by stripping, douching, dancing, displaying her vagina, and gagging realistically after simulating oral sex on a row of rubber phalluses.[23] That some art shocks does not elevate everything shocking into art.[24] The invocation of art to justify the harms of speech merely shifts debate from an arbitrary boundary to an ineffable essence. We certainly can have no confidence in the judgements of contemporaries. When Eduard Manet's "Olympia" was first exhibited Théophile Gautier sneered: "[I]t can be understood from no point of view, even if you take it for what it is, a puny model stretched out on a sheet . . . . Here there is nothing, we are sorry to say, but the desire to attract attention at any price." The Salon jury rejected Manet's "Déjeuner sur l'herbe," refusing to reconsider at the request of Napoleon III.[25] The Nazis equated expressionist portraiture with the physiognomy of deformed mental patients, labelled Jewish art degenerate to justify banning it, and launched a House of German Art and an annual Great Exhibition.[26] Most of what the Soviet Union lauded as socialist realism remains of interest only to historians. These controversies continue unabated. In 1977 a state legislator condemned the California Arts Council for supporting a musician who performed underwater to entertain migrating whales and composed a piece to accompany kangeroo rats dancing in Death Valley.[27] In 1992 Catalonia's greatest artist, Antoni Tapies, sculpted a 60-foot sock with a hole in the heel as the centerpiece of the new National Museum of Catalan Art. Although the government was furious, Oriol Bohigas, a well-known architect, insisted: "It is Tapies's most important work."[28]

Artists resist state regulation not only to preserve their autonomy but also because of art's irreducible ambiguity. Leonard Freed declared: "The more ambiguous the photograph is, the better it is. Otherwise it would be propaganda."[29] John Gardner agreed: "Morality is infinitely complex, too complex to be *knowable*, and far too complex to be reduced to any code, which is why it is suitable matter for fiction, which deals in understanding, not knowledge."[30] Meaning depends on context, yet law decontextualises the determination of guilt and liability.[31] Although memory can aggravate or ameliorate the hurtfulness of speech, law takes a shallow view of history. It is uninterested in the characteristics of the parties, their relationship, or the environment within which they interact. It imposes an artificial symmetry on the real asymmetries of social life. The film "White Men Can't Jump," which unfavourably compared the character and athletic prowess of a white basketball hustler with his black counterpart, was a commercial and artistic success, but it would no longer be acceptable to make a movie entitled "Women Can't Add."[32]

## The Excesses of State Regulation

How would the law handle a sexual harassment complaint brought by Rudolphe against Emma Bovary or by Mildred Rodgers against Phillip Carey for his obsessive pursuit in "Of Human Bondage"?[33] Motive defines the moral content of speech but remains opaque to outsiders—and sometimes to the speaker as well.[34] Law's contortions in attributing motive produce some of its least satisfactory performances: degrees of homicide, actual malice in tort, contractual meeting of the minds, undue influence on a testator, landlord or employer discrimination, even legislative intent. The historical shift from subjective to objective standards is an admission of failure. Psychiatric resistance to forcing the nuances of medical diagnosis into the legal dichotomy sane-insane should caution us against obliterating the subtleties of literary and artistic production and criticism by labelling a text pornography or hate speech. Whereas mens rea usually aggravates or mitigates heinousness along a continuum of culpability, the speaker's motive can render the contemptible praiseworthy. Canadian authorities disregarded or misunderstood motive when they banned the feminist documentary "Not a Love Story" for presenting pornography in order to criticise it.[35] "Paris Is Burning" walked a fine line between sympathetic portrayal of New York's transvestites and transsexuals and homophobic voyeurism. In order to mobilise their co-religionists, British Muslims reproduced, translated, and read aloud the most offensive passages in *The Satanic Verses*. Most viewers who condemned the racist speech of the Ku Klux Klan and the White Aryan Resistance applauded the public television programme in which a panel of academics analysed the prosecution of a white racist for killing an Ethiopian immigrant in Portland, Oregon. But motives always are mixed. On his talk show Geraldo Rivera not only paired the White Aryan Resistance with CORE's Roy Innis but also encouraged Innis to assault the racist by shouting "Go ahead, Roy!," then made further shows about the fistfight, and allegedly taped yet another about Innis and the KKK to augment his audience during the television rating sweeps.[36] I cannot vouch for the purity of my own motives in choosing a sensational topic for these lectures and spicing it with racy examples.

Were legal regulation to take account of motive, even the speaker's stated intent would be inconclusive. American Jews accuse Philip Roth of fueling anti-Semitism by disseminating stereotypes; feminists identify John Updike, Saul Bellow, and Arthur Miller with their chauvinistic protagonists; Muslims heard Rushdie's voice in every one of the fantastic creatures who populate the 547 pages of

*The Satanic Verses.*[37] Each author might have echoed Bret Ellis's defence of *American Psycho.*

> I would think most Americans learn in junior high to differentiate between the writer and the character he is writing about. . . . Bateman is the monster. I am *not* on the side of that creep. . . . the murder sequences are so over the top, so baroque in their violence, it seems hard to take them in a literal context. And there are dozens more hints that direct the reader toward the realization that for all the book's surface reality, it is still satirical, semi-comic and—dare I say it?—playful in a way.

This did nothing to placate his critics, who despatched 13 death threats, containing photographs with his eyes poked out and an axe through his head. Los Angeles National Organization of Women president Tammy Bruce reiterated her commitment to a boycott. "This is not art. Mr. Ellis is a confused, sick young man with a deep hatred of women who will do anything for a fast buck."[38] The viewers who charged Spike Lee with anti-Semitism in the portrayal of two Jewish nightclub owners in "Mo' Better Blues" were equally dissatisfied with his retort: "Why is it that there can be no negative Jewish characters in films . . . [yet] we have black pimps and black drug dealers?"[39] Such philistinism may explain Antoni Tapies's refusal to "explain" his 60-foot sock: "I have always felt that works of art are like delicate flowers: the more you handle them, the more they are harmed. . . . I have made 7,000 works of art. I wonder how far I would have gone if I had submitted each one to a referendum."[40]

Authorship can profoundly shape reader response. When Doris Lessing submitted a book manuscript under the pseudonym Jane Somers her two regular British publishers rejected it. After Michael Joseph published the book, no Lessing authority would read it and no serious journal reviewed it.[41] Salvador Dali and Andy Warhol represent the opposite extreme, casually valorising the worthless by appending their signatures.[42] The speaker's identity similarly affects the harmfulness of words. Subordinated peoples neutralise slurs through banter within the contemned group, as when African Americans "play the dozens." They deflate insults by appropriating them as titles, as in the black rap group Niggaz With Attitude or the gay activists in Queer Nation, who plastered Greenwich Village with posters crying "Queers Be Ready" to protest the homicide prosecution of a gay man. Images that would be pornographic become feminist erotica when crafted by women, as when Judy Chicago's "Dinner Party" honoured 39 great women by decorating dinner plates with vaginas.[43] A Connecticut casino dressed cocktail waitresses as Pocahantas, with feathers in their hair and beaded miniskirts slit to the thigh. Imagine the outcy had it been owned by Anglos rather than Pequot Indians.[44] The difference between the golliwog on the Robertson's jam jar and a "Black Is Beautiful" doll depends not just on the images but also on who produces them for whom.

Audiences can disagree utterly and unpredictably about the meaning of a message. Sexual texts may be particularly open to conflicting interpretations, exemplified by the feminist split over lesbian sado-masochistic pornography, but political statements also permit diametrically opposed readings. Anselm Kiefer, one of the first post-war German artists to risk using Nazi symbols, published photos of himself giving the Sieg Heil salute in a variety of Roman amphitheatres, in a volume ambiguously entitled "Besetzungen" (occupations). Germans initially saw him as a Nazi sympathiser and have remained wary. But Americans, especially Jews, embraced him as an anti-Nazi German, elevating him above Marc Chagall as their favourite purveyor of Jewish themes.[45] When the fall of the Berlin Wall exposed Hitler's bunker the city's chief archaeologist wanted to incorporate it into the new German Parliament being built above the site: "It's an important and provocative memory, especially for people who will be working in the new ministry buildings. It would remind them every day of how evil governments can become." But at a public hearing one Berliner said: "This is a continuity of history that I don't want. I'm all for honoring the victims of Nazism, but this plan sounds like a way of honoring the perpetrators."[46]

The relationship between speaker and audience can colour the message. The Congregation for the Causes of Saints is said to be considering canonising its first African American—a Haitian who accompanied his impoverished master to New York after the late eighteenth-century slave revolt, cared for and supported him even though emancipated, and turned to good works after his master's death, tending cholera victims, building an orphanage, and helping the poor. Rev. Lawrence E. Lucas of the Resurrection Catholic Church in Harlem was contemptuous: "The man was a perfect creature of his times. He was a good boy, a namby-pamby, who kept the place assigned to him." Princeton religion professor Albert Raboteau was equally dismissive: "It calls out the sarcastic, 'Gee, thanks for finding us a hero' response."[47] A change in both speaker and audience can render an otherwise offensive message merely silly. Each year thousands of Germans dress up as Indians, Huns, Vikings, and Africans for the Cologne pre-Lenten Karneval. Some groups call themselves man-eaters, jungle brothers, and cannibals and wear blackface. With typical Teutonic thoroughness one man visits American Indian reservations every other year to buy artifacts and learn more about the culture. "Indians . . . say 'You're European. Go be Vikings.' They think we're crazy. . . . Hey, I can't help it. I just don't dream about being a Bavarian."[48]

Law is the construction of boundaries, which always are over- and under-inclusive. But when the state regulates speech, every categorisation is a hard case, not just those at the edge. Bans against pornography, hate speech, or blasphemy are forced to admit exceptions for politics, art, literature, and scholarship that are capable of engulfing the rule. Aesthetic criteria are inescapably political. All symbols are irreducibly ambiguous. Context, history, identity, audience, relationship, and motive can invert the moral quality of speech. But law decontextualises, aspires to universalism, and finds motive hopelessly elusive.

## III. Confused Consequentialism

Because utilitarianism is the dominant contemporary justification for criminal justice—indeed, the foundation of the modern state—the regulation of speech requires consequentialist arguments.[49] Robin Morgan gave the feminist campaign against pornography a central slogan: "pornography is the theory, and rape the practice."[50] The first newsletter of Women Against Violence in Pornography and Media cited convicted rapists' recollections of being aroused by pornography to argue that "even the most banal pornography objectifies women's bodies. An essential ingredient of much rape and other forms of violence to women is the 'objectification' of the woman."[51] Judith Bat-Ada contended: "Saturation with straightforward female sexual stimulus leads slowly but inevitably to the need for, and the acceptance of, such things as child molestation, incest, and sexual violence."[52] All the empirical research actually finds, however, is that exposure to violent images elicits aggressive *feelings*, not acts; and sexualising violence has no independent effect.[53] Supporting bills pending in Massachusetts and the U.S. Congress (despite the unconstitutionality of the Indianapolis ordinance), Catherine MacKinnon argued:

*The Excesses of State Regulation*

It's for the woman whose husband comes home with a video, ties
her to the bed, makes her watch, and then forces her to do what
they did in the video. It's a civil rights law. It's not censorship. It
just makes pornographers responsible for the injuries they cause.

Leanne Katz, executive director of the National Coalition against
Censorship, disagreed: "It negates all that we know about the . . .
ambiguity of the human animal, and all that we love about the
complexity of visual images and the written word."[54] Some anti-
porn campaigners buttress fears of rape with solicitude for pornographic actors, repeating atrocity stories about women actually
killed in snuff films. There is no evidence, however, that the
pornographic film industry is any riskier than mainstream studios
making horror movies, westerns, war stories, action films, or murder
mysteries.[55] Furthermore, society glamorises many more dangerous
occupations, such as ballet dancer, athlete, and police or fire
officer.[56] Nor does pornography necessarily degrade: some actors
are exhibitionists who enjoy performing sex in public to excite
others.[57]

Taking consequentialism seriously would require us to trace the
harmful effects back to the totality of causes, rather than contenting
ourselves with those that appear more susceptible to regulation but
may be less powerful. Because legal proscriptions can entail serious
penalties they must be framed narrowly, focusing on the aberrant
extreme: hard core pornography, neo-Nazi hate speech. Indeed, the
entire regulatory apparatus of the modern state is predicated on the
dubious strategy of seeking to compensate through intensity of
punishment for the impossibility of correcting more than a tiny
fraction of all deviance. But if the evils of pornography are objectification and violence, surely the beauty industry is a far greater villain.
On a randomly chosen day the *Los Angeles Times* contained nine
advertisements for weight loss, filling more than three pages with
photos of women in sexually provocative poses and captions like:
"Lose Up to 3 Dress Sizes in 10 Weeks," "Body of the '90's," "Now
I can wear the clothes my skinny sister wears."[58] A study of white
high school girls found only 22 per cent satisfied with their physical
appearance—not surprising, given that fashion models are 16–23
per cent thinner than the average woman. College students are avid
readers of women's magazines, of which *Cosmopolitan* has been the
most popular for 14 of the last 15 years. Almost half said the
magazines made them less confident, more than two-thirds felt
worse about their looks, and three-fifths said the magazines hurt

women. Although all were normal weight, four-fifths had dieted, and 10 percent had had eating disorders. Half of all American women say they would consider cosmetic surgery. There were 643,910 such operations in 1990, including 89,402 breast augmentations and 109,080 liposuctions. Even (perhaps especially) women whose bodies are envied or desired by millions—Cher, Mariel Hemingway, and Jane Fonda—have had breast augmentations. As a result, the American cosmetic surgery industry earns $300 million a year, the cosmetics industry $20 billion, and the diet industry $33 billion.[59] Advertising also reproduces racial subordination. African American women use skin lighteners, which may be linked to cancer. These have become popular in Africa, where they contain much higher concentrations of the active ingredient, greatly increasing the risks. One of the many illustrations of the impaired racial self-image is the preference by darker adoptive parents for lighter adopted children—a finding reported in *Ebony* magazine opposite an ad for Vantex Skin Bleaching Creme.[60]

The consequentialist case against speech dates to the early postwar decades, when critics blamed rising crime rates on television.[61] But just as the critique of pornography implicates all advertising, so the attack on media violence incriminates movies, comic books, and much of literature, including the Bible, Shakespeare's histories and tragedies, and Tolstoi's *War and Peace*. This debate has acquired racial overtones as commentators have attributed the violent response of some audiences to the content of films by African American directors about inner-city life: Ernest Dickerson's "Juice," Mario Van Peebles's "New Jack City," and John Singleton's "Boyz N the Hood."[62] "New Jack City" star Wesley Snipes regretted the violence but disavowed responsibility: "This film is anti-drug, anti-violence and anti-fratricide right across the board. If it was the film, then why don't we have a melee at each of the 800 plus theaters where it's showing?"[63] The producers maintained:

> Some of the films we have made attract black youths. What happens when they get together is not the films' fault. They take their beefs with them.
>
> . . .
>
> The media has begun a pre-release witch hunt with black films. You see cameras setting up outside theaters waiting for violence to happen. Sometimes, it's a self-fulfilling [prophecy].[64]

Just as African Americans have complained that black rappers are accused of obscenity for saying no more than white performers, so they can point to far more violent movies by Bruce Willis, Arnold Schwarzenegger or Clint Eastwood.[65] But some black filmmakers may be guilty of false naïvete. The poster advertising "Juice" depicted four young black men with the caption: "Juice. Power. Respect. How far will you go to get it?"[66] An independent producer who worked on marketing the film commented: "The vocabulary of film and television entertainment is dominated by sex and violence. To address real social issues in a marketable way, it is hard to avoid the reality of that vocabulary."[67] The writer and director of "Boyz N the Hood" insisted that the trailer focus on violence: "I wanted that action crowd." Had he promoted the film as a story about relationships, no one would have seen it.[68] The stakes are high: African Americans are twice as large a proportion of movie-goers as they are of the population.[69]

Scepticism about sweeping generalisations blaming violence on the media does not preclude causation in specific instances. Using stringent standards of causality the criminal law of conspiracy holds speakers responsible for their words. Parents have sued when their 9-year-old daughter was raped with a soda bottle a few days after television portrayed a rape with a plumber's helper, and when their adolescent sons attempted or committed suicide after listening to heavy metal recordings by Judas Priest and Ozzy Osbourne.[70] The Southern Poverty Law Center won a $7 million judgement against the Alabama Ku Klux Klan on behalf of a black woman whose son was lynched, and a $12.5 million award against Tom Metzger and the White Aryan Resistance for the murder of an Ethiopian immigrant by Portland, Oregon skinheads.[71] The sons of a contract murder victim won a $4.4 million judgement against *Soldier of Fortune* magazine, through whose advertisement the killer had been hired.[72]

Yet the relationship between life and art usually is too complex to reduce to unidirectional causality. At John Gotti's recent trial a taped telephone conversation recorded the mobster saying: "He didn't rob nothin'. You know why he is dying? He's gonna die because he refused to come when I called." One prosecutor said Gotti was copying Al Capone in "The Untouchables." A scriptwriter for "Married to the Mob" based the protagonist, Tony (the Tiger) Russo, partly on Gotti's performance at his 1986 racketeering trial. Dean Stockwell, who played Russo, stayed in character off the set: "I would get the most extraordinary reactions. Waiters, cabbies, they would do anything for me; I was like a king." Salvatore Locascio, the son of a Gotti co-defendant in the 1992 sequel, expressed outrage when Judge I. Leo Glasser disqualified one of his father's lawyers: "This is America; haven't they ever heard of the Bill of Rights? We have a Bill of Rights in this country. It's right over there, on the wall. Tell them to go over there and read it." One reporter was struck by the resemblance to Rod Steiger playing Al Capone in the 1959 movie: "We have a constitution in this country. The Constitution—ever heard of it? I suggest that when you go to your office you read it." Joseph Colombo Sr., the capo di tutti capi, agreed to help film "The Godfather" if some of his people were hired as extras and the words "Cosa Nostra" never were mentioned. James Caan, who played Sonny Corleone in the film, spent so much time hanging out with Carmine (the Snake) Persico that undercover agents once mistook him for the mobster. Henry Hill, a real gangster, whose biography was the basis for Martin Scorsese's "Goodfellas," said "the dress, the manner, the cockiness—a lot of it comes from the movies." When he was growing up, the older neighbourhood "wiseguys" "walked round like actors—it was like being a movie star." He described the first time he had seen Gotti, 30 years earlier. "John was at the card table" and suddenly started beating up a man. "I mean there was blood splashing over the walls." Asked if he was not confusing memory with a scene in "Goodfellas," Hill replied no, it was much closer to "The Untouchables."[73]

Although there may be rare instances in which we can confidently locate the genesis of action in expression, the relationship usually is far more complex. An image may be stimulus, but it may also evoke revulsion, represent fantasy, or offer catharsis. The attribution of causality tends to disregard the speaker's moral tone. Life may imitate art as often as art imitates life, but each is an improvisation, a variation on the other. Were we to take consequentialism seriously, we would have to accuse mainstream culture rather than scapegoating vulnerable targets on its fringe.

## IV. Perverse Penalties

Many of the legal system's generic problems are exacerbated when it regulates speech. Because formal procedures are costly—to the state as well as the parties—law is mobilised only against egregious offences.[74] The British Attorney General refuses to prosecute most complaints about race hatred, such as the Holocaust revisionist pamphlet "Did Six Million Really Die?" or Wing Commander Young's fulminations in "Deadlier than the H. Bomb": "Millions of

Negroes and Asiatics have been brought into Britain to pollute and destroy our Celtic-Anglo-Saxon race by mongrelisation."[75] The severity of sanctions diverts attention away from the heinousness of the crime and toward procedural niceties. American death penalty litigation offers an extreme example; the electric chair, to paraphrase Samuel Johnson, concentrates the mind wonderfully, but on the wrong issues. Like prosecutors, juries find legal penalties disproportionate to the wrong and rarely convict.[76] Because 1500 reports of racial hatred in Austria between 1984 and 1992 produced only 21 convictions, the government has drastically reduced the minimum sentence.[77] Law's glacial pace distorts and diminishes the remedies eventually awarded. Nearly five years after a professor allegedly began to sexually harass a student the University of Washington finally settled a complaint that had consumed hundreds of hours of hearings in four separate proceedings.[78]

All regulation encourages evasion, but the very ambiguity of speech that makes law such a crude response further facilitates evasion. A gamut of poetic techniques is readily available to disguise and multiply meanings: simile, metaphor, conceit, personification, hyperbole, litotes, synecdoche, metonymy, paradox, and irony. Effective advertising cleverly manipulates ambiguity to suggest what it cannot or will not declare. A romantically out-of-focus photograph of a couple embracing by a fountain is captioned: "The Art of French Kissing. Pour two glasses of Martell Cognac: one for you and one for someone you love. Then proceed to kiss in whatever manner pleases you."[79] Similar devices can convey proscribed political messages. When General Jaruzelski banned Solidarity, slogans appeared on walls, pamphlets, and banners throughout Poland in the distinctive script of Solidarność. Sympathisers of the PLO, ANC, IRA and other outlawed groups express defiance by displaying the colours of their organisations. Forbidden songs are given new words or the tunes simply hummed. Chinese youths revive memories of Tiananmen Square by wearing t-shirts bearing slogans like: "I'm bored" or "I'm the emperor." One simply displayed a black cat, elliptically referring to an epigram by the discredited 1960s reformer Deng Xiaopeng: "It doesn't matter if a cat is black or white. As long as it catches mice, it's a good cat."[80]

Commercial speech uses similar strategies to stymie regulation. When Quebec outlawed any language but French on outdoor signs a billboard advertising a self-storage operation in English sought protection as political speech by adding: "Before Bill 101, This Sign

Was Legal. Vote to Make This Legal Again."[81] In autumn 1991 a full-page advertisement ran in major British newspapers:

> This commercial has been banned from British television. As usual, it all comes down to a question of taste. Voice over: "For years we had a love affair. We thought it was over. But now passions are soaring once again since we discovered the taste of . . . 'I Can't Believe It's Not Butter!' . . . the new spread flavoured with buttermilk for that fresh, butter-like taste. High in polyunsaturates, low in saturates . . . with virtually no cholesterol." Looks innocent enough, doesn't it? Well, believe it or not, our commercial's got some people—including a certain food lobby—very hot under the collar.

The next day's variation partly obscured the still-legible word "butter," noted that the product could be promoted in the United States, and commented: "Now America is the land of free speech. If you want to say 'I can't believe it's not butter!' you can come right out and say so. . . . But not in Britain."[82]

When American television banned all tobacco advertising in 1971, Philip Morris initiated the Virginia Slims women's tennis tournament and R.J. Reynolds launched the Winston Cup auto race. They soon had many imitators: Vantage's Golf Scoreboard, Salem's Pro-Sail races, Lucky Strike bowling competitions, Winston's rodeo, Benson & Hedges ice skating, and Marlboro horse races. In 1988/89, 22 of the 24 major league baseball stadiums displayed cigarette advertisements in locations likely to be televised during games. By sponsoring the 1986 World Cup in Mexico City, R.J. Reynolds was able to erect four 20-foot signs next to the playing field, which were seen by the 650 million television viewers.[83] Philip Morris regained access to television for the first time in nearly two decades by subsidising the National Archives' bicentenary celebration of the Bill of Rights. Seeking to identify the right to smoke and to advertise cigarettes with civil rights, feminism, and artistic expression, it also bought advertisements occupying two-thirds of a page in leading American newspapers featuring the head and shoulders of Judith Jamison, the black director of the Alvin Ailey American Dance Theatre, accompanied by a quote skillfully chosen to imply an analogy to smoking:

> If anyone loses even a single right, we risk losing them all. . . . We cannot assume that the individual rights spelled out so succinctly

99

in the Bill of Rights will always be ours to enjoy. We must keep a watchful eye, a sharp mind, and most of all, a willingness to ensure that everyone is afforded the same freedom.[84]

The producers of blasphemy, pornography, and hate speech are no less inventive. Salman Rushdie's parody was sufficiently subtle to escape most early reviewers; had he not named the protagonists after historical characters his critique of Islam might have passed unnoticed and certainly would have gained less notoriety. Pornographers portray sex as mutual and call it erotica. Novel technologies offer new means of dissemination. When the French government launched its electronic conferencing system on Minitel, more than 20 per cent of the messages were sexually charged. America Online invites computer users to meet electronically in a series of public rooms—"Naughty Girls," "Romance Connection," "Gay Room"— and then adjourn to private rooms for confidential conversations; participants can use faxes to transmit sexually explicit photographs. Sierra On-Line offers an interactive version of the best-selling adult software program, Leisure Suit Larry, in which participants can configure the appearance of their characters and engage in sexual adventures with each other.[85] Madonna clothed (or rather exposed) her brand of striptease in the mantle of patriotism and civic duty by giving rap performances urging young people to register and vote. Wearing red panties, bra and combat boots and literally wrapping herself in the flag, she incanted:

Dr. King, Malcolm X
Freedom of speech is as good as sex.
. . .
We need beauty, we need art
We need government with a heart.
Don't give up your freedom of speech.
Power to the people is in our reach.

Backed by two flag-waving male dancers in tight shorts and army boots, who were paddling her, she warned: "If you don't vote, you're going to get a spankie." Although a VFW spokesman denounced this as "border[ing] on desecration," Madonna's publicist boasted that more than 10,000 college students had registered as a result.[86]

Racists translate hate into pseudo-science, substituting regression analyses for vulgarities. The Nation of Islam has published *The*

*Secret Relationship Between Blacks and Jews*, which claims to document Jewish responsibility for slavery in 1275 footnotes.[87] Holocaust revisionists mimic the apparatus and objectivity of scholarship. Their deceptively misnamed *Historical Review* extols the academic travesties of fellow travellers: "a truly comprehensive and scholarly compendium of primary research that challenges all the major orthodox 'Holocaust' claims," "hundreds of critical commentaries on the Nuremberg Trials by leading western military men," "personal systematic research that culminated in his well-documented refutation of the entire Holocaust story."[88] Emulating David Duke's sanitised racism, Colorado KKK head Shawn Slater ran for city council in a Denver suburb on the slogan: "Equal rights for all; special privileges for nobody." "I'm not a white supremacist," he claimed, forbidding his followers to use racial epithets or wear Nazi insignia. National leader Thomas Robb insisted that the Klan does not hate blacks, it just loves whites.[89] In a pamphlet misleadingly titled "Jewish Tributes to Our Child Martyrs," Lady Jane Birdwood used such "conciliatory tones" to repeat the blood libel that "Christian children . . . were crucified, tortured and bled to death all over Europe in mediaeval times to satisfy Jewish religious rituals" that the Attorney General refused to prosecute. Condemning the Talmud for "incitements to hatred of gentiles in general and Christian people in particular," which "are *still* a part of the catechism of Jewish belief propounded in Rabbinical colleges the world over," Lady Birdwood asked rhetorically: "Could these awful texts have prompted the child murders?" She commended Jews for seeking Christian "forgiveness and trust" and hoped that "the commemoration was but a first step by decent Jews to eradicate the mephitic odours of anti-Christian hatred which waft through the writings of their ancestral 'learned sages' . . . ." A reader of this pamphlet would be surprised to discover that the events she described as "an unprecedented display of Jewish contrition and humility" for a "mass suicide of Jews" actually were an apology by *Christians* for the *massacre* of hundreds of Jews 800 years ago.[90]

Commercial speakers have perfected the strategy of hiding their profit motive behind a hypocritical attachment to principle. The tobacco industry is notorious for pretending to defend freedom rather than sell poison. In October 1991 it placed daily full-page advertisements in many British papers, beginning with a quotation attributed to St. Augustine: "Hear the Other Side."

When fundamental freedoms are at stake it's particularly vital to hear the other side. . . . In a judgement delivered at the end of July, a Canadian court ruled that there was no proven connection between tobacco advertising and overall tobacco consumption. And no proof that banning advertising reduces consumption. In fact, the Court struck down Canada's tobacco advertising ban as "a form of censorship and social engineering which is incompatible with the very essence of a free and democratic society."

The ad neglected to mention that the judgement is on appeal. A week later the industry raised the spectre of Puritan intolerance, quoting Cromwell: "Not what they want but what is good for them" and adding: "there's something inherently anti-democratic in imposing upon people your view of what's best for them." A third ad invoked Juvenal: "Let my will replace reasoned judgement" and sought to inflame British resentment against Eurocrats: "That's not fair or democratic. But that seems to be Brussels' view when it comes to tobacco advertising."[91]

With considerably less sophistication, racists have presented themselves as champions of free speech victimised by state oppression. We saw earlier how the National Socialist Party of America shifted public debate from the hatefulness of its message to its constitutional right to march in Skokie. Tom Metzger of the White Aryan Resistance insists: "I believe everything I publish is protected by the First Amendment."[92] Justifying the invitation of Holocaust revisionists to a conference, the head of a black Los Angeles group, declared: "It's time we hear all sides of this thing of holocausts. And that is what the 1st Amendment is all about . . . ."[93] The revisionist California Institute for Historical Review bought advertisements in a number of university student newspapers under the heading "Committee for Open Debate on the Holocaust."[94] Electoral politics also offers a protected arena. IRA members otherwise silenced by British television can speak as political candidates.[95] Well before George Bush's 1988 campaign ad featured a rape by a black prisoner on weekend leave, the British National Party used elections to propagate racism. A candidate for the Loughton, Essex local council pictured a 75-year-old white woman "savagely beaten by two young black thugs who raided her flat in Brixton." The Tower Hamlets branch condemned "Asian racial violence directed at the white community" and warned: "The Moslems are taking over our East End."[96]

If state regulation of speech were merely ineffective it might be a harmless diversion. But punishment can be positively perverse. Civil litigation over defamation or invasion of privacy typically pits celebrities against the tabloid press in a battle each side both wins (publicity and circulation) and loses (reputation, emotional distress, and money).[97] Just as women are raped twice—the second time by defence counsel—so speech victims may suffer more from the repetition, elaboration, proof, rebuttal, and publicity of the trial. Indeed, only the legal regulation of speech reenacts the crime verbatim, usually before a much larger audience. Bill Roache, who played Ken Barlow on "Coronation Street" for 31 years, sued *The Sun* for a centre-page article entitled "Boring Ken was girl-crazy stud," which portrayed him as smug, boastful, wooden, lucky not to have been fired, a joke to scriptwriters, and universally hated by the cast. Roache testified: "I felt humiliated and so embarrassed that I didn't want to see people or talk about it"—but of course he did both in the courtroom. Although he had disregarded certain accusations to spare his wife, newspapers covering the trial reported in salacious detail his alleged one-night stand with the late Pat Phoenix and his "seduction" of Jennifer Moss on the floor of his house after a party. Full of emotion, Roache reproached *The Sun's* counsel "for behaving like *The Sun*. I didn't bring this [up] . . . and I don't see why I should have to go through it." Awarded £50,000 and costs estimated at £200,000, Roache complained "We've been through hell and back." *The Sun's* legal officer was unrepentant: "We offered Bill Roache £50,000 about a month ago. He could have had an apology and could have had his costs paid. I think he has been through this last week's ordeal . . . for little or no reason."[98]

Even when legal regulation does not court evasion or aggravate harm it constructs and encourages deviance. Ever since the Edenic myth we have known that prohibition arouses desire.[99] Iran has banned all videotapes except children's cartoons, and the Force to Combat the Corruption of Society confiscated more than 20,000 unlawful tapes in Teheran in a seven-month period, but Iranians still can buy anything, including hard-core porn.[1] Regulation confers moral salience. Skinheads flaunt swastikas; German youth sing "Deutschland über Alles," wear Nazi insignias, and give the Sieg Heil salute; the KKK dresses in white hoods and burns crosses—all because the state response evidences public outrage. The editor of the National Front *Bulldog* challenged the government to prosecute him, warning that otherwise "we will print a special victory issue . . . with even more racialist articles."[2] True ideologues welcome punishment as martyrdom, which can only enlarge their entourage. After losing his house to satisfy a $12.5 million damage award for inciting skinheads to murder a black immigrant, White Aryan Resistance leader Tom Metzger vowed to continue his racist propaganda.[3] Punishment confers visibility.[4] Frank Collin and his pitiful band of neo-Nazis would have languished in obscurity had Skokie not tried to stop them from "marching." When the KKK demonstrated at the Colorado statehouse to vilify Martin Luther King's birthday as a "Day of Infamy for America," 400 police had to protect the hundred Klansmen from a thousand opponents, who fought the cops and trashed nearby stores, producing extensive media coverage. The state Klan leader welcomed the incident as "a million dollars worth of publicity." Each weekend, when Klansmen drop *The White Patriot* and other racist literature on residential doorsteps, "somebody usually gets mad and makes a few calls. And bingo! We're back on television."[5] Sentenced to six months imprisonment for 18 counts of racist slander on the Stockholm Community radio network, Ahmed Rami emulated Hitler's *Mein Kampf* by writing a 500-page book about his persecution, entitled "Jewish Witch-Trial in Sweden."[6] Jean-Marie Le Pen and the National Front gained publicity and even sympathy during regional French elections when demonstrators prevented their plane from landing, mayors banned their gatherings, and police disrupted marches.[7]

Black rappers have capitalised on the repression of their outrageous lyrics. When 2 Live Crew were prosecuted for obscenity after performing at a Florida nightclub, group leader Luther Campbell used the trial to promote their next video, soon to be premiered on MTV: "It's about how 2 Live Crew gets punished and sent to Cuba and Castro is waiting for them." Sales of the album on which their nightclub act was based had peaked at 1.2 million until born-again Miami lawyer Jack Thompson began a campaign against it, sending copies of the lyrics to Florida Governor Bob Martinez and the sheriffs of 65 counties. Sales promptly jumped to 2 million. Broward County Sheriff Nick Navarro—nicknamed "Prime Time" for his frequent media appearances—put undercover deputies on the case. The rapper and the sheriff appeared on Geraldo Rivera's television talk show, while Phil Donahue paired the rapper with the Christian lawyer. 2 Live Crew responded with a new album, "Banned in the USA," described as "a rap ode to the First Amendment."[8] The lyrics of Ice-T's "Cop Killer," recorded a year before the Rodney King beating trial, seemed to foreshadow the Los Angeles riots: "I got my 12-gauge sawed off/I got my headlights turned off/I'm 'bout to bust some shots off/I'm 'bout to dust some cops off." After the worst civil disturbance in twentieth-century American history the Combined Law Enforcement Association of Texas, the Los Angeles Police Protective League, and the Fraternal Order of Police declared a boycott of the record. A Latina Los Angeles city councillor running for Congress urged Time Warner to withdraw it and local radio stations to stop playing it. The California Attorney General wrote to the executives of 18 record chains. The Houston city council denounced the lyrics. Three record store chains with more than a thousand outlets pulled the song. Ice-T bristled: "What they're really trying to do is shut down my platform. They do not want to let me be able to speak to the masses. . . . I'm going to talk about this record on the next record." Predictably, the campaign had the opposite effect. Sales jumped 60 per cent in Los Angeles, 100 per cent in Austin, San Antonio and Dallas, and 370 per cent in Houston; the album climbed from 62nd to 49th on the charts, selling 330,000 copies in 17 weeks. Ice-T sold out a live performance in Los Angeles. When he unexpectedly withdrew the song six weeks after the controversy began, to prove he was not motivated by profits, there was a run on the 150,000 unsold records. He continued to maintain that "Cop Killer" "is not a call to murder police. This song is about anger and the community and how people get that way."[9]

## V. Conclusion

Governmental bans on speech suffer the problems common to all state regulation and some that are unique. Law dichotomises experience, rupturing its inherent continuities. Boundaries are arbitrary and therefore indeterminate. It is impossible to distinguish unlawful speech from the routine opportunism of politicians pandering to popular prejudice: an Enoch Powell, Jean-Marie Le Pen, Patrick Buchanan, David Duke, Dan Quayle, or George Bush emphasising the "costs" of immigration, calling for "law and order," depicting AIDS as divine retribution, attacking racial quotas, or extolling family values. Legal distinctions elevate form over substance: sceptics may attack religious belief as long as they do not mock the believer; filmmakers may exploit sex if they portray the behaviour as mutual or add an artistic veneer; racists and anti-Semites can indulge their hatred in the language of pseudo-science or history.

Legal efforts to regulate speech founder on the ineradicable ambiguity of meaning. The significance and moral valence of symbols vary radically with speaker and audience and can reverse rapidly, even instantaneously, like the optical illusion that flips between a vase and two profiled faces. Whereas circumstances only aggravate or mitigate the heinousness of other crimes, they can transform speech from abhorrent to commendable and vice versa. Subordinated groups play with their stigmata in order to neutralise them; lesbians enjoy erotica that would be pornography if produced or consumed by men. Legal formalism aspires to a universalism that must willfully ignore context, as illustrated by the prosecution of British black power advocates under the 1965 Race Relations Act. Yet law's attempt to frame exceptions encounters great difficulty in dealing with black anti-Semitism, minority homophobia and misogyny, and female racism. Although the moral quality and hurtfulness of symbols depend on the creator's motive, this is singularly difficult to discern. Author or critic may insist that extreme misogyny turns into parody, as Bret Ellis protested about his novel *American Psycho* and Henry Louis Gates Jr. said of 2 Live Crew. And even the best intentions may only mitigate, not excuse. The equally pivotal audience response is unpredictable, divided, and fickle. The history of art, literature, politics, religion, morality, and even science should inspire healthy scepticism about the durability of contemporary judgements.

The severity of legal remedies can be justified only by exaggerating the consequences of speech, but consequentialist reasoning is fatally flawed. Causation is complex and the responsibility of speech unsubstantiated. All audiences actively engage in interpretation and criticism—even young children seemingly mesmerised by television cartoons. Preoccupation with the extremes—which alone provoke sufficient outrage to mobilise the political support necessary for prohibition—diverts attention from the quotidian—which inflicts far greater harm. Hard-core porn and neo-Nazi ranting contribute much less to reproducing attitudes toward race, ethnicity, gender, and sexual orientation than do the mass media, advertising, popular culture, political rhetoric, childrearing practice, education, and religion. But legislators and judges openly refuse to confront modal behaviour.

If the consequences of speech are too indeterminate to justify punishment, the effects of punishment are positively perverse. The severity of legal punishment, combined with uncertainty and disagreement about the moral quality of speech, make prosecutors reluctant to charge, juries unwilling to convict, and judges hesitant to punish. Formal law diverts attention from the content of speech to the procedures used to suppress it, delaying the outcome and

*Conclusion*

thereby distorting and diminishing the impact of legal remedies. The ambiguity of symbols facilitates evasion, allowing speakers to cloak their motives in the garb of art, science, or politics—forms that law's literalism cannot penetrate. Regulation may fail most when it appears to succeed. Because speech is the offence, a repeat performance at trial aggravates the injury. The greatest perversion, however, is that law, far from silencing harmful speech, rather encourages, valorises, and publicises it, transforming offender into victim and offence into romantic defiance.

## Notes

[1] Except where otherwise noted, my source is Gordon (1982: 1–22). For documentation of racial hatred, abuse, and violence, see Lawrence (1987); Waller (1981/82); Hytner (1981); Gordon (1990a); Klug (1982; 1988); Hiro (1971); Tompson (1988); Bethnal Green (1978); Gilroy (1987); Macdonald et al. (1989); Gifford et al. (1989); Brown (1984); Hall (1985); CRE (1984; 1987; 1988a); GLC (1984a; 1984b; 1984c; 1984d; 1984e); Layton-Henry (1984); Pulle (1973). Scotland Yard recorded 3373 incidents of racial assault or abuse in London in 1991, 16 per cent above the previous year. Civil rights groups reported 6459 in England and Wales in 1990, up a third since 1988. *New York Times* (August 20, 1992). On racial attacks throughout Europe, see European Parliament (1985); *Searchlight*.

[2] House of Commons Debates, vol. 711, col. 940 (May 3, 1965), quoted in Dickey (1968: 490).

[3] *The Times* (December 22, 1966), rev'd, (1967) Q.B. 51 (GBM leaflet); *The Times* (January 26, 1967) (Colin Jordan).

[4] Home Office (1975).

[5] *Daily Telegraph* (July 25, 1978).

[6] *Daily Telegraph* (October 31, 1978).

[7] Home Affairs Committee (1980).

[8] Green Paper (1980).

[9] We saw in the second chapter that Henry Louis Gates Jr. defended 2 Live Crew as self-parody. Fiske (1989) has offered a similar reading of Madonna's sexual stereotypes.

[10] *Jacobson v. U.S.*, 118 L.Ed.2d 174 (1992); *New York Times* s.1 p.8 (April 19, 1992).

[11] *New York Times* s.4 p.4 (January 19, 1992).

[12] On the history of blasphemy, see Jones (1980); Webster (1990).

[13] Steinem (1980: 37); see also Longino (1980). On the difficulty of bounding pornography, see Barthes (1976); Sontag (1982). For the dismal history of the American attempt, see de Grazia (1992); on Britain, see Barker (1984). Responding to criticism of rap lyrics, 67 record companies took a full page ad citing examples of earlier bans: Cole

*The Excesses of State Regulation*

Porter's "Love for Sale" (1940), The Doors' "Unknown Soldier" (1968), Neil Young (criticised by Vice President Spiro Agnew 1970), Bob Dylan (banned 1971). *Los Angeles Times* F? (July 17, 1992). Sholem Asch's play "God of Vengeance" was banned in New York in 1923. *New York Times* s.2 p.6 (October 18, 1992). A Japanese court banned Nagisa Oshima's "In the Realm of the Senses," although it could not define obscenity. Oshima (1992); *New York Review of Books* 40 (October 8, 1992).

[14] *Guardian* 5 (November 13, 1991).

[15] Matsuda (1989: 2357, 2367). How would she deal with a Hebrew translation of *Mein Kampf*? Shocken Books refused the project: "we suffered too much as a result of this man and this book, and should not perpetuate his ideas." So did Yad Vashem (the memorial to Holocaust victims) because "it still is emotionally difficult." The translator, an Austrian Jew who fled the Nazis and whose parents were killed in the camps, persisted despite a dozen rejections. "It's a sad episode but a historical fact, and the younger generations must know what really happened and why. You have to know who your enemy is and what he is." Akadamon ultimately printed 400 copies of an annotated version of one-fifth of the original book, in plain black and white covers without illustrations. *New York Times* B2 (August 5, 1992).

[16] Eysenck (1971); Jensen (1969); Herrnstein (1971); U.S. News & World Report (1965). For a critique of racist biology, see Gould (1981). Shockley was a physicist who donated his sperm to a Nobel-prize winner sperm bank and won a $1 damage award for defamation when his racist theories were challenged. *National Law Journal* 6 (September 24, 1884), 8 (October 1, 1984).

At City University of New York, philosophy professor Michael Levin has written articles for academic journals contending that "there is now quite solid evidence that . . . the average black is significantly less intelligent than the average white." *Levin v. Harleston et al.*, SDNY 90 Civ 6123 (KC) (September 4, 1991); Rohde (1991). On the other side, Black Studies chair Dr. Leonard Jeffries Jr. has called Europeans "ice people"—materialistic and intent on domination—in contrast with the humanistic "sun people" of African descent. He claims that extra melanin gives blacks intellectual and physical advantages. *Chronicle of Higher Education* A4–5 (September 25, 1991), A19 (November 6, 1991), A19 (February 5, 1992); *New York Times* A13 (April 20, 1990), A18 (March 27, 1992). Within the "Afrocentric" movement Michael Bradley's *The Iceman Inheritance: Prehistoric Sources of Western Man's Racism, Sexism, and Aggression* argues that whites are so vicious because they are descended from brutish Neanderthals, of whom Jews are the "purest" example. It was recently reissued with endorsements from two members of the City University Africana Studies Department. *New York Times* A13 (July 20, 1992) (op ed). Bradley purported to rely on Carleton Coon, whose *The Origin of Races* (1962) has been exposed as unscientific and wrong. *New York Times* 14 (August 29, 1992) (letter to the Editor from Ashley Montagu, August 15). How would Matsuda distinguish between *The Satanic Verses* and the long tradition of debunking religious belief, e.g., Fox (1992); Wilson (1992).

[17] The *Harvard Lampoon* produced a parody of the May 1992 issue of the conservative *Dartmouth Review*, substituting it for the real thing at campus distribution points. A fictitious editorial writer apologised for the *Review*'s gaffe of quoting from *Mein Kampf* in a 1991 issue while hailing the Führer's "rhetorical flair unsurpassed in German literature since Nietzsche." A "Spring Fashion" section showed Hitler posing in the woods in preppy attire. The Dartmouth administration refused the *Review*'s request to condemn the Harvard prank. *New York Times* B8 (May 13, 1992).

[18] The Ku Klux Klan used to march openly on Long Island in the 1920s, winning popularity contests at county fairs. The trophies it awarded volunteer fire departments remained on display in the fire houses for 70 years. They disappeared only when black community groups sought to integrate the departments in 1992. White firefighters were surprised at the outrage their retention provoked. *New York Times* A13 (August 11, 1992).

[19] Quoted in Edwards (1991). The language is strikingly similar to Rushdie's open letter to Rajiv Gandhi, quoted in Chapter One.

[20] Kappeler (1986: 83).

[21] Gardner (1978: 170).

[22] *Guardian* 27 (November 9, 1991) (the verdict was overturned because the judge overreached in summing up).

[23] *Guardian* 33 (October 10, 1991).

[24] Pop star Marky Mark dedicated his recent book to his penis and opened with a frontispiece picturing him holding it. *New York Times* B2 (September 28, 1992). Madonna's MTV teaser for her single "Erotica" and $49.95 picture book *Sex* showed her with eyes masked, dressed in leather, being ridden like a horse; pulling the reins of bondage boys; and in a lesbian love scene and a ménage à trois—all shot in grainy black-and-white reminiscent of snuff films. The "Erotica" album comes in a "adult" version with a parental advisory sticker. The track "Where Life Begins" celebrates her pleasure in being orally gratified. *Los Angeles Times* F4 (October 5, 1992); *New York Times* s.2 p.28 (October 18, 1992).

[25] Friedrich (1992).

[26] Paintings bore titles like "Insults to German Womanhood" and "Nature as Seen by Sick Minds." Opening the 1937 exhibition in Munich, Hitler called for the imprisonment or sterilisation of artists who continued the "practice of prehistoric art stutterings." *New York Times* B3 (March 5, 1992); *The New Yorker* 32 (October 5, 1992). See also Peter Cohen's documentary movie "The Architecture of Doom" reviewed in *Los Angeles Times* F14 (March 27, 1992).

*The Excesses of State Regulation*

[27] Svenson (1982: 207).

[28] *New York Times* B1 (March 24, 1992).

[29] Fried (1991); *Guardian* 25 (November 21, 1991). Sally Mann's photographs of her children (7, 10, and 12 years old) are a perfect example (1992). They appear nude, poor, and abused but insist they enjoy posing for her. A psychologist found them "well adjusted and self-assured," Ms. Mann gave them a veto, which they exercised against some pictures: "They don't want to be geeks or dweebs," she said, but "nudity doesn't bother them." Some of the most troubling pictures—"The Wet Bed," "Jessie Bites"—are posed reconstructions. Mann says she would stop if she thought she were harming them. "I don't think of my children, and I don't think anyone else should think of them, with any sexual thoughts. I think childhood sexuality is an oxymoron." A Cardozo Law School professor maintained: "There isn't the slightest question that what she's doing is art . . . " But religious conservatives have sought to close her shows, and a federal prosecutor warned her against exhibiting some photos and urged her to look out for strangers who see them and ingratiate themselves with the family. *New York Times Magazine* 29 (September 27, 1992).

[30] Gardner (1978: 135). A Stasi officer once shouted at the East German writer Lutz Rathenow: "I forbid you to write poems with double meanings! Also poems with triple meanings! We have experts who can decipher everything!" Kinzer (1992: 50).

Should the ambiguity of art protect Andres Serrano's "Piss Christ" (a crucifix submerged in the artist's urine), "Stigmata" (a nude female with white leather cuffs and bloodied hands), "Cabeza de Vaca" (a calf's head on a pedestal but also the name of a 15th century Conquistador), "Heaven and Hell" (a cardinal turned away from a bloody nude woman whose hands are bound and head is flung back), "Ejaculate in Trajectory" (self-explanatory), and the "Red River" series (close-ups of sanitary pads)? Serrano "explains": "I've always had trouble seeing things as black or white. I've always accepted that duality in myself. My work is a reflection of it." Lippard (1990).

[31] Abel (1973).

[32] An American Indian recently entitled an article "White Men Can't Drum," complaining (humourously) about the appropriation of his people's culture and symbols by the fringe of the men's movement that seeks to recapture manhood in the wilderness. *New York Times Magazine* 30 (October 4, 1992).

[33] Perhaps with humour. A cartoon in the inaugural issue of *The New Yorker* under the editorship of Tina Brown (formerly of *The Tatler* and *Vanity Fair*) shows a man walking by a construction site, from which four women workers taking a coffee break give wolf whistles and yell catcalls like "Yo! Nice Butt!" "I think I'm in love!" and "Looking for me, Sweetie?" *The New Yorker* 114 (October 5, 1992).

[34] Ellen Burstyn and the entire cast of "Shimada" protested that the critics

saw only the surface, literal aspects of the play. We were shocked and stunned that they had missed what the play was about, that it was designed to stimulate questions, not give easy answers, to encourage people to look at their own prejudice, the old wounds on both sides. . . . please do not impugn our honor by calling us prejudiced when we employ our God-given gifts to tell our deepest truths about the moral failure of prejudice.
New York Times A18 (May 8, 1992) (letter to The Editor, April 26).

[35] Lacombe (1988); King (1985); Callwood (1985).

[36] *Los Angeles Times* F1 (February 5, 1992). In August, Rivera taped a Klan rally in Wisconsin. When Klansmen started calling him spic and dirty Jew and throwing things he fought back and was arrested but secured his release from jail in time to film the cross burning. *Los Angeles Times* A12 (August 17, 1992).

What was the motive of Bill Buford (expatriate American author and *Granta* editor) in hanging out with British neo-Nazis and writing "objectively" about their thuggery? Buford (1992a; 1992b). Or the *Weekly Mail*, South Africa's prize-winning progressive paper, in publishing an article entitled "Too Many Tits, Not Enough Text" illustrated with four pictures of topless women, ostensibly to criticise the government's hypocrisy in banning the local porn magazine *Scope* while admitting its American competitor *Penthouse*. *Weekly Mail* 6 (September 4, 1992).

[37] "How can one possibly accept that a writer could distance himself from the words his characters speak? Indeed, how can he not be responsible for his entire representation?" Bharucha (1990: 64). This commentator is an Indian drama critic.

[38] *New York Times* B1 (March 6, 1991); Edwards (1991).

[39] *Los Angeles Times* F6 (February 26, 1992).

[40] *New York Times* B1 (March 24, 1992).

[41] Lessing (1984: vii–xii); Kappeler (1986: 125–26).

[42] 80 years ago Marcel Duchamp "found" art, transforming ordinary objects into "ready-mades" by appending his signature. In the overheated art market of the 1980s, identity was the philosopher's stone. Salvador Dali's lobster-claw telephone sold for $110,000 in 1988; one of Joseph Beuys's 100 identical felt suits for $75,360 in 1989; and in November 1991 Dan Flavin's diagonal fluorescent light commanded $148,500 and Jeff Koons's vacuum cleaners in plastic boxes $198,000. In February 1992 auctioneers expected to get $50–60,000 for Willem de Kooning's five-hole privy seat and $80–120,000 for Robert Gober's pair of urinals. *New York Times* s.2 p.37 (February 23, 1992).

[43] Kappeler (1986): 39) citing English (1980). See also Kensington Ladies' Erotica Society (1984); Barbach (1984; 1986); Chester (1988); Scholder & Silverberg (1991); Grace (1991); Kiss & Tell (1991); Shepherd (1992); Gordon (1984).

In-group membership does not guarantee immunity from criticism. When the Israeli rock group Duralex Sedlex accepted an invitation to

*The Excesses of State Regulation*

Poland, hoping to play the song "Zyklon B" at Auschwitz to symbolise Jewish survival, many Israelis protested. One Auschwitz survivor found this "a desecration of the memory of the victims." *New York Times* B2 (August 5, 1992).

[44] *New York Times* A8 (January 29, 1992), s.1 p.15 (February 16, 1992); *Los Angeles Times* E1 (February 21, 1992).

[45] Flam (1992). The prestigious Documenta IX exhibit in Kassel removed four of the five paintings by Filipino-American artist Manuel Ocampo because they contained swastikas, although he denied advocating fascism and claimed they were an ancient mystic symbol. *Los Angeles Times* F8 (June 15, 1992). Soon thereafter the Galería Otra Vez at a Latino art centre in Los Angeles removed Ocampo's "Vade Retro"—a cartoonish black man with gigantic genitals urinating on the cross—from its "Monster! Monster?" exhibit for the Columbus quincentennial. The gallery refused Ocampo's offer to post a statement explaining his intentions. *Los Angeles Times* F1 (October 10, 1992).

Two Columbia College seniors argued strongly that "Batman Returns" was anti-Semitic. *New York Times* A17 (July 2, 1992) (op ed).

[46] *New York Times* A5 (February 29, 1992); *Los Angeles Times* A3 (July 25, 1992).

[47] *New York Times* s.1 p.1 (February 23, 1992).

[48] *Los Angeles Times* E1 (January 28, 1992).

[49] For consequentialist justifications for regulating hate speech, see Riesman (1942); Delgado (1982); Matsuda (1989: 2327). When Goethe published *The Sorrows of Young Werther* in 1774, a fictionalised account of his own love triangle, some communities banned it, blaming it for several suicides that followed. *New York Times* B1 (August 7, 1992).

Roger Coggan, director of Los Angeles Gay and Lesbian Community Services, deplored the threefold increase in attacks on gays and lesbians between 1989 and 1991 and blamed California Governor Pete Wilson's veto of AB101, which would have outlawed employment discrimination against gays and lesbians. "The veto . . . sends a message that gays and lesbians are not entitled to basic government protection. It's a message that fans the flames of gay-bashing and bigotry." *Los Angeles Times* B1 (January 23, 1992).

During his first bout as presidential candidate, Ross Perot followed the dubious lead of Dan Quayle by attacking a "Doogie Hawser" episode in which the eponymous character and his girlfriend, both 18, lost their virginity. "Some 15-year-old girl that's been thinking about it hadn't done it yet. 'Hell, Doogie's girl did it. It must be all right.' " *New York Times* A9 (June 8, 1992).

[50] Morgan (1977: 169).

[51] Russell and Lederer (1980: 24–26).

[52] Lederer (1980d: 122).

[53] Childress (1991). It is more plausible that tolerating pornography increases its prevalence. Porn stars are appearing in mainstream films (Traci

112

Lords in "Crybaby") and as fashion models (Jeff Stryker for Thierry Mugler). Madonna has persuaded model Naomi Campbell and rap star Vanilla Ice to pose for *Sex*, her erotic coffee table book. Comedian Sandra Bernhard posed for *Playboy*. Vanessa Williams, the black 1984 Miss America who was forced to resign when nude photos were published, made the cover of *McCall's* magazine. Even the notorious Koo Stark appeared at Leo Castelli's table at the 35th anniversary party for his trendy art gallery at Industria. *New York Times* B4 (May 11, 1992). The success of "Basic Instinct" has produced a rash of imitative erotic thrillers: "Caged Fear," "Sunset Heat," "Fatal Instinct," "Animal Instincts," and "Red Shoe Diaries." *New York Times* B5 (October 8, 1992). But when hard-core porn star Amber Lynn participated in the Youth AIDS Foundation of Los Angeles fund raiser, advisory board members Tori Spelling ("Beverly Hills, 90210") and Corin Nemec ("Parker Lewis Can't Lose") discovered they had other engagements. *New York Times* B2 (August 31, 1992).

Violent behaviour among children is correlated with the number of hours they watch television but not with programme *content*, suggesting that the causal link may be deprivation of play or failure of parental discipline. Winn (1985); *New York Times* s.4 p.16 (August 9, 1992) (letter to The Editor by Winn, July 31).

54 *New York Times* s.1 p.10 (March 15, 1992).

55 The deaths in the filming of "The Twilight Zone" did not shut down television, or even end that show.

56 Burstyn (1985b); Gordon (1983); *New York Times* A18 (August 12, 1992) (letters to The Editor from two women doctors about the effect of gymnastics on women: delay or suspension of menses, early osteoporosis, stress fractures, and chronic pain).

57 Stoller (1991); L. Williams (1989); Delacoste & Alexander (1987). In both D.H. Lawrence's *Sons and Lovers* and Philip Roth's *Goodbye Columbus* lovemaking couples court discovery to heighten erotic pleasure. Clive Secker, 27, and Amanda Broomfield, 25, stripped naked and had sexual intercourse in daylight on a roundabout in Frome, Somerset. Both said they had dared the other. Secker is the son of the former mayor of Frome. *Guardian* 2 (November 22, 1991).

What should one make of San Francisco's "modern primitives," who engage in "body modification" or "body play," subjecting themselves to enormous pain for their own pleasure? Nikki Chandle explains: "Every tattoo and every piercing signifies some pain I have experienced in my life. Piercing is just like life. It hurts. It heals. And then you live with it. Forever." Christine S. adds: "I'm a masochist, so I'm really into the pain of it. With piercing, when the needle is going through, it's agonizing. You get an incredible rush of endorphins. You feel like God's daughter." At the DNA lounge on lower Haight, "Fakir Musafar" (formerly Roland Loomis of Aberdeen, South Dakota) hangs from hooks inserted in holes through his nipples. Marchand (1992). Such activities are going mainstream.

Universal Studios in Florida is considering showcasing the Jim Rose Circus sideshow at Halloween. Rose swallows razor blades, lies on a bed of nails, and hammers spikes into his nose. Mr. Lifto hangs heavy objects from his pierced nipples, while the Torture King puts pins through his; an ageing dwarf feeds live slugs to the Sword Swallower, while Matt (The Tube) Crowley drinks several quarts of beer, chocolate sauce and ketchup through a tube in his nose and then regurgitates the mixture. Fans queue for front-row seats to see the tears in Mr. Lifto's eyes. *New York Times* B4 (June 15, 1992); *Los Angeles Times* E1 (September 1, 1992); cf. Bogdan (1988).

[58] *Los Angeles Times* A6, A8, A10, A12, A14, A17, A18, A19, A22 (March 25, 1991).

[59] Implants enhance the attractiveness of breasts to men while eliminating them as a site of female pleasure. Wolf (1991); Faludi (1991); *New York Times* A1 (February 6, 1992); *Los Angeles Times* E1 (August 18, 1992); 254(5) *The Nation* 155 (February 10, 1992). To reduce sexual harassment, women in the U.S. Navy have adopted the opposite strategy, gaining weight, eschewing makeup, and wearing uniforms several sizes too large to make themselves unattractive. *Los Angeles Times* A1 (February 10, 1992). On the role of advertisements in constructing gender images, see Goffman (1976); Steele (1985: 65–67); Goldman (1992).

Male bodies are being similarly fetishised. A Los Angeles bookstore reported a 25–30 per cent increase in sales of health and fitness books to men in 1991. Male celebrities in *People* magazine have waists under 30 inches. The head of the men's division at LA Models explained: "Ultimately, we're selling sex, and women like to see men with nice bodies, broad shoulders, and the V-shape." The proportion of cosmetic surgeries performed on men has increased from 5 per cent a decade ago to 20 per cent today. They include hair, calf, and pectoral implants, chest-hair dying, and face patterning. Men's cosmetic sales now total $2.5 billion. More male anorexics and bulemics are seeking treatment. Glassner (1993); *Los Angeles Times* E1 (August 7, 1992).

[60] *New York Times* B7 (February 26, 1992); *Los Angeles Times* E1 (April 17, 1992).

[61] Critics who should know better repeat the calumny of the religious right and politicians like Dan Quayle—that the media are to blame for most contemporary social ills. Medved (1992). An article in the prestigious *Journal of the American Medical Association* just reiterated the claim that television causes violence, based on correlations between the white homicide rate and the introduction of television in the United States, Canada, and South Africa! Centerall (1992); *New York Times* A12 (July 27, 1992) (editorial). South Africa seems to take such nonsense seriously. The SABC is cutting scenes from children's shows like "The Real Ghostbusters," "Bionic Six" and "Robotech" because they contain occult, satanic, and other "dubious signs and symbols." Examples include the peace sign (broken cross or crow's foot), the Taoist yin-yang symbol, the

Egyptian symbol of life (Ankh), and the pentagram. The stimulus was a recent tragedy: "a four-year-old boy in a Superman outfit shot his father dead with a .38 revolver, shouting: 'Dad, I'm Robocop. You are under arrest.' After the incident, he declared: 'Batman shot Daddy dead.' " *Weekly Mail* 5 (September 18–24, 1992).

[62] *Los Angeles Times* B6 (March 9, 1991); *New York Times* A10 (March 13, 1991).

Police attacked rapper Ice-T's "Cop Killer" (discussed below) as a threat to their safety. That campaign was intensified when rapper Tupac Amaru Shakur's "2Pacalypse Now" was found in the tape deck of a car stolen by Ronald Ray Howard, a black 19-year-old Texan charged with murdering Bill Davidson, a white state trooper who had pulled him over after a high-speed chase. Howard had two prior convictions for car theft.

Shakur appeared in "Juice" and will appear in John Singleton's "Poetic Justice." His mother was a member of the Black Panther Party and his godfather is former Panther leader Elmer "Geronimo" Pratt. Shakur had recently sued the City of Oakland after two policemen allegedly beat him while arresting him for jaywalking. Shakur's record had sold 400,000 copies. Half a dozen of its songs described killing police—for instance, "Soulja's Story":

Cops on my tail, so I bail till I dodge them,
They finally pull me over and I laugh,
Remember Rodney King
And I blast this punk ass
Now I got a murder case . . .
What the fuck would you do?
Drop them or let them drop you?
I choose droppin' the cop!

The president of the Combined Law Enforcement Association of Texas declared: "If it's illegal to produce physical pollution, it ought to be illegal to produce mental pollution." Davidson's widow Linda has sued Shakur and Interscope Records (a Time Warner subsidiary), declaring: "There isn't a doubt in my mind that my husband would be alive if Tupac hadn't written those violent, anti-police songs and the companies involved hadn't published and put them out on the street." Her lawyer said "our goal is to punish Time Warner and wake up the executives who run the music business." Col. Oliver North promised the help of his Freedom Alliance: "This case provides us with a painfully vivid example of why this kind of music is so dangerous." Dan Quayle chimed in with a call to withdraw the record. Howard's lawyer also plans to use the record in the penalty phase to argue for life imprisonment instead of death. But the president of the Recording Industry Association of America warned that any damage award "would not only restrict free speech in the future, it would turn the concept of what we consider to be artistic freedom completely on its head." *Los Angeles Times* A1 (September 17, 1992), A12 (September 23, 1992), F1 (October 13, 1992).

[63] *New York Times* 7 (April 13, 1991).

[64] *Los Angeles Times* F1 (February 22, 1991).

[65] *New York Times* A14 (February 4, 1992). "Lethal Weapon 3" earned $140.9 million in the summer of 1992, the second highest gross, and "Terminator 2" was the highest grossing film the previous summer, earning $183.1 million; both far outdistanced black films. *Los Angeles Times* F1 (September 1, 1992).

[66] *New York Times* B1 (January 22, 1992).

[67] *New York Times* A14 (February 21, 1992) (letter to The Editor).

[68] *Los Angeles Times* F1 (February 22, 1991).

[69] 24 versus 12 per cent. *New York Times* A14 (February 21, 1992).

[70] *Olivia N.* v. *National Broadcasting Co.*, 126 Cal.App.3d 488, 178 Cal.Rptr. 888 (1981), cert. denied, 458 U.S. 1108 (1982) (rape; liability rejected on First Amendment grounds); *Waller* v. *Osbourne*, 763 F. Supp. 1144 (M.D. Ga. 1991); *McCollum* v. *CBS, Inc*, 202 Cal.App.3d 989, 249 Cal.Rptr. 187 (1988); *New York Times* B4 (August 3, 1992) (suicide; case pending); B1 (September 23, 1992) (all three cases against Ozzy Osbourne dismissed). After Denise Barnes was assaulted she sued members of the rap group Niggaz With Attitude for $22.75 million for giving interviews to *Rolling Stone* and *The Source* in which they said: "[t]he bitch deserved it" and we "hope . . . it happens again." *National Law Journal* 3 (January 27, 1992) (suit dismissed). The family of an adolescent who died of autoerotic asphyxiation sued *Hustler* for an article entitled "Orgasm of Death," which was found at his feet. *Herceg* v. *Hustler Magazine Inc.*, 814 F.2d 1017 (5th Cir. 1987), cert. denied, 485 U.S. 959 (1988). The family of a youth who committed suicide sued the publisher and manufacturer of the game Dungeons & Dragons. *Watters* v. *TSR, Inc.*, 715 F.Supp 819 (W.D. Ky. 1989), aff'd, 904 F.2d 378 (6th Cir. 1990) (dismissed). Parents sued when their son was killed by another youth who had just seen "The Warriors," a film about gangs. *Yakubowicz* v. *Paramount Pictures Corp.*, 404 Mass. 624, 536 N.E.2d 1067 (1989) (dismissed). Parents sued when their son accidentally hanged himself after watching a professional stuntman perform a similar trick on "The Tonight Show." *DeFilippo* v. *NBC*, 446 A.2d 1036 (R.I. 1982) (dismissed).

[71] *New York Times* s.1 p.10 (February 23, 1992); 190 *Searchlight* 18 (April 1991).

[72] *New York Times* A12 (August 19, 1992). The jury originally awarded $12.4 million. Another case against the magazine was settled out of court, and a third was dismissed because the judge found the advertisement's language, "high risk assignments," too ambiguous. *Ellmann* v. *Soldier of Fortune Magazine, Inc.*, 680 F.Supp. 863 (S.D. Tex. 1988). California courts have held a radio station liable for encouraging teenagers to race around the San Fernando Valley in pursuit of a prize, in the course of which another driver was killed. *Weirum* v. *RKO Gen. Inc.*, 15 Cal.3d 40, 123 Cal. Rptr. 468 (1975).

In an ironic footnote to the Skokie case, a California court upheld an information charging a Jewish Defense League member with solicitation to murder by addressing a Los Angeles press conference five weeks before the planned march and offering $500 to anyone "who kills, maims, or seriously injures a member of the American Nazi Party." *People* v. *Rubin*, 96 Cal. App. 3d 968, 158 Cal.Rptr. 488 (1979), cert. denied, 449 U.S. 821 (1980).

[73] *New York Times* B1 (February 21, 1992); Pileggi (1986). James Caan appeared at the 1985 trial of Carmine Persico and publicly kissed him on the cheek. "I would never deny that my friend is my friend. Where's the morality in that?" In 1992 Caan pledged his house as collateral for the release of Ronald A. Lorenzo, charged with cocaine trafficking, robberies, and kidnappings. He had met Lorenzo 15 years earlier during the filming of "Chapter Two" and now calls him his "best friend." *Los Angeles Times* F1 (September 30, 1992). After Lorenzo was convicted, a juror commented that it was "a little ironic, this guy in the 'Godfather' movie testifying here." *Los Angeles Times* B1 (October 16, 1992). Caan received favourable reviews for his latest role as the big-time gambler who loses the girl in "Honeymoon in Vegas."

There are endless examples of post-modernist confusion between image and "reality," including Quayle's attack on "Murphy Brown" and Perot's on "Doogie Hawser." The cast of "L.A. Law" are invited to address lawyers on the fine points of advocacy and legal secretaries on sexual harassment in the office. Dana Carvey's impersonation of Bush on "Saturday Night Live" led to an invitation to the White House and a request by the President's speechwriter for hints about Bush's mannerisms. *New York Times* s.2 p.20 (August 16, 1992). Seeking to publicise a movie in the 1930s, a producer hired a $5 a day extra, dressed her in black, and sent her to the statue of Rudolph Valentino in Hollywood, telling the press she mourned his death every year. Enjoying the attention, she returned the following year, only to encounter a rival. Now, almost 60 years later, several women still appear annually, each accusing the others of seeking publicity; they sometimes fight, grabbing each other's veils and bouquets. *Los Angeles Times* B1 (August 17, 1992). Ozzy Osbourne maintained: "All the stuff on stage, the craziness, it's all just a role that I play, my work. The closest I ever came to witchcraft is a Ouija board. And believe it or not, I can't even watch slash films." *New York Times* B1 (September 23, 1992).

Viewers might have been forgiven some scepticism when Woody Allen denied any similarities between his personal life and "Husbands and Wives": "Movies are fiction. The plots of my movies don't have any relationship to my life." Defending his relationship to Mia Farrow's adopted daughter Soon-Yi Previn, Allen told *Time*: "The heart wants what it wants. There's no logic to those things." In the film he says about his relationship to Rain, a college student the same age as Soon-Yi, "my heart does not know from logic." Conflating man and *auteur*, audiences booed trailers for the movie in Los Angeles and New York. *New York Times* B1 (August 31, 1992), s.2 p.6 (September 6, 1992), B1 (September 14, 1992). Farrow then felt compelled to issue a press statement declaring that her relationship with Allen had *not* broken down before the movie was completed, she knew nothing of his romance with Soon-Yi, and she was not taking drugs during the shooting. ''Her behavior on screen is all acting.'' *Los Angeles Times* F2 (September 22, 1992). On television viewers' confusion of character and actor, see Gitlin (1986); *New York Times* B1 (September 25, 1992).

[74] On the pervasiveness of racial slurs in ordinary speech, see Davies (1982); van Dijk (1987); Essed (1991).

[75] 102 *Searchlight* 3 (August 1990); Gordon (1990a: 34–35).

[76] GLC (1984d: 21).

[77] *New York Times* A3 (January 24, 1992).

[78] *Chronicle of Higher Education* A1 (October 31, 1991).

[79] ''Home Design,'' *New York Times Magazine* pt.2 p.7 (April 5, 1992); see also Lee (1990: 61) (use of colour purple to evoke packaging of Silk Cut cigarettes).

Appealing to a different audience, Van Halen's recent album was titled ''For Unlawful Carnal Knowledge.''

Seeking verisimilitude, the serious play ''Melody Jones,'' set in a 1970s New Jersey strip club, hired a real stripper. Stephanie Blake is proud of her body—she works out every day—and her skill.

Nowadays, strippers come out and dance one song, take off a piece of clothing. The art is gone. So we're trying to bring that back—the teasing part. . . . I'm known for being kind of an acrobat. It's good to have a gimmick. I used to do one number where I took a bath in a big glass of champagne.

*Los Angeles Times* F2 (August 29, 1992).

[80] *New Statesman and Society* 17 (October 4, 1991).

American family planning clinics responded to the Bush Administration's gag rule prohibiting them from using federal money to discuss abortion by dividing the time of advisers between federal and state support; if a woman tested pregnant when the counsellor was being paid by the federal government, she was advised to return when the state was paying salaries. *Los Angeles Times* A1 (October 2, 1992).

Ambiguity also can be used to repress. In South African treason trials the state constantly tried to show similarities between innocuous behaviour and the political line of the banned ANC and SACP. Bruce Herschensohn, far-right California Republican candidate for the U.S. Senate, reproduced in his autumn 1990 newsletter a picture of the recently released Nelson Mandela raising his clenched fist at the London rock concert in his honour and called it ''the communist salute.'' *Los Angeles Times* A3 (October 12, 1992). This news report was accompanied by a photograph of Dan Quayle at a campaign appearance in Los Angeles in autumn 1992—making the same gesture!

[81] *Los Angeles Times* A1 (January 21, 1992). When the Children's Television Act of 1990 required stations to increase the number of educational programmes, they simply characterised whatever they were showing as educational. WGNO (New Orleans) said of one cartoon: "Good doer Bucky fights off the evil toads from aboard his ship. Issues of social consciousness and responsibility are central themes of the program." A Durham (North Carolina) station said "Superboy" "presents GOOD as it triumphs over EVIL." WDIV in Detroit said that "Super Mario Brothers" taught self-confidence because "Yo Yogi" captures the thieving cockroaches, thereby demonstrating the value of "using his head rather than his muscles." The Bush Administration had opposed more precise language as infringing the First Amendment. *New York Times* A1 (September 30, 1992).

[82] *Guardian* 5 (October 29, 1991), 7 (October 30, 1991).
Politicians are past masters at the insinuation that asserts by denying. Mary Matalin, a leading publicist in the Bush campaign, declared that Clinton was "evasive and slick. We've never said to the press that he's a philandering, non-smoking draft dodger." "The way you just did?" the interviewer asked? "The way I just did," she conceded. *New York Times* A14 (August 5, 1992). The U.S. Treasurer accused Clinton of being a "skirt chaser" and then apologised. Bush campaign chair Robert Mosbacher said that marital fidelity "should be one of the yardsticks" by which candidates are measured" and then apologised. Both accusation and apology served to spread the dirt. *New York Times* A7 (August 20, 1992).

[83] *New York Times* s.4 p.5 (March 4, 1990). The Marlboro logo is on television during half the Grand Prix race and has appeared some 6000 times. *New York Times* A16 (August 25, 1992) (letter to The Editor, August 7, reproving Mayor Dinkins for signing a 10-year contract to host the Grand Prix after calling for removal of tobacco ads from sports complexes).

[84] *Los Angeles Times* A17 (May 8, 1990).
In December 1989 Pepsi showed video clips of the Berlin Wall coming down, with its logo and the caption "Peace on Earth." Benneton has attained notoriety through its ambiguous advertisements featuring catastrophe and tragedy: a bombed-out car, Albanian refugees climbing an overcrowded ship, and an Indian couple wading through flooded streets, a young man dying of AIDS in his father's arms, a murdered Mafia victim in a pool of blood. *New York Times* s.2 p.33 (May 3, 1992).

[85] *New York Times* s.4 p.5 (March 22, 1992).

[86] *New York Times* 7 (October 20, 1992). MTV has used Aerosmith to similar effect as part of its $1 million "Choose or Lose" campaign. Lead guitarist Joe Perry shouts "Freedom is the right to use handcuffs for friendly purposes . . . freedom to wear whipped cream as clothing," while he licks whipped cream off the chest of a blonde woman. Two other women wearing American flag suits hold the rim of a gigantic

condom while an off-camera voice intones: "Freedom to wear a rubber all day—if necessary." Lead singer Steven Tyler adds: "Hey! Protect your freedoms. Vote!" "Rock the Vote" during the New Hampshire primary registered 10,000 young adults. A free concert in Seattle by grunge-rock group Pearl Jam signed up 2400. *New York Times Magazine* 30 (October 11, 1992).

[87] *New York Times* A13 (July 20, 1992).

[88] 185 *Searchlight* 17–19 (November 1990).

[89] *New York Times* s.1 p.10 (February 23, 1992).

[90] 182 *Searchlight* 3 (August 1990); 183 *Searchlight* 5 (September 1990).

[91] *Guardian* 9 (October 14, 1991), 5 (October 23, 1991), 9 (October 28, 1991). During the 1992 Democratic National Convention an anti-abortion activist stopped Clinton in the street and thrust a foetus in his face. If this "speech" should be protected, what about the British artist who made freeze-dried foetuses into earrings? The Young Unknowns Gallery in London was fined £350 for displaying them. *R v. Gibson and Another* [1990] Criminal Law Review 738, [1991] Criminal Appeals Reports 341. An appeal is pending before the European Commission for Human Rights.

[92] Bill Moyers's PBS documentary "Hate on Trial" (February 5, 1992).

[93] *Los Angeles Times* B1 (January 31, 1992).

[94] *New York Times* A27 (December 11, 1991), A14 (December 30, 1991).

[95] Lee (1990: 120).

[96] 179 *Searchlight* 7 (May 1990), 189 *Searchlight* 5 (March 1991).

[97] See, *e.g.* Ernst & Lindey (1936); Dean (1953); Lewis (1992).

[98] *Guardian* 1–2 (October 30, 1991), 2 (November 1, 1991), 1 (November 5, 1991).

[99] Tobacco Institute campaigns ostensibly designed to discourage children from smoking do just the opposite. *New York Times* A13 (September 2, 1992).

[1] *New York Times* 12 (March 28, 1992).

[2] GLC (1984d: 21).

[3] Bill Moyers's PBS documentary "Hate on Trial" (February 5, 1992).

[4] The Brooklyn Museum opened an exhibit entitled "Too Shocking to Show," featuring artists censored by the NEA, including Holly Hughes (whose performance art depicts female sexuality), Tim Miller (on gay male sexuality), Scarlet O (whose masturbation caused the Franklin Furnace performance space to lose its 1992/93 grant), and Saphire (whose poem "Wild Thing," about race and sexuality, was called blasphemous by Rev. Donald Wildmon). The museum director commented: "We feel very strongly about freedom of artistic expression. The issue of censorship is not going to go away. . . . it's a matter of standing up and being counted." *New York Times* B8 (June 19, 1992). The exhibit catalogue was published with an explanatory essay. Freedberg (1992).

Dan Quayle's attack on "Murphy Brown," already CBS's highest-rated entertainment series, allowed the network to raise its price 114 per cent to an average of $310,000 for a 30-second spot, the most expensive on any regular network programme. Before the 1992/93 season began, commercial time was virtually sold out through December. When writer Diane English accepted her Emmy for the best comedy series she thanked "the sponsors for hanging in there when it was getting really dangerous." The admiration was mutual; the ad agency for her regular sponsor said: "I love being associated with 'Murphy Brown.' . . . the controversy has worked in a positive sense." *New York Times* C8 (September 17, 1992). The hour-long premiere showed Murphy Brown watching Quayle criticise her. 44 million people saw the episode—4 million more than watched the Republican convention. Quayle was among them, accompanied by several single mothers. Newspapers carried pictures of Quayle watching Murphy Brown watching Quayle talking about Murphy Brown. *New York Times* A17 (September 23, 1992).

⁵ *Los Angeles Times* A14 (January 21, 1992); *New York Times* s.1 p.10 (February 23, 1992).

⁶ 186 *Searchlight* 10 (December 1990).

⁷ *New York Times* A8 (March 10, 1992).

⁸ *New York Times* A1 (October 17, 1990); *Los Angeles Times* A20 (October 20, 1990). When Gustave Courbet's painting "Return From the Conference" was rejected by the Salon in 1863 he boasted: "I painted the picture so it would be refused. I have succeeded. That way it will bring me some money." Quoted in Barnes (1992: 3). When Howard Stern debuted as disk jockey on KLSX-FM in 1991, 50 advertisers withdrew because he attacked gays, women, blacks, Latinos, and the homeless and used scatological humour. The FCC cited him for indecent broadcasting. A year later he had become the most popular morning radio personality among male listeners in New York, Philadelphia, Washington, and Baltimore, and the advertisers had returned. *Los Angeles Times* F1 (July 30, 1992).

⁹ *Los Angeles Times* F1 (June 13, 1992), F1 (June 16, 1992), F1 (June 18, 1992), F1 (June 19, 1992), D1 (July 4, 1992), B3 (July 25, 1992), A1 (July 29, 1992), D1 (July 30, 1992); *New York Times* B1 (July 8, 1992). Ice-T managed to keep the controversy alive. At a San Diego concert he read a letter from the 1900 member San Diego Police Officers Association denouncing him, stuffed it in his crotch, and sang the song defiantly while a mostly white crowd yelled "Die, pig, die." *Los Angeles Times* A3 (October 1, 1992).

Shortly thereafter the New York State Sheriff's Association, which had joined the campaign against "Cop Killer," sought to suppress a forthcoming album by San Francisco rapper Paris, whose cover showed a man with an automatic weapon about to ambush President Bush (the topic of one song). The track "Coffee and Doughnuts and Death" included these lyrics:

As an example so all the blue coats know
Ya get poached when ya fuck with black folk

## The Excesses of State Regulation

. . . Black folk can't be nonviolent now.
I'd rather just lay ya down, spray ya down
Till justice come around
Cuz without it, there'll be no peace.
White House Press Secretary Marlin Fitzwater asked "appropriate legal authorities to take a look at this case . . ." *Los Angeles Times* A33 (July 3, 1992).

# 4. Taking Sides

I began these lectures by analysing controversies over pornography, hate speech, and blasphemy as struggles for respect between status groups. Contemporary western societies respond by oscillating between the extremes of liberalism and authoritarianism, uncritical tolerance and perfectionist control, idolatry of the market and fealty to the state. Liberalism demands faith that truth and justice will triumph in the long run; but Keynes reminds us that in the long run we will all be dead. Politicians court fickle publics by promising the quick fix of more laws and heavier penalties. Both sides construct moral panics. Liberals warn that any restraint on speech is a step down the slippery slope toward fascist and communist totalitarianism; governmental partisanship revives memories of state religion and agitprop. Prohibitionists justify bans on pornography and hate speech by raising the spectre of physical attacks on women and racial, religious and sexual minorities. In the second and third lectures I criticised both extremes: civil libertarianism cannot inform a principled stance toward speech, yet state regulation inevitably invites excesses and errors. This final lecture attempts the formidable task of charting a path that reduces one harm *of* speech—the reproduction of status inequality—while minimising the harm *to* speech from state regulation. I begin by arguing the need to take sides, drawing lessons from other particularistic experiments. I briefly consider efforts to liberate and amplify silenced voices but focus on responses to harmful speech. Although I do not claim to have eliminated the inescapable tension between freedom and authority, I am hopeful that modest steps to redress status inequality will enlarge our vision of the just society and lead us toward it.

# *I. The Evasions of Neutrality*

Liberal political theory is enthralled by the chimera of neutrality, hoping to avoid the responsibility of political choice by finding a principled basis for the exercise of power. But the search is doomed to fail and entails high costs. The "haves" come out ahead not only in the pursuit of justice, the contest for power, and the competition for wealth, but also in the struggle for respect.[1] Authority that is willfully blind to real inequality perpetuates and magnifies it. The explosive growth of homelessness has rendered Anatole France's century-old aphorism even more timely: "The law, in its majestic equality, forbids the rich as well as the poor to sleep under bridges, to beg in the streets, and to steal bread."[2] Defending the denial of political asylum against a charge of racism, British Home Secretary Kenneth Baker offered an unwitting paraphrase: "Our policy is colour blind. It applies to people wheresoever they come from, whether it is Africa, Asia, or Eastern Europe."[3] It clearly was irrelevant that North Americans and West Europeans were not clamouring at the gates. Baker's boss displayed greater candour. Opposing changes in the inheritance tax, John Major declared: "I want to see wealth cascading down the generations. We do not see each generation starting out anew, with the past cut off and the future ignored." For the same reason he supported educational inequality.[4]

Daily experience reveals the myriad ways in which formal equality creates substantive inequality. Gender-blind allocation of toilets in theatres produces much longer queues during the interval outside the women's than the men's. When the Law Lords invalidated the Fares Fair campaign and London Regional Transport terminated the "Just a Ticket" scheme women suffered more than men because they were more likely to travel by bus than underground and much less likely to drive.[5] Programmes intended to overcome class differences may inadvertently exaggerate race and gender. When medical condition is held constant among elderly Americans, whites receive 4–7 times as many heart bypasses as blacks and black women almost 50 per cent more than black men.[6] Among poor Americans with kidney disease, whites are significantly more likely to obtain transplants.[7]

Liberal theory rationalises the persistence of inequality under conditions of political freedom as the outcome of individual "choice."[8] But the state is not the only constraint on freedom, or even the greatest, as the fall of communism vividly illustrates. In

Poland, a British entrepreneur offering "free" sporting activities to pre-adolescent boys in exchange for participation in homosexual pornography and prostitution found plenty of takers.[9] Berlin's East European community allegedly kidnaps or buys babies and young children for adoption in the West, where fair-skinned merchandise can fetch up to £24,600.[10] Estonian prostitutes migrate to Finland and Yugoslav to the Netherlands, while Poles are lured into Swedish prostitution by fraudulent advertisements for marriage.[11] Moscow teenage girls' *first* choice of a career is "escorting" foreigners for hard currency, *i.e.* becoming high-class call girls.[12] Sasha Kazachkova, a Jewish émigré, exchanged her job as attendant in the men's room of Moscow's National Hotel for one as attendant in the men's room of New York's Laura Belle Supper Club.[13] Despite their facade of self-righteous prudery, the Reagan and Bush administrations' market fetishism also stimulated sexual exploitation. Between 1987 and 1992 "quality" topless clubs multiplied from 800 to 1100, becoming a $3 billion a year industry. Tara Obenauer, who dances at the up-scale Stringfellows, postponed her entry to NYU Law School because "the money here is just so good." Performers earn up to $1000 a night in tips.[14] "Choice" is even more illusory in the third world. During 1991, 249 Nigerian "mules" were arrested at Kennedy Airport for smuggling heroin by swallowing small amounts wrapped in condoms, which they later excreted; those who escaped detection (and long prison terms) earned 16 times their annual incomes.[15]

Material need and greed do not exhaust the constraints of civil society. Cultural hegemony is at least as powerful. The television program "American Gladiators," featuring five men and five women who fight challengers, appears on 156 stations nationwide. 15,000 people have auditioned for the chance to brawl in public. One woman watches it regularly with her 4-year-old daughter because she prefers its role models—"five women out there, kicking butt, just like the men"—to the cartoon stereotypes of stupid women obsequiously following dominant men.[16] The year after Princeton admitted women, male undergraduates began "streaking" through town to celebrate the first snowfall. A senior explained why she and other women joined the event 16 years later: "My first thought was, here's a male tradition. I not only wanted to be part of it, I wanted to try to take it over. Running in the Nude Olympics is not wise, but it's fun." The Women's Center and the Sexual Harassment and Assault Advising Resources and Education Office encouraged participation. But Sandra N. Silverman, assistant dean of students, was appalled: "I can't think of a more ultimate vulnerability for women. I'm somewhat surprised that women feel so strongly about participating in a men's event, rather than attempting to come up with an event that addresses women's needs."[17]

If neutrality is willful blindness and individual choice is always constrained, the responsibilities of power cannot be fulfilled by simple deference to the oppressed. Contrary to Arnold Toynbee's naïve faith, they are not always morally superior. Quite the contrary, subordinate people typically express their powerlessness by directing resentment away from the dominant, who are too remote or frightening, to more vulnerable targets: rural Southern whites and urban ethnics at African Americans, African Americans at Jews and now Koreans, West European workers at immigrants, East Africans at East Indians, Southeast Asians at Chinese. Middle class women cope with the patriarchal division of labour by hiring working class women, often women of colour, as housekeepers, thereby reproducing class and racial inequality. Black men respond to racial subordination by oppressing black women in popular music, blaxploitation films, and of course sexual and domestic behaviour. Black women feel doubly degraded when black men enjoy white female pornography—or even form romantic relationships with white women.[18] And people of colour are not immune to homophobia. When the GLC "Positive Images" campaign sought to increase respect for gays and lesbians in schools in 1987, a spokesman for the Haringey Black Pressure Group on Education retorted that "homosexuality is something that has been introduced into our culture by Europeans; it is an unnatural set of acts that tend toward genocide." Some members joined with the neo-fascist New Patriotic Movement under the banner "Gays=Aids=Death."[19]

Some oppressed not only participate in the subordination of others but also are complicit in their own, internalising and legitimating the dominant rationalisations for privilege. If women did not support Phyllis Schlafly's patriarchy the feminist movement would have made greater progress.[20] Clarence Thomas's racial self-hatred and meritocratic apologetics echo those of other racial minorities who have made it.[21] Sometimes betrayal reflects overwhelming pressure. After joining the Derbyshire police at 19, Shaun hid his homosexuality for 17 years: "I called it the canteen culture. Heavy drinking, womanising and doing all the things that heterosexual males are expected to do." He married at 24, fathered two children, and maintained the family facade, although his wife knew he was gay. For seven years he was a vice squad detective, often entrapping gay men into soliciting sex. "I knew what to look for and what sort of places to investigate—that's possibly why I was so good."[22] For other collaborators, however, the goad is pure ambition. As a professor at San Francisco State University, S.I. Hayakawa helped form the Faculty Renaissance Committee to combat campus radicals. A grateful state chancellor recommended him as acting president to then Governor Reagan, who responded with typical tact: "Tell him if he takes the job, we'll forgive him Pearl Harbor." On his first day in office Hayakawa crushed the students' strike by jumping on their soundtruck and ripping out the loudspeaker wires. As senator for California he opposed bilingual education and ballots as "foolish and unnecessary" and sponsored a constitutional amendment to make English the official language. Spared wartime internment (as a Canadian citizen), he called it "perhaps the best thing that could have happened" to Japanese-Americans because it forced them to assimilate. "I am proud to be a Japanese-American, but when a small but vocal group demand a cash indemnity of $25,000 for those who went to relocation camps, my flesh crawls with shame and embarrassment."[23]

Despite its professed loyalty to formal equality, collective neutrality, and value agnosticism, the liberal state cannot avoid choices. If one is free speech, another is abridging speech when the state feels threatened. In December 1991 the Islamic Front won 189 out of 430 seats in the first free Algerian election in years and was expected to win enough runoffs to gain a majority. Fundamentalists in Lebanon, Sudan, Jordan and Yemen rejoiced. Demanding immediate segregation of the sexes in schools and workplaces and a ban on alcohol, Mohammed Said told a huge crowd it was time Algerian women went back to veils and stopped looking like "cheap merchandise that is bought and sold." The Front proclaimed its intent to introduce an Islamic state under the slogan: "No laws. No constitution. Only the laws of God and the Koran." When the Algerian military nullified the results and barred all demonstrations western nations breathed a sigh of relief; none criticised this blatant suppression of democracy.[24] The day after a nearly successful coup in Venezuela an association of retired military officers took full-page advertisements in major newspapers, condemning the regime for corruption and poor administration. President Carlos Andrés Pérez immediately prohibited newspapers from publishing photographs of the plotters or articles or advertisements suggesting that they enjoyed popular support or military backing, and seized defiant papers. "We have said, don't exalt the man who attempted the military coup."[25]

*Taking Sides*

Poland banned "Party X" of Canadian émigré businessman Stani-
sław Tyminski because its xenophobia and general lunacy were
embarrassing the fledgling democracy. Although the excuse was
10,000 forged signatures on electoral registration documents,
Tyminski claimed that similar abuses by other parties were overlooked. Expelled from the country, his parting words were: "I don't
want to be in a Poland transformed into a Jewish colony." Of course,
almost all the Jews had been murdered half a century ago by the
Nazis, with the complicity of many Poles.[26] Soon after succeeding
Gorbachev, Yeltsin outlawed the Communist Party. Such responses
are not limited to shaky third-world or ex-communist governments.
The U.S. Supreme Court refused to intervene when the Republican
Party prevented David Duke from running in its Florida and Georgia
presidential primaries.[27]

Forced to express preferences about speech, the liberal state
typically emphasises form over content. But the time, manner and
place restrictions that even First Amendment devotees accept inevitably favour those who can comply and still be heard. As we have
seen, regulation often targets extremes, hoping that stylistic excess
will foment enough anger to generate a consensus for restraint. As
religious fervour declined, blasphemy laws punished only the worst
insults. As sexual taboos fell, only the portrayal of violent sex was
proscribed. Racism, anti-Semitism and homophobia are so pervasive that only the most virulent forms are regulated. As I argued in the
previous lecture, however, preoccupation with the extremes toler-
ates and appears to condone quotidian harms. In any case, outrage
is not a neutral quality. It varies with the audience, as even the U.S.
Supreme Court acknowledges in enforcing community standards of
decency.[28] Furthermore, the very novelty that causes offence is an
essential aesthetic ingredient.[29] In one of his most striking dances,
Merce Cunningham jumped into a plastic sack and propelled himself across the stage like a fish on land. He no longer performed it,
however, "because I was in it once."

> Every artist should ask, "What is the point of doing what you
> already know?" . . . Dance, like any work of art, is not interesting
> unless it provokes you—where you say, "I never thought of that,"
> and have some new experience. When I see dances where I can
> perceive from the first five minutes what they're going to be, my
> interest drops 50 per cent.[30]

Artists delight in shocking the bourgeoisie: Salvador Dali paints a moustache on the Mona Lisa; Andres Serrano photographs a crucifix submerged in his urine; Robert Mapplethorpe poses a man with a broomstick up his anus; in a video shown after he had died of AIDS, Freddie Mercury dressed in the royal crown and cape for a rendition of "God Save the Queen."[31] Yet artistic pretensions do not necessarily justify the harms of expression. Helmut Newton photographs sexually provocative nudes, often in sadomasochistic positions. "I love vulgarity. I am very attracted by bad taste— it's a lot more exciting than supposed good taste, which is nothing more than a standardised way of looking at things."[32] In his autobiography, John Osborne boasted of his homophobic dislike of "poofs" and his chauvinistic contempt for pretentious French, short Italians, provincial Australians ("natives of a suspicious, benighted land"), and Jews and Irish ("cold-hearted" races, whose abundant "sentimentality . . . is the sugar-ornament of the hard of heart").[33]

Just as those without a presidential podium, religious pulpit, media megaphone, or advertising budget must take to the streets and shout in order to be heard, so political dissidents may have to use guerrilla tactics to unsettle conventional beliefs or grab the attention of listeners suffering from information overload. Anti-war activists burn draft cards and flags, anti-abortion demonstrators display pickled fetuses, neo-Nazis flaunt swastikas, graffiti artists deface walls and advertisements. Hoping "to revive the 'zap action' tactics of the early women's liberation days," a group of performance artists got into *Life* magazine by appearing at a conference at New York's Plaza Hotel barefoot, chained together, wearing voluminous black maternity garments padded to make them look pregnant, and accompanied by others in black jumpsuits and shocking pink headbands carrying a huge pink banner reading "Forced childbearing is a form of slavery."[34] Overshadowed by hundreds protesting the first California execution in 25 years, two "good old boys" in a pickup truck demonstrated for the death penalty with a poster showing the condemned man and an "Alka-Cyanide" capsule being dropped into a glass of sulfuric acid, above the caption: "Plop Plop Fizz Fizz, Oh, What a relief it is!"[35]

There is no escape from politics. Some messages should be encouraged and others discouraged for *what* they say, not how they say it. The task is made acutely painful by millenia of religious intolerance, philistine censorship, and political and sexual repression. My goal is to reduce subordination based on gender, race, ethnicity, religion, and sexual orientation. But that amorphous ideal leaves difficult questions unanswered. If feminists campaign against pornography because it subordinates women, why should not the religious right attack sexual permissiveness as subordinating believers? How could we criticise Salman Rushdie while venerating such notorious blasphemers as Moses, Socrates, Jesus, Luther, Galileo, Darwin, and Freud? Or while tolerating protests against sabbatarianism, religion in schools, or the sexism and homophobia of denominations that refuse to ordain women or celebrate the union of homosexuals? Cannot Catholics argue that advocacy of abortion, contraception, and divorce subordinates them?[36] When Sinéad O'Connor appeared on "Saturday Night Live," shouted "Fight the real enemy," and tore up a photo of Pope John Paul II after singing Bob Marley's "War," the California Chapter of the Catholic League for Religious and Civil Rights declared: "Millions of Catholics in California are incensed at this blatant defamation of the leader of the Catholic Church . . . [and] this blatant hatred shown toward the Catholic religion."[37] Cannot Muslims say the same about critiques of polygyny or patriarchy? Is Dan Quayle right that "Murphy Brown" and the entire media élite diminish him by mocking his values? One answer would be that he does not belong to "a historically oppressed minority."[38] But oppression is contingent, mutable, and ambiguous. Could neo-Nazis argue that they have been oppressed for almost half a century? Jews are historically oppressed but now oppress Palestinians. Who is oppressing whom in Rwanda, Estonia, Yugoslavia, Armenia or Azerbaijan? As I noted above, "historically oppressed minorities" sometimes are complicit in their own oppression and collaborate in oppressing others. In the end we will have to justify difficult prudential choices with full awareness of context, history, identity, relationship, and motive.

## II. Experiments in Particularism

Recognising that all forms of inequality—class, race, religion, gender, and sexual orientation—outlast conscious discrimination, liberals acknowledge an obligation to take remedial action favouring victimised categories. Reconstruction sought to redress centuries of American slavery. After World War II, West Germany paid reparations to Holocaust victims, Japan to the countries it invaded, and the United States to Japanese-American internees. The former communist regimes are besieged by claims from those they deprived of property or freedom.[39]

Yet liberal ideology has great difficulty reconciling solicitude for victims with fidelity to universalism, as the British experience illustrates. In 1943, as Holocaust rumours were confirmed and local fascists parroted Nazi anti-Semitism, the government considered outlawing incitement to hatred against Jews (who were one percent of the population). Home Secretary Herbert Morrison (a socialist member of the coalition government) rejected the proposal because "it would be contrary to public policy to single out one section of the community for preferential treatment and protection . . . we must maintain the principle that our law is no respecter of persons."[40] Half a century later, some have grown more sensitive to past injustice. The Labour Party allows constituencies to exclude male candidates from short lists and has declared that women will be at least 40 percent of the national executive by the mid-1990s.[41] Embarrassed that only 23 of its 12,000 drivers are women, British Rail advertises openings in women's magazines.[42] Sometimes the particularism is implicit. Among those charged with killing a spouse or lover between 1982 and 1989, women were nearly twice as likely as men to be charged with manslaughter rather than murder, four times as likely to be acquitted or found unfit to plead, only two-thirds as likely to be imprisoned, and sentenced to terms just over half as long.[43]

Yet preferential treatment elicits strong resentment. After the Metropolitan Police changed its height and weight requirements because of their discriminatory effects—only 1.6 percent of officers were black compared to 15 percent of London's population, and none was Chinese—a majority of officers protested that *they* were victims of race and sex prejudice.[44] When Cambridge announced an affirmative action plan affecting less than a dozen of its 10,000 undergraduates, Harrow headmaster Ian Beer condemned the university for embarking "on a dangerous road of social engineering" and complained that "it is not the fault of Harrow boys that they are well taught."[45] The Bar Council narrowly voted to urge chambers to offer five per cent of their vacant seats to minorities; and Lord Mackay, noting that no High Court judges and only two circuit judges are black, began monitoring the ethnicity of applicants for silk. But the Master of the Rolls attacked a proposed judicial appointments commission. "Why," asked Lord Donaldson, "is there a right number of barrister or solicitor judges or men or women judges?" He simply recommended the best person for the job.[46]

The United States, which embraced affirmative action earlier, more explicitly, and with greater commitment, displays an equally incoherent mix of rhetorical posturing and political struggle. The

Ninth Circuit rejected a constitutional challenge to reparations for Japanese Americans by a man interned with his German-born parents in Texas during World War II, noting that two-thirds of the 120,000 Japanese Americans detained without trial were citizens, whereas virtually all the 14,426 German and Italian Americans detained were aliens, each received an individual hearing, and they constituted only about 10 percent of all European enemy aliens.[47] Sometimes the equivalences are patently absurd. Representative Ray McGrath (R-LI) opposed participation by gay Irish-Americans in the St. Patrick's Day parade "for the same reason I wouldn't want the Ku Klux Klan in the Martin Luther King Day Parade."[48]

Affirmative action is most controversial in employment and education, with the races splitting along predictable lines. Black youths are almost 50 per cent more likely to believe that universities should give "special consideration to minority students for enrollment," while whites are two and a half times more likely to feel that *they* suffer discrimination in scholarships, jobs, and promotions.[49] When the Denver Police Department administered a preliminary examination to select 40 out of 892 applicants, the 86 per cent of whites and 91 per cent of Hispanics who failed were furious that all the black examinees passed—clearly reflecting the fact that only 6 per cent of the officers were black.[50] The Bush Administration has outlawed the practice of ranking candidates taking federal civil service examinations within each ethnic group in order to equalise representation.[51] It also banned race-exclusive university scholarships and then rescinded the ban under intense public pressure; but a constitutional challenge to the practice is pending.[52] A white high school student wrote to the U.S. Department of Education to denounce "the most overlooked travesty in our nation's colleges and universities: reverse racial discrimination" when Duke University rejected her and accepted a black classmate with what she claimed were lesser credentials. The black woman responded: "I am so mad right now, tears are streaming down my face. I'd like to think I was picked because I was qualified and because I had a little bit more I could offer to someone else."[53] Conservative faculty are even more vitriolic. At a University of Michigan conference on "Deconstructing the Left," David Horowitz pronounced that "affirmative action amounts to racism pure and simple. It's exactly what's being dismantled in South Africa."[54] When the Middle States Association of Colleges and Schools, one of six regional accrediting bodies, deferred approving Bernard M. Baruch College of CUNY for doing too little to hire minority faculty and administrators or retain minority students and threatened to disapprove Westminster Theological Seminary unless it put women on its board of governors, the U.S. Secretary of Education forced it to back down by delaying its own reauthorisation. An adviser to the Secretary denounced the Middle States diversity standard as "taking a side" and "impos[ing] a moral or political litmus test."[55]

Subordinated peoples increasingly reject integration as a strategy of collective mobility in favour of protected spaces within which to develop their distinctive strengths.[56] Because this appears to reinforce or revive the very separation liberals have fought for more than a century through coeducation and desegregation it causes considerable unease. The British Muslim Education Co-ordinating Committee advocates "separate educational institutions for male and female pupils in accordance with the principles of Islam," although the government has refused to grant voluntary-aided status to the several dozen Muslim schools.[57] Such initiatives can attract embarrassing support from conservative groups like Parental Alliance for Choice in Education, the Social Affairs Unit, and the Adam Smith Institute and even the racist National Front. Some Muslims strongly disavow them. Southall Black Sisters denounced the Labour Party for "abandon[ing] the principle of equality where black women are concerned . . . [and] deliver[ing] us into the hands of male, conservative and religious forces within our communities, who deny us the right to live as we please."[58] In the United States the ACLU vigorously challenged a Milwaukee plan to create elementary and middle schools exclusively for black boys. The New York Civil Liberties Union condemned a proposed New York high school, which, though nominally open to all, would emphasise the experience and culture of black and Hispanic men and be located in a largely minority neighbourhood. Dr. Kenneth B. Clark, the noted black psychologist who had testified for the plaintiffs in the 1954 desegregation case, was appalled:

> It's isolating these youngsters and telling them "You're different. We're having this school because black males have more social and crime problems than others." . . . This is an approach that stigmatizes rather than educates.[59]

Feminists have defended girls' schools, pointing to the success of their graduates and the tendency of teachers in coeducational settings to favour boys and assign textbooks with sexual stereotypes.[60] A British scientist noted for discovering that the hypothalamus of gay men is half as large as that of heterosexuals has established the West Hollywood Institute for Gay and Lesbian Education (Whigle). A local gay activist who initiated the proposal explained: "We need to unite and come together, developing our culture. Once we've done that, we can integrate and become full participants in a transformed society."[61] Defenders of separatism point to the vital role of homogeneous fraternities, sororities, and religious organisations in easing the entry of Jews and Catholics into American higher education a generation earlier.[62] Yet all anti-subordination strategies must expect to be attacked as particularistic and resented by those whose privilege they threaten.

## III. Equalising Voices

Respect is the latest prize in the unending struggle against subordination. The bourgeois revolution sought to free markets and equalise access to political power. Workers demanded control over the means of production but usually settled for token participation and a larger slice of the pie. Resistance to patriarchy, racism, and homophobia has had to repeat some of these contests, but it focuses on new spheres: families, education, and culture. We might see this as extending the social democratic project of material equality (employment, housing, and health) to reproduction, the principal battleground of post-industrial society. On this new field, antagonists in the cultural wars deploy proactive and reactive strategies, prescribing the future and judging the past. Texts and curricula, advertising, mass entertainment, news reporting, public rituals, religion and high culture all transmit collective messages about status; insults and sexual harassment are particular instances of status degradation. The former act extensively, the latter intensively; each reinforces the other.

Because all cultural phenomena are associated with particular status groups, expression is inescapably partisan. The creators of symbolic goods may rationalise their behaviour as the response to hypostatised market forces; but some consumers always are more equal than others, and supply shapes consumer demand while purporting to satisfy it. Those who produce or sponsor records, concerts, plays, exhibitions, movies, television, radio, and printed matter also have a moral responsibility for their content, if not the same as the creative artist's. Audiences are accountable for what they patronise, which makes the boycott of creators, producers, and sponsors not just legitimate but obligatory. Invoking market failure, the state and private philanthropy subsidise cultural production. School teachers and university instructors consciously shape the minds of future generations.

The belief that the existing distribution of cultural messages is apolitical—just the way things are, indeed, the only way they could be—epitomises Gramsci's notion of hegemony. A counter-hegemonic strategy must encourage new voices to speak and secure them a hearing. Its goal is to equalise cultural capital—access to and position within symbolic space—through affirmative action in the industries that produce and disseminate information and values.[63] Some will condemn this as the dilution of standards, the contamination of art by politics. Yet the participation of silenced voices will transform judgements about quality; and all art is inescapably political.

Examples of cultural affirmative action abound.[64] Schools encourage girls in science and maths and boys in cooking, postpone single-sex sports, and resist the sexual division of labour, both among their staff and in the career choices of their pupils.[65] Women, racial, ethnic and religious minorities, and gays and lesbians have sought inclusion in the collective tradition transmitted by literature and history courses in schools and universities, with mixed success.[66] Media workers demand a hearing for excluded voices while fighting stereotypes.[67] When the "Committee for Open Debate on the Holocaust" sought to disseminate its revisionist lies, student newspapers at Harvard, Yale, Brown, Pennsylvania and USC refused to sell them space. Rutgers ran the ad as an opinion column with a note detailing its mendacity and offered to print other rebuttals.[68] The Arab-American Anti-Discrimination Committee persuaded a television station in Detroit, which houses the country's largest Arab-American community, not to rebroadcast "The Little Drummer Boy," a 1968 children's show that stereotyped Arabs. The programming director explained: "I think that this is a case where, in the years since this show was made, we have become more aware of some things we didn't see before."[69] Public authorities face similar choices. When the Labour-controlled Lancaster Council, which had staged the Miss Great Britain beauty contest for decades, decided to terminate it, the female chair of the arts and events committee explained:

> We were all so naive in our 20s and 30s, but when women started going on to platforms to protest, I started thinking. Those women

changed ideas. We woke up and asked ourselves what were we doing, spending time watching women being paraded like this? And then it seemed bygone, outdated and boring. It didn't take a revolution, it was dead and the audiences were gone.[70]

The success of publishing houses, magazines, and newspapers for subordinated groups encourages mainstream competitors to appeal to those audiences.[71] Public platforms welcome new speakers. The U.S. House of Representatives asked Imam Siraj Wahaj to give the invocation in 1991; the Senate heard Imam Wallace D. Mohammed do so the following year.[72] The Brooklyn Historical Society has organised exhibitions about black churches and black women, Hispanic culture, and the Italian festival in Williamsburg.[73] Entrepreneurs have redesigned prosaic artifacts that powerfully shape consciousness of relative worth. When Yla Eason's 3-year-old son cried because he could not grow up to be master of the universe since he was black, she began manufacturing dolls and action figures with ethnically authentic features: Imani (a high-fashion model) and Sun-Man (a Star Trek character). Although major toymakers initially rebuffed her approaches, they soon became interested in reaching the 34 per cent of children under 10 who are Black or Hispanic.[74] As these (and earlier) examples show, attacks on racial subordination may perpetuate or even intensify gender stereotypes. To counter these, Cathy Meredig designed an anatomically correct doll, with a shorter neck, higher waist, and larger feet than Barbie. Little girls did not notice the difference, but mothers exclaimed: "Wow! a doll with hips and a waist!"[75]

## IV. Addressing the Harms of Speech

At the same time that the hegemonic culture moulds what is said and heard, profoundly affecting collective reputation, particular exchanges enact status inequalities. In response, the struggle against subordination seeks to sensitise speakers to the harm they cause. Although civil libertarians may recoil from any interference with speech, it is always constrained, as I argued in my second lecture.[76] Speakers could be "free" of their social environment only if the audience were absent or indifferent—which would render speech pointless. Speakers always engage in dialogue with their audiences, even when the latter are silent.[77] In intimate settings, couples choose their words with care, thinking and feeling much they never verbalise; marriage counselling often focuses on problems of communication.[78] Parents and teachers socialise children to address siblings and friends without inflicting unnecessary hurt.[79] Speech codes at American and British universities have been condemned by conservatives and invalidated by courts, but academic institutions could not function if their members "freely" hurled racist slurs, homophobic taunts, or sexist innuendoes at each other, or if pornography covered the walls of the senior common room or the co-ed toilets of residence halls. All performers—especially the most successful—cultivate their audience. While writing *The Last Chronicle of Barset* in the drawing room of Athenaeum, Anthony Trollope heard two clergymen disparaging his characters, with particular animus toward Mrs. Proudie. He declared "I will go home and kill her before the week is over" and promptly did so.[80] When 500 million people in 27 countries saw the première of Michael Jackson's video "Black or White," many protested a scene showing him rubbing his pelvis and unzipping his fly and another in which he smashed up cars. Although he had already edited the tape for violence, Jackson immediately agreed to cuts. "I've always tried to be a good role model [a strange claim given his deliberately ambiguous sexual and racial identity] . . . . I deeply regret any pain or hurt that the final segments of Black or White has [sic] caused children, their parents or any other viewers."[81] When Americans and Japanese collaborated on a television programme about World War II, a scene of Chinese being shot in a ditch was narrated differently. The English text read: "Japan's claim it was liberating China was ludicrous to Americans, particularly when hundreds of thousands of Chinese men, women and babies were murdered in what was called the Rape of Nanking." The Japanese version did not mention Nanking, saying rather: "in a totalitarian attempt to grab land and wealth, the Japanese military had led the country into an eight-year war in Manchuria and China."[82]

## A. Measuring the Injury

Because the effect of speech on status is contextually specific, we need a framework for analysing its harms in order to calibrate the response. This section begins that task.

*1. Speaker Identity* Public officials purport to speak for the collectivity, endowing their message with formal authority and apparent consensus. Although James Watt, Reagan's first Secretary of the Interior, could wreak havoc on the environment with impunity, he was forced to resign after indelicately declaring that he had appointed a Jew, a Negro, and a cripple to a committee. Political candidates quickly learn that visibility brings responsibility. American Jews have never forgiven Jesse Jackson for calling New York "Hymietown" during his 1988 Presidential campaign; Italian-Americans were similarly incensed by Bill Clinton's suggestion to Gennifer Flowers that Mario Cuomo acted as though he had Mafia connections.[83] Celebrity gained through artistic, athletic, or entrepreneurial prowess also enhances a speaker's impact. J. Peter Grace, chairman and CEO of the chemicals conglomerate W.R. Grace & Co. and director of Reagan's Private Sector Survey on Cost Control, was forced to apologise when he praised Wisconsin's Republican Governor Tommy G. Thompson by saying: "He doesn't have much competition. Where I come from we have Cuomo the homo, and then in New York City, we have Dinkins the pinkins."[84] Recognising that the disciplinary powers of police, prison warders, and teachers add weight to their words, American courts uphold limits on their speech, despite the First Amendment.[85] Responsibility is diluted when the speakers are collective: committee reports, mass entertainment, demonstrations. Reputation also can undercut a message. When Patrick Buchanan sought to revive his failing Presidential campaign by maligning a public television programme about gay black men, the response was strangely muted. An ActUp spokesman explained: "Buchanan is just so vile it's almost redundant to say it." Another activist added: "Buchanan . . . is not a new homophobe; he's an established homophobe."[86]

*2. Motive.* Although motive is elusive, unstable, and opaque, it has enormous influence on the effects of speech. Worse motives always aggravate harm, although good motives may not prevent it—as defamation law acknowledges. Students at Pierce College in Los Angeles complained about an AIDS awareness poster showing HIV-positive victims being bashed by bigots, losing weight, developing cancer, and dying—even though it declared: "no disrespect is intended by this depiction of human suffering."[87] Advocates of state regulation usually make exceptions for the good motives presumed in scholarly inquiry, news reporting, art, or political debate. Yet audience interpretation remains critical; because motive can be feigned, the speaker's avowal is never conclusive. Ambiguity increases the risk of discordant interpretations.

Context can invert motive totally: compare the 1937 Nazi exhibition of "Entartete Kunst" (Degenerate Art) with its reconstruction half a century later in Los Angeles and Berlin.[88] Blacks, especially women, were insulted when white fraternity members put on black-face, fright wigs, and padded breasts and buttocks for a skit in the George Mason University student refectory. Did women feel equally insulted when gay men calling themselves the West Hollywood Cheerleaders marched in the eighth annual AIDS Walk Los Angeles wearing mini-skirts, padded tops, and oversized wigs?[89]

*3. Target.* Abstract assaults on collectivities affect larger numbers, while concrete insults to individuals inflict more intense harm. Compare pornography with sexual harassment, blasphemy with desecration of religious sites or disruption of rites, mass media stereotyping with face-to-face taunts. The higher the target's status, the less likely it is to be impaired. If unredressed, the harms of speech cumulate, transforming tendentious allegation into unquestioned stereotype, alerting speaker and audience to the victim's vulnerability. Characteristics deemed volitional are more likely to seem fair game: sexual orientation rather than gender, religion rather than race.

*4. Relationship between Speaker and Target.* Group members can use language that would be intolerable from outsiders. An image that is erotic if created by and for lesbians becomes pornographic if produced by or for men. Blacks distinguished sharply between Paul Robeson's portrayal of Othello and Laurence Olivier's. Consider the decision to cast Denzel Washington as Steve Biko and add Whoopi Goldberg to the film version of "Serafina." Lenny Bruce made a career out of telling anti-Semitic jokes to mostly Jewish audiences. Eddie Murphy satirised Jesse Jackson on "Saturday Night Live." Hanif Kureishi can make films about Pakistani immigrants and Spike Lee about African Americans, Maxine Hong Kingston can write about Chinese Americans and James Welsh about American Indians in ways that outsiders cannot.[90] Subordinated groups neutralise the sting of epithets by domesticating them: one woman calling another a "bitch," a black describing another as a "bad nigger," Larry Kramer titling a play "Faggots." A publisher explained why he had named his magazine NYQ: "The word queer started up as a way to say it's not derogatory to be a homosexual. It is also a way of defining yourself as a political person."[91] Yet community membership can intensify the sense betrayal when insiders address the outside world, as shown by the response of Muslims to Salman Rushdie, Jews to Philip Roth, and African American men to Alice Walker. The impact of speech varies with the parties' relative status. Cheekiness in an inferior can be reproved or ignored; contempt from a superior reinforces subordination.

The interplay between speaker, target, and audience greatly complicates meaning. David Hammons, a black artist, painted a 14x16 foot portrait of a white-skinned, blond, blue-eyed Jesse Jackson, captioned "How Ya Like Me Now?" While white workers were installing it, two black men attacked the painting with hammers. The black curator defended the portrait as "an important image that had to be seen, concentrated upon, talked about. . . . contemporary art in general is not to be embraced or understood upon immediate perusal." Jackson had the last word: "I understand that it was an interpretation. I encourage artistic expression and full artistic freedom. Sometimes art provokes. Sometimes it angers, which is a measure of its success. Sometimes it inspires creativity. Maybe the sledgehammers should have been on display too."[92] Contrast the Hammons incident with the response when a white student at the School of the Art Institute of Chicago painted the African American Mayor Harold Washington dressed in a frilly white bra, panties, garter, and stockings, and called it "Mirth and Girth." When it was displayed at a private show shortly after the mayor died of a heart attack, three black Aldermen stormed into the Institute and ordered the police to confiscate the painting, warning that it "increased tensions in the African-American community to the point where violence on the scale of the 1960's West Side riots was imminent."[93]

The history of a relationship can influence the interpretation of new messages. Trust can increase tolerance, while prior injuries rankle. The Crusades, colonialism, and the rancorous Middle Eastern conflict coloured Muslim reaction to *The Satanic Verses*. Jewish memories of the Holocaust underlay fear of the threatened Nazi demonstration in Skokie as well as anger at Germany's failure to nominate "Europa, Europa" for an Academy Award and its hospitality to Austrian President Kurt Waldheim.[94] Absent any prior relationship, otherwise offensive speech may be risible. Anti-Semitism thrives in Japan without an ostensible target. Den Fujita, an enormously successful Osaka businessman whose books "The Jewish Way of Doing Business" and "How to Blow the Rich Man's Bugle Like the Jews Do" have sold millions of copies, claims to be a philo-Semite. "I'm trying to do something good for the Jewish people. Most Jewish people speak two or three different languages. They're good at mathematics. The Japanese should learn from that. . . .

Business people in and out of Japan call me a 'Ginza Jew.' I am satisfied with that.'' A board member of the Japanese-Israel Friendship Association commented cryptically: "In Japan, there is no anti-Semitism. But many Japanese accept this Nazi-style stereotype that Jews control the world."[95]

*5. Style.* Texts occupy a stylistic continuum from the clarity of propaganda through the double entendres of advertising to the irreducible ambiguity of art. Authors are not their protagonists nor actors their characters, even if audiences and critics constantly conflate the two. Echoing classical theories of the cathartic function of tragedy, Bruno Bettelheim has argued that fairy tales must elicit fear and anger if children are to work through those emotions.[96] Messages vary from demotic to esoteric: compare tabloids with scholarly journals, soap opera with literary criticism, television commercials with modern poetry. The esoteric reaches fewer people but claims greater authority.

*6. Dissemination and Reception.* Even if the medium is not the message it may be equally important. Writing is more permanent than speech but less immediate. With declining literacy, visual images become more powerful than words and appear more truthful. Still images can be consulted at will and displayed permanently, but moving images offer greater verisimilitude. Direct interaction increases emotional power, but reproduction allows the speaker to address a larger audience. Live performances are unique and transitory; recording allows repetition but may reduce impact. Cultures imbue media with different weight: peoples of the book revere writing; oral traditions respect rhetoric and story-telling. Environment may affect emotional tone: compare the intimacy of the bedroom with the impersonality of the street. Spontaneity may be excused, while deliberation aggravates: compare insults exchanged after a road accident with premeditated affronts. A message expressing the hegemonic culture has greater influence than a frontal attack on received wisdom. Group dynamics can reinforce or undermine the message. Audiences may be critical or credulous, attentive or distracted. We have developed a protective carapace against the media's massive assault; all writers know how little their readers absorb or retain. How much do you remember of the last five pages?

B. Encouraging Complaints
If speakers are to become more sensitive to the ways they reproduce

status inequality, somebody has to educate them. Those with the greatest incentive are their victims. Yet the weakest link in all regulatory processes is not detection, conviction, and sentencing (as the media and politicans insist) but the failure of victims to complain. Within any remedial system attrition is greatest at the early stages: naming an experience as harmful, blaming another, and claiming redress.[97] Because such decisions are private and invisible, inequality flourishes.[98] These problems are compounded when the injury is to dignity, not just property or person. Shame and guilt deter rape and incest victims from reporting.[99] A British study of sexual harassment at work found that only 25 percent of victims complained to a third party, and only 2 per cent took legal action.[1] According to the National Gay and Lesbian Task Force, only one out of six hate crimes reported to victim assistance groups in six major American cities was communicated to the police.[2] An even smaller proportion of those targetted by racial hatred in Britain seek redress—probably less than 5 per cent.[3]

Consciousness is the first obstacle and possibly the greatest. Victims may have internalised the dominant culture so thoroughly that they cannot feel the hurt or blame themselves. Women accept male definitions of love, sex, and beauty. Gays and lesbians try to pass. Ethnoreligious minorities assimilate, changing their customs, language, accent, clothes, even skin, nose, eyes, and hair. The more pervasive the affront, the harder it is to challenge. We should not be surprised that dignitary harms go unrecognised when for decades workers endured serious physical disabilities, such as lung impairment from exposure to coal, cotton and asbestos. Even after victims have acknowledged their injuries and externalised responsibility, expressing anger can be a frightening admission of vulnerability and dependence.[4] Further publicity may aggravate dignitary wrongs: the repetition of defamation or invasion of privacy, the humiliation of rape and sexual harassment victims. William Kennedy Smith's lawyer cast aspersions on the complainant's motives; although Mike Tyson could have KO'd Desiree Washington with the back of his hand, he claimed to have been overwhelmed by her superior brains and education.[5] Anita Hill was maligned as a woman scorned, seeking revenge and celebrity. The separation of work and family, impersonality of most interaction, privatisation and commercialisation of leisure, declining social significance of residential neighbourhoods, and increasing geographic mobility all encourage victims to exit from conflict rather than voice grievances.[6] The American victims' rights movement has failed to involve complainants in prosecuting offenders, despite the investment of considerable resources.[7] Even New Yorkers, notorious for aggressive self-assertion, swallow most insults.[8]

Collective efforts are necessary to encourage subordinated peoples to complain about the harms of speech. Although such partisanship might seem to violate liberal theory, it is no different from state intervention to remedy market failure (restrictive practices and consumer protection laws), electoral failure (campaign financing rules), and juridical failure (legal aid). The state has already assisted vulnerable and reticent victims through institutions like the Freedmen's Bureau (during Reconstruction), protective services for women and children, and labour inspectorates.[9] The Law Society's Accident Legal Aid Scheme helps tort victims seek compensation, thereby reducing the underrepresentation of women and the unwaged.[10] South Yorkshire police have provided mobile telephones so that racial and sexual harassment victims can summon assistance quickly.[11] The British Department of Education helpline for the 120,000 boarding school pupils received 10,000 calls in its first nine months; over the next three months its successor received 2000 complaints about bullying, three-fourths of them from girls.[12] Since the state is unlikely to be a vigorous ally of speech victims, they must seek support from other groups--the functional equivalent of trade unions or the ad hoc aggregations of victims of drunk driving accidents or mass torts.[13] Because hurtful speech often occurs in a private setting—home, residence hall, or office—the audience may be non-existent or unsupportive. Other members of the subordinated category—all of whom suffer status loss—represent the most promising allies, another reason to defend such groups against charges of separatism. Because most victimised groups are minorities, they must form coalitions with other principled opponents of subordination (political, religious, civil rights and civil liberties groups).[14]

Victims also need norms that confirm their sense of violation, enhance their feeling of empowerment, elicit audience sympathy, and help legitimate the complaint in the offender's eyes. Despite the complexity of the relationship between norm, morality, and action no one could deny that laws against discrimination on grounds of race, gender, age, and disability have had salutary consequences. Successful complaints can have a cumulative effect. Like any behaviour, complaining is learned; visible rewards encourage the victim to repeat and others to imitate.[15] When a Chicago woman went on television to describe the damages she won for being strip-searched during a routine traffic citation—a humiliation long accepted as the cost of driving in that city—many women telephoned the station with similar stories.[16] When Anita Hill testified before hundreds of millions of viewers about her sexual harassment by Clarence Thomas, innumerable women felt their anger validated for the first time.[17] In Hollywood, many who had accepted harassment as the occupational hazard of an industry that marketed sex have challenged it and sued perpetrators.[18]

Such insubordination is more likely to be punished than rewarded, however. The same factors that discourage complaints also render status victims particularly vulnerable to retaliation.[19] An English doctor who exploded at the male doctor with whom she shared a surgery, shouting "I'm fed up with you brushing against me and having my breasts touched and my bum touched as you go by," was ordered to pay £150,000 damages—the highest slander verdict ever recorded—and an estimated £100,000 costs. The judge had instructed the jury not to be miserly, referring to the just completed Clarence Thomas hearings.[20] When a black man was insulted and assaulted in Norwich by white racists, the judge sentenced him and his white rescuers to the same two-year prison sentence as the assailants, declaring: "I can see no basis for differentiating between you in the matter of penalty."[21] It is essential, therefore, to protect complainants against further victimisation.

C. Processing Disputes Informally

In what forum should speech victims complain, through what procedures, and toward what end? State regulation should be minimised for all the reasons I advanced earlier: procedural fetishism, severity, formalism, inaccessibility, and delay. Instead, the state should encourage the communities of civil society to redress speech harms.[22] What constitutes a self-regulating community will vary across time and place, but possible locales include schools and universities,[23] workplaces,[24] trade unions,[25] residential neighbourhoods,[26] libraries,[27] shops, public transportation, voluntary associations, sports teams, political parties and movements, and religious congregations. Only communities whose diversity reflects that of the larger society can address the reproduction of status inequality. The community has several obvious merits as a locus of struggle. Because it constructs status, the community can alter it. Because members are joined by significant social bonds, they can influence each other through informal sanctions like gossip, cooperation and obstruction, deference and contempt, inclusion and ostracism. By enhancing civility, the redress of speech harms strengthens community. The plurality of communities offers a safety valve for dissent; those who cannot or will not offer the respect demanded in one community can move to another. For the same reason, some social spaces should remain unregulated by any community—a speech frontier for the incurably disaffected.

Communities should regulate speech informally. A decade ago I criticised informalism for simultaneously extending unwarranted power to the state and false hope to the powerless.[28] Informal community responses to speech harms do just the opposite, exercising influence in situations where power is inappropriate and indifference unacceptable. The ambiguity of symbols, nuances of meaning, opacity of motive, and complexity of history and context—all of which make the dichotomies of formal law an intolerably crude instrument for regulating speech—are the essential grist for informal processes, giving the parties space to negotiate. The process must be initiated and controlled by the victim—not lawyers, police or prosecutors—since a principal purpose is empowerment. Because victims belong to subordinated groups, they require support from former victims, group members, and others. For the same reason, any third party must also be partisan, openly acknowledging the social asymmetries that formality hypocritically obscures. The goal is substantive justice not procedural neutrality, status equality not conflict resolution. Indeed, the purpose is to give voice to grievances borne silently, hurts suffered mutely. For this reason the process must be accessible and speedy, since it lacks the in terrorem effect of loss of freedom or wealth. The process is the punishment.[29] The absence of coercive authority becomes an advantage, obviating the procedural fetishism that distracts from the real issues. Informal community responses are not limited to the lowest common denominator of societal consensus; enclaves can prefigure a more inclusive equality. Because the norms governing status relations are inchoate and mutable, informalism legislates while adjudicating—a conflation of roles that embarrassed legalists try to hide. The norms that emerge from the experience of processing complaints empower subsequent victims.

What do status victims want? Individuals want offenders to acknowledge the harm and apologise. Groups want that personal response to elevate collective status. The remedy must be speech, not punishment or monetary compensation.[30] Just as insults are performative utterances, raising the speaker's status at the expense of the victim's, so the only corrective is more speech. Even the First

Amendment denies protection to "fighting words"; what it fails to recognise is that words do not just provoke fights, they *are* fights. This theorisation avoids some of consequentialism's uncertainties about the effects of speech and the efficacy of deterrence. The goal is an institutionalised but informal conversation between victim and offender.[31] First the offender must be allowed to offer an account, an alternative interpretation of ambiguous words and impenetrable motives. To the extent that the victim honours this account the wound may be salved.[32] But few accounts are entirely credible, and some are wholly implausible. Lingering resentment must be mollified and persistent status inequality corrected by an apology.

Unlike accounts, which are limited only by the speaker's imagination, apologies are highly structured ceremonies. In these degradation rituals offenders must affirm the norm, acknowledge its violation, and accept responsibility. Such a social exchange of respect can neutralise the insult.[33] The offender owes, offers, or gives an apology, thereby acknowledging moral inferiority; the offended accepts it, thereby restoring the offender to a plane of moral equality, or rejects it, preserving the moral imbalance. Thus the victim not only initiates the remedial process but also controls its outcome, becoming the arbiter of the offender's rehabilitation. Police at a white suburban mall held two African American shoppers at gunpoint: Gerald Early, a professor at Washington University, and his wife Ida, vice-president of the St. Louis Junior League. When the officer and police chief refused to apologise, a letter-writing campaign and threatened commercial boycott prompted the mayor to say: "I very much regret that Prof. and Mrs. Gerald Early felt uncomfortable and unwelcome . . . ." The Urban League responded: "That's no apology. [The mayor] could have simply said, 'We apologize to Professor Early and his family, not for their uneasiness but for their treatment.' "[34] Like this failure to affirm the norm and admit its violation, disavowal of responsibility can defeat the apology. In recognition of Black History month John Cardinal O'Connor declared in New York's St. Patrick's Cathedral: "If there is one place in the whole world in which [racism] should not exist, it is in the Holy Roman Catholic Church . . . . And yet we know in our hearts, we know in our shame, that it continues to exist." But he qualified this abasement by speaking of "bilateral racism" and placing on blacks the burden of making Catholicism one church.[35] In order to redefine status relations, an apology often is witnessed by an audience, who independently judge its adequacy. The third party might play this role—a truth-telling function similar to that of an ombudsman.[36] At a minimum, the audience for the apology must be as large as that for the insult. To amplify its impact, French law compels those convicted of racial hatred to pay substantial sums to publish the retraction and apology repeatedly in several national newspapers.[37]

There is unavoidable tension in this process since accounts seek to disavow responsibility while apologies must embrace it. Unless they are separated, the former can undermine the latter. Nixon characteristically conflated the two in his resignation speech: "I regret deeply any injuries that may have been done in the course of events that led to this decision. I would say only that if some of my judgments were wrong, and some were wrong, they were made in what I believed at the time to be the best interest of the Nation." When it was disclosed in 1992 that Elisabeth Noëlle-Neumann, a German political scientist visiting at the University of Chicago, had displayed anti-Semitism in her dissertation and newspaper articles in the 1930s, she mixed justification with apology:

> Anyone who has dealt with texts written under a dictatorship knows that certain phrases serve an alibi function and are a necessity if one is to be able to write what is in fact prohibited. I am terribly sorry if any hurt was caused by what I wrote 50 years ago. I certainly can say that when I wrote that passage at the time, I had no intention of doing any harm to the Jews.

The department chair was not satisfied: "Knowing what we know about the Holocaust, there is no reason for her not to apologize. To ask somebody who played a contributing role in the greatest crime of the twentieth century to say 'I'm sorry' is not unreasonable."[38]

The realignment of status is highlighted when apologies are exchanged between groups. Signing the bill authorising reparations to Japanese Americans interned during World War II, President Reagan declared: "No payment can make up for those lost years. What is more important in this bill has less to do with property than with honor. For here we admit wrong." When three young Japanese radicals massacred Jews at Lod Airport in 1972 many ordinary citizens visited the Israeli embassy in Tokyo to offer apologies, while the Japanese ambassador said on Israeli television in halting Hebrew: "Dear citizens of Israel, it is my wish to express my sorrow and apologize for this terrible crime perpetrated by Japanese nationals" and then burst into tears. Sometimes no words may be commensurate with the harm inflicted. In 1986 the moderator of the United Church of Canada told a gathering of native Canadian elders:

> We ask you to forgive us. In our zeal to tell you about Jesus Christ, we were blind to your spirituality. We imposed our civilization on you as a condition for accepting our gospel. As a result, we are both poorer. . . . These are not just words. It is one of the most important actions ever taken by the church.

"[T]he happiness felt in the council teepee was almost unbelievable" according to the chairman of the church's National Native Council. When the church's biennial General Council reconvened in 1988, however, the All-Native Circle Conference acknowledged the apology but refused to accept it.[39]

In the conversations just summarised the offender listens to the victim's grievances, advances an account, and apologises. But what about those who refuse to participate, proffer flimsy excuses and hypocritical regrets, or repeat the offence? Some are emotionally or ideologically committed, others motivated by political ambition or greed. Communities can mobilise various forms of persuasion, including publicity, withdrawal of privileges and benefits, and ostracism. Universities have been particularly inventive. A male student who called a female residence hall supervisor a "cunt" for denying him entry without the requisite invitation was excluded from women's residence halls for the rest of the semester and ordered to perform 30 hours of community service.[40] UCLA students who sexually harassed women were required to establish programs to educate fraternities about sexual harassment. Two white Harvard Medical School students who aped Clarence Thomas and Anita Hill by attending a party in blackface had to prepare a course on medicine in a multi-ethnic society.[41] Ultimately, however, no community can survive without the ability to expel incorrigibles.[42] Schools and universities, employers, trade unions, and housing estates all have done so.

This approach to the harms of speech leaves two intractable problems: bad communities and extra-communal life. Many communities are indifferent to status inequalities, and some affirm them. Dominant religions oppose heterodoxy, religious conservatives condemn homosexuals, patriarchal communities repress women, and white communities assert racial superiority. Yet this fear may be exaggerated. The liberal consensus against discrimination has been growing, if its strength diminishes as we move from race through religion to gender and sexual orientation. Successful community efforts to redress the harms of speech will broaden and deepen that consensus, allowing the state to extend the expectation of equality, as it has been doing since the Enlightenment. The second problem—harmful speech that escapes communal regulation—seems less troubling. Each nation will have to decide whether to tolerate it on the margins—in Hyde Park, for instance, or the streets of Skokie. An essential virtue of pluralistic regulation by partial overlapping communities is that it allows everyone to hear many messages and speak in several fora; those discontent with one community can join another. As the regulatory jurisdiction expands, the consequences of silencing dissent become more momentous. The case for suppressing speech strengthens with its danger: where the harm to subordinated groups is greatest, the audience receptive and growing, the message least ambiguous, and the motive clearly evil. I support laws against such harmful speech, if mainly because their mere enactment elevates the status of those protected, but I would not expect the inevitably compromised enforcement to play a major role in redressing inequality. The real answer to both questions—bad communities and communal interstices—is that there is no safe place, no escape from politics to persuade communities of their error and prudence to guide communities and states in exercising power. There is no one best solution to the tension between freedom and authority.

## V. The Perils of Pluralistic Regulation

If communal efforts to redress status inequality are limited by pluralism, their success also generates risks: backlash and trivialisation, the self-indulgence of identity politics, revolutionary excess, and damage to civil libertarian bulwarks. Conservatives denigrate the struggle for respect with the epithet "political correctness"—a redundant tautology, since politics are omnipresent and all actors believe theirs are correct.[43] Dominant groups confound challenges by concocting reverse atrocity stories that ridicule victims or transmute them into oppressors. California kooks are a favourite target. After Governor Wilson vetoed a bill outlawing employment discrimination on the basis of sexual orientation, the Santa Cruz Body Image Task Force proposed to prohibit discrimination based on height, weight, and appearance. Although respectable jurisdictions like Michigan and the District of Columbia had similar laws, the media quickly fixated on Cooper Hazen, recently fired as a psychiatric aide for having a post in his pierced tongue, purple hair, five earrings, and a nose ring; a short Mexican American lesbian who complained of being "vertically challenged"; and Sara "Hell," who wore black leather and a dangling skeleton earring and had tatooed her shaven head to highlight a long lock of fuchsia hair.[44] Similarly, the *Guardian* had a field day when a Berkeley waitress refused to serve breakfast to a man reading *Playboy*, generating irate phone calls from male and female soft-porn fans, a boycott, and a "read-in" at the diner, with free copies from the publisher.[45]

If the dominant trivialise the harm they inflict, the subordinate abuse their moral leverage by playing identity politics, claiming exclusive rights to speak for or about their group. Identity always has been salient in electoral politics, as evidenced by the ethnic machines of American cities, gerrymandering, and the gender gap. Women recently defeated liberal men for the Democratic nominations for both California Senate seats. Although Gray Davis urged voters not "to make their choice based . . . on a chromosome count," the California vice-president of the National Women's Political Caucus promoted Diane Feinstein, asserting: "A man cannot speak for a woman in Congress." Barbara Boxer, the other victor, declared: "The U.S. Senate needs a dose of reality, and that dose comes in this package."[46]

Subordinated groups increasingly assert their claims to cultural territory.[47] Thirty years ago William Styron was condemned for daring to write *The Confessions of Nat Turner* and Laurence Olivier criticised for portraying Othello.[48] By the 1990s only an Asian could play the lead in "Miss Saigon." When Warner Brothers decided to produce a biography of Malcolm X it hired Norman Jewison, the white director of "A Soldier's Story," a highly acclaimed film about a Southern black regiment during World War Two. After being deluged with up to 100 protest letters a day the studio substituted Spike Lee. Although Lee denied orchestrating the campaign, he acknowledged: "I had problems with a white director directing this film. Unless you are black, you do not know what it means to be a black person in this country." Malcolm's former friends and associates would not have cooperated with a white director. "Most black people are suspicious of white people and their motives. That's just reality."[49]

Identity, however, is neither necessary nor sufficient for authenticity. When white jazz critic Leonard Feather bet that black trumpeter Roy Eldridge could not distinguish black and white musicians on records, Eldridge did worse than chance. After Danny Santiago won an Academy of Arts and Letters award for his moving portrayal of Chicano life in the East Los Angeles barrio in his novel *Famous All Over Town*, he embarrassed many admirers by revealing that he was Daniel L. James, a 70-year-old Jew educated at Andover and Yale.[50] *The Education of Little Tree*, promoted as the true story of a 10-year-old orphan who learned Indian ways from his Cherokee grandparents, sold 600,000 copies, won the American Booksellers Association award for the title they most enjoyed selling, and was displayed on gift tables in Indian reservations and assigned as supplementary reading in Native American literature courses. Studios competed for the right to film it. *Booklist* praised its "natural approach to life." In Tennessee, where the story was situated, the *Chattanooga Times* called it "deeply felt." Declaring that it captured a unique vision of native American culture, an Abnaki poet lauded it as "one of the finest American autobiographies ever written" and compared it to "a Cherokee basket, woven out of the materials given by nature, simple and strong in its design, capable of carrying a great deal." *The New Mexican* reviewer raved: "I have come on something that is good, so good I want to shout 'Read this! It's beautiful. It's real.' " But it wasn't. The pseudonymous author Forrest Carter actually was the late Asa Earl Carter, "a Ku Klux Klan terrorist, right-wing radio announcer, home-grown American fascist and anti-Semite, rabble-rousing demagogue and secret author of the famous 1963 speech" in which Alabama Governor George Wallace promised "Segregation now . . . Segregation tomorrow . . . Segregation forever."[51] If identity can be successfully feigned, biology does not guarantee acceptance. When Julius Lester criticised James Baldwin in 1988, 15 colleagues in the African American Studies Department forced the University of Massachusetts to reassign him to Judaic Studies. Many blacks repudiate conservatives like Clarence Thomas or Thomas Sowell; many women disavow Phyllis Schlafly.[52]

Like any political conflict, the struggle for equal status will foster excesses. Some feminist critics of pornography have entered unholy alliances with conservative moralists and religious prudes, threatening valuable art and literature as well as misogynist trash and inhibiting sexual expression by women as well as men, homosexuals as well as heterosexuals.[53] As long as gendered power inequalities persist, complaints against real sexual harassment may also inhibit love. The *fatwa* against Salman Rushdie is a grave injustice to him and a terrible blot on the reputation of Islam. Suspicion contami-

151

nates discourse across status boundaries. Fear of inflicting harm may discourage research on genetic and biological differences, or investigation of the darker history of subordinated groups.[54] Propaganda may displace art. The unity necessary to struggle for enhanced status may breed internal intolerance, painful separatism, and external distrust.[55]

Abandonment of an absolutist civil libertarianism may deprive citizens of weapons valuable in resisting state oppression. Yet efforts to evade political responsibility by seeking refuge in illusory principle violate intellectual integrity. And it is unclear that communal or even state regulation of speech that reproduces status inequality encourages the suppression of religious or political dissent, intellectual or artistic creativity. There is little evidence that either the public or their officials tolerate speech they abhor because speech they value is tolerated by those who abhor it.[56]

Let me conclude on a more positive note by stressing how far we have come, how many forms of status degradation once taken for granted have lost their legitimacy. Racist, anti-Semitic and sexist slurs that pervaded polite discourse have been banished to the margins of deviance. Crude media stereotypes now startle and shock by their rarity. Hegemonic religion is yielding to pluralistic tolerance. Public disapproval is curtailing sexual harassment. The differently abled, long forced to beg or display their differences as "freaks," have greater access to public life. Even homophobia is in retreat. Communal regulation of harmful speech builds on these small victories in the unending struggle for a more humane society.

## Notes

[1] Galanter (1974).
[2] France (1927: ch.7).
[3] *Guardian* 8 (November 14, 1991).
[4] *Guardian* 6 (October 12, 1991).
[5] GLC Women's Committee (nd: 5, 9).
[6] All are eligible for Medicare. *New York Times* A14 (March 18, 1992).
[7] All are eligible for Medicaid. *Los Angeles Times* A3 (January 31, 1992).
[8] Soon after California gassed its first convicted criminal in 25 years the legislature authorised the lethal injection as an alternative. The news headline read: "California Inmates Get Choice in Executions." *New York Times* A7 (August 31, 1992).
[9] *Guardian* 8 (October 12, 1991).
[10] *Independent* 10 (October 15, 1991).
[11] *Guardian* 28 (November 1, 1991).

[12] *New York Times* A19 (January 25, 1991). A Moscow brokerage house advertisement for women secretaries, 18–21 years old, told them to wear a mini-skirt to the interview. An advertising firm seeking a receptionist asked women to submit full-length photos, preferably in a bikini to display their "full super-attractiveness." *New York Times* 13 (September 12, 1992) (op ed).

[13] *New York Times* B12 (December 11, 1991).

[14] *New York Times* B1 (April 15, 1992).

[15] *New York Times* 1 (February 15, 1992).

[16] *New York Times* B1 (January 23, 1991).

[17] *New York Times* s.1 p.69 (December 15, 1991). Dalma Heyn's *The Erotic Silence of the American Wife* (1992) was much ballyhooed as a call for eliminating the double standard by ending monogamous fidelity for women as well as men.

It's about time women gave voice to all their dimensions, including the erotic, without shrinking in guilt. (Gail Sheehy)

Dalma Heyn has shown us a new reality and a tantalizing hint of the future—and neither women nor marriage will ever be the same. (Gloria Steinem)

Heyn reminds us . . . that women are sexual beings and that, for women as well as men, sex is a fundamentally lawless creature, not easily confined to a cage. (Barbara Ehrenreich)

Dalma Heyn exposes the lie that men, by nature, play around and women, by nature, are monogamous. (Louise Bernikow)

*New York Times* B2 (June 17, 1992) (advertisement).

Male actors, singers, and athletes have always been sex objects. Women law students comment on cute male professors in teaching evaluations and bathroom graffiti. Now other male performers are seeking to exploit their sexuality. EMI Classics promoted Tzimon Barto's "Chopin Preludes" with publicity photos showing him without a shirt. The female vice president of marketing explained: "What we are trying to do is represent the artist as a whole person. Not only does he play the piano beautifully, but he's also a body builder . . . " Trying to make a Swiss harpist "a sex symbol of classical music," the company photographed him in bed with his harp. The performer conceded: "we try to use the fact that I'm young, that I do sports, I lift weights, whatever to catch the attention of the people to listen." *New York Times* B4 (September 14, 1992).

[18] Walker (1980); Teish (1980); Crenshaw (1991). Consider the reaction of black men to Alice Walker's *The Color Purple* (both the novel and film), or of the black women in Spike Lee's "Jungle Fever" to the interracial love affair. See also Campbell (1992) and the reader response. *New York Times Magazine* 12–13 (September 13, 1992) (letters to The Editor).

[19] Mercer (1990: 45–49).

[20] Camille Paglia has cynically pursued an academic and media career by attacking feminism. She recently wrote that "every woman must take

*Taking Sides*

personal responsibility for her sexuality" and must be "cautious about where she goes and with whom." If raped, she "must accept the consequences, and, through self-criticism, resolve never to make that mistake again." Rape "does not destroy you forever. . . . It's like getting beaten up. Men get beat [sic] up all the time." Anita Hill is not a "feminist heroine," and Clarence Thomas emerged from the hearings "with vastly increased stature." Paglia was "delighted that [William Kennedy] Smith was acquitted" of rape. (1992; see also 1990).

21  Stephen L. Carter (Yale Law School); Shelby Steele (San Jose State University English department); Linda Chavez (Equal Employment Opportunities Commission); Glenn C. Loury (Boston University economics department); Thomas Sowell (Hoover Institute, economics); Walter E. Williams (George Mason University economics department); Randall Kennedy (Harvard Law School). See, *e.g.* Carter (1991).

22  *Guardian* 3 (November 21, 1991).

23  *Los Angeles Times* A1 (February 28, 1992) (obituary).

24  *New York Times* s.1 p.3 (December 29, 1991), A4 (December 31, 1991), A3 (February 10, 1992). The government banned political activity in the mosques and closed three independent daily newspapers for "endangering the nation's interest." *New York Times* A16 (August 20, 1992).

25  *New York Times* A3 (February 10, 1992).

26  *Guardian* 6 (September 18, 1991), 6 (October 21, 1991), 26 (November 22, 1991).

27  *New York Times* A10 (February 6, 1992), A7 (February 25, 1992).

28  Repohistory, a group of 65 artists, installed 39 signs in lower Manhattan with the approval of the Department of Transportation. The one on Maiden Lane showed a doll with an illustration of a hymen taken from a medical textbook, explaining that the street got its name from the young girls who did the laundry along a stream in the 17th century. A 40-year old woman said: "It's disgusting. Everyone's taste in art varies, but I just think this particular thing is offensive to women." *New York Times* A14 (August 27, 1992).

29  Hughes (1980).

30  *New York Times* s.2 p.10 (March 15, 1992).

31  If a charge of blasphemy against Islam has terrorised Salman Rushdie for nearly four years, Gore Vidal's publisher has exulted in similar accusations against his novel *Live from Golgotha* (1992), reproducing them in newspaper advertisements:

It's too funny to be condemned simply as a blasphemous novel that should be added to the Vatican's Index of banned works and censored by the book police anywhere. Like it or not, its assault on the New Testament prophets or their modern successors and on religion in general is in a bawdy and anti-hypocritical tradition that goes back to Chaucer, Rabelais, Balzac and our own Sinclair Lewis. (Herbert Mitgang, *New York Times*)

Bracingly blasphemous. Vidal still hasn't gone respectable: Christians and Jews, p.c. gays and uptight straights will all find plenty to offend them. (*Newsweek*)

Despite every Rushdie-like blasphemy he can think of . . . what he achieves is a serious argument about the birth and meaning of Christianity. (*Chicago Tribune*)

I will not read the book, and I will not spend money on it. (Dr. Michael Harty, Bishop of Killaloe)

*New York Times* B3 (September 23, 1992), B2 (September 24, 1992), B2 (October 2, 1992).

At the end of a rave review of "Glengarry Glen Ross," Vincent Canby observed that the movie "which has been rated R . . . is stuffed with language that is vile, obscene and gratuitously vulgar, which is its method." *New York Times* B1 (September 30, 1992).

[32] *Guardian* 33 (November 14, 1991).

[33] Osborne (1991), reviewed in *Guardian* 27 (October 31, 1991).

[34] Harvey (1984).

A Jersey City group (whose name the *New York Times* would not print because it contained an obscenity) made a statue of Jesse Helms filled with fertilizer (bullshit), gave it a mock trial for censorship, and smashed it on the Capitol steps during an anti-censorship rally. They disrupted rush-hour traffic by chaining a 46-foot banner of headless suits across Wall Street to protest "the mindless omnipotence of corporate America." They hung sculptural corpses named for art movements to street lights near SoHo galleries to demonstrate that "art is dead." They changed smiles into grimaces and faces into skulls on 42 billboards before two members were arrested. The Gannett Corporation, which owned the billboards, dropped the charges and gave the group its own to produce a message for the Women's Health Action Mobilization on AIDS. Like Guerrilla Girls (feminist artists who wear gorilla costumes to gallery openings to protest male hegemony), they wear black clown outfits to accuse galleries of playing it safe. *New York Times* s.1 p.34 (April 26, 1992).

Robbie Conal's posters display Chief Justice William Rehnquist over the caption "Gag Me With a Coat Hanger" and the six male justices likely to vote against abortion over the caption "Freedom of Choice" in which "of" has been crossed out and replaced by "from." Guerrilla Matrons mysteriously plaster them across Los Angeles, following a two-page guide to "Guerrilla Etiquette and Postering Technique." *Los Angeles Times* E1 (June 9, 1992).

[35] *Los Angeles Times* A10 (April 23, 1992). During the Sixties we shouted: "Hey, Hey, LBJ/How many kids did you kill today?" When Clarence Thomas wrote an opinion shortly after his confirmation holding that the repeated beating of a federal prisoner did not constitute cruel and unusual punishment, the political cartoonist Conrad pictured him (and Justice Scalia) beating a bound, gagged, and manacled black prisoner with their gavels. *Los Angeles Times* B7 (March 3, 1992).

[36] Commenting on the proscription of swearing in British family and

children's television programmes, Ian Curteis said: "As a Christian, I find the casual expletive 'Jesus' or 'Christ' momentarily sickening . . . . To most ordinary people, sex remains a private, almost secret thing, verging on the miraculous. A sudden crude blow to such feelings can produce the same sort of shock as a religious based swear-word." *Guardian* 31 (October 28, 1991). A survey by the Broadcasting Standards Council ranked swear words from the least objectionable (blast—49 per cent objected) to the most (piss—72 per cent objected). *Guardian* 2 (October 25, 1991).

When George Bernard Shaw presented *The Adventures of the Black Girl in Her Search for God* to Dame Laurentia McClachlan of Stanbrook Abbey she was so upset that she broke off a long and valued friendship, refusing to speak to him for a year, according to Hugh Whitemore's "The Best of Friends" (an adaptation of their letters for theatre and television). A.N. Wilson's *Jesus* (1992) seems to be provoking a similar storm more than half a century later.

[37] *Los Angeles Times* F1 (October 6, 1992). What about Francis Bacon's portraits of Popes, some of them sitting on the toilet?

[38] Matsuda (1989: 2357).

[39] Hungary has declared its intent to compensate the victims of state oppression, from the first law against Jews passed on March 11, 1939 to the fall of communism on October 23, 1989. *New York Times* A4 (May 14, 1992). The Jewish Restitution Organization (uniting eight groups) plans to claim payment for schools, hospitals, synagogues, art, and ritual objects seized by Nazis and communists, worth an estimated $10 billion. *Los Angeles Times* A4 (August 4, 1992). Chief Moshood Kashimawo Abiola, a major Nigerian capitalist and close friend of the president, is seeking reparations to Africans from all the countries involved in the slave trade. *New York Times* A2 (August 10, 1992).

[40] Morrison's permanent secretary, quoted in Lester (1987: 21).

[41] *New Statesman & Society* 20 (October 4, 1991).

[42] *Guardian* 2 (November 22, 1991).

[43] *Guardian* 7 (November 11, 1991). The Minnesota Supreme Court has invalidated a criminal statute imposing heavier penalties for possession of crack than powdered cocaine because almost all of those caught with crack were black (96.6 per cent), while most of those found with cocaine were white (79.6 per cent). The state had not shown that crack was more dangerous. *New York Times* 8 (December 14, 1991).

[44] 190 *Searchlight* 7 (April 1991); 187 *Searchlight* 8 (January 1991) (sample of 3000).

[45] *New York Times* A4 (March 4, 1991).

[46] *Guardian* 2 (October 14, 1991) (Bar Council), 6 (September 19, 1991) (Lord Chancellor), 5 (October 12, 1991) (Master of the Rolls).

[47] *Los Angeles Times* A29 (March 28, 1992).

[48] *New York Times* s.4 p.16 (March 22, 1992). In South Africa, which certainly has as much experience as any country with de facto inequality,

a reviewer for the leading liberal weekly ridiculed the argument that pornography degrades women by arguing that "hideous stereotyping of nightclub owners, plumbers who leave their bodies lying out from under the sink and newspaper boys who knock on the door, also occurs." Stober (1992).

[49] *New York Times* A10 (March 17, 1992) (margin of error +/-4%).

[50] *New York Times* A8 (October 9, 1990).

[51] *New York Times* 1 (December 14, 1991).

[52] *New York Times* B16 (December 4, 1991), A7 (February 6, 1992); *Podberesky* v. *Kirwan*, 956 F.2d 52 (4th Cir. 1992). Only about 1500 minority students hold such scholarships, less than 0.03 per cent of the 5,200,000 university students receiving financial aid. *Los Angeles Times* A5 (March 17, 1992). The Regents of the University of California recently accepted a $500,000 bequest for scholarships for "very poor American Caucasian" students, observing that the testator "was well-intentioned." *New York Times* A11 (September 22, 1992). There are now enough minority alumni at many universities to donate significant funds for minority scholarships—$1.4 million at Syracuse University in the last four years. *New York Times* A6 (August 31, 1992).

[53] *Chronicle of Higher Education* A38 (February 5, 1992). The U.S. Justice Department's Office of Civil Rights has just required the UC Berkeley law school to change its affirmative action admissions programme dramatically. *Los Angeles Times* A1 (September 29, 1992); *New York Times* A15 (September 30, 1992).

India's half-century effort to alleviate religious, caste, and ethnic inequalities has stimulated even more violent responses. In 1990 six students in Haryana, Punjab and Andhra Pradesh committed suicide to protest affirmative action for the scheduled castes and indigenous peoples; there were three more attempts in New Delhi, and trains and cars were attacked in Allahabad. *New York Times* A4 (October 9, 1990). See generally Galanter (1984).

[54] *Chronicle of Higher Education* A15 (November 27, 1991).

[55] *New York Times* 1 (April 13, 1991); *Chronicle of Higher Education* A24 (January 8, 1992), A24 (February 12, 1992). The panel member was an anti-feminist woman philosophy professor, Christina Hoff Sommers.

[56] University students with physical disabilities enthusiastically supported the creation of their own cultural centre. A counselor explained: "a cultural center is saying we have a culture we want to share. The culture is part of the disability that distinguishes us, the same as people of color organize around their culture." One of the organisers, who is blind, added: "For years we have been asked to live in this able-bodied world, trying to become able-bodied people. The idea here is, I'm proud of my disability and I don't need to be fixed." *New York Times* s.1 p.45 (April 26, 1992).

[57] *Guardian* 29 (November 5, 1991). Since 1988 the Dutch government has supported Islamic primary schools, with single-sex physical education

classes; Muslim leaders now have asked for separate secondary schools. *Los Angeles Times* A1 (February 8, 1992). African American converts to Islam increasingly are sending their children to private Muslim schools; there are eight in the New York area and more than 60 nationwide. *New York Times* A14 (October 6, 1992).

[58] 183 *Searchlight* 7, 18 (September 1990), 182 *Searchlight* 4 (August 1990); Weeks (1990: 93–94).

[59] *New York Times* A17 (January 10, 1991), s.1 p.15 (January 13, 1991). The very day the New York proposal was announced a front-page headline declared: "South Africa Desegrates Some White Public Schools." *New York Times* A1 (January 10, 1991). Detroit has established an all-male primary school; although formally nonracial, more than 90 per cent of Detroit schoolchildren are minority. *New York Times* A12 (March 1, 1991). Most "historically black" public universities want to retain that identity. Hacker (1992: 154–58). Even in integrated institutions, some minority instructors admit only minority students to their classes. *New York Times* A20 (January 29, 1992) (Leonard Jeffries's African history course at CUNY's City College). Some whites have responded by establishing white student unions to defend their privileges and assert their cultural superiority. *Chronicle of Higher Education* A37 (September 11, 1991).

[60] *Independent on Sunday* 8 (November 3, 1991) (70 per cent of a sample of successful women had attended girls' schools; but dubious methodology); Wellesley College Center for Research on Women (1992); *New York Times* A1 (February 12, 1992); *Los Angeles Times* A1 (February 12, 1992) (review of more than 1000 studies). A recent book, however, suggested that women teachers in girls' schools may encourage obedience, conformity, passivity, and niceness. Brown & Gilligan (1992).

[61] *Los Angeles Times* B1 (February 28, 1992). The Lesbian Herstory Archives in Brooklyn bars men from some files (in accordance with the donor's wishes) and encourages them to send female researchers. 3(1) *Ms.* 59 (July/August 1992).

[62] *Chronicle of Higher Education* B1 (September 25, 1991) (Prof. Troy Duster, an African American sociologist at UC Berkeley).

[63] Bourdieu (1991); Curran et al. (1986). Dutch and Danish experiments with schools and the mass media offer examples.

[64] The developer of Colonial Village, a 640-unit condominium in Arlington, Virginia, just outside the District of Columbia, has been fined $850,000 for using only white models in its ads from 1981 to 1986, in violation of the 1968 Fair Housing Act. *New York Times* s.1 p.10 (May 17, 1992). At their annual conference, American Methodists adopted the first new "Book of Worship" in 25 years. An optional prayer described God as "our Mother and Father," "bakerwoman" leavening hopes, and giving "birth to our world." It included a Mexican Christmas eve service, many Native American prayers, and a Korean rite. *New York Times* s.1 p.14 (May 17, 1992). The co-chair of the Eleanor Roosevelt Monument Fund observed

that there are no statues of American women in New York City. A 3-foot high statue of Gertrude Stein in Bryant Park (behind the Public Library) will be the first; an 8-foot statue of Eleanor Roosevelt is planned for Riverside Park. *New York Times* 14 (August 29, 1992) (letter to The Editor, August 14). The New York City Board of Education adopted the ''Children of the Rainbow'' curriculum guide for first grade, which urges teachers to be ''aware of varied family structures, including . . . gay or lesbian parents . . .'' *New York Times* s.4 p.16 (September 27, 1992) (editorial). Hurricanes, which used to be named exclusively after women, now alternate between men's and women's names.

[65] ILEA (1982).

[66] Reinhold (1991); Bromwich (1992); Berman (1992); Aufderheide (1992); Schlesinger (1992); *Partisan Review* (1991); *New York Times* s.1 p.65 (December 15, 1991).

[67] Dickey and CPBF (1985) (Working Group against Daily Mail Racism; TUC; National Union of Journalists Code of Conduct; Association of Cinematograph, Television and Allied Technicians Code of Conduct); GLC Women's Committee (nda: 13) (London Transport Code of Conditions of Acceptance of Advertising).

[68] *New York Times* A27 (December 11, 1991), A14 (December 30, 1991). I question *The Nation*'s judgement in accepting an advertisement from a Los Angeles group called Positive Realism.

Gay to Straight. It Can Be Done? Sexuality derives from personality. Just as you make personal changes in your life, so heterosexuality can become a *natural*, self-fulfilling, joyous experience. How? You don't need to be converted or insulted. Instead, you can use a proven, well thought-out, positive and understanding approach. Any gay or bisexual man or woman can do it even if they've never experienced a heterosexual desire. Many already have.

Although the editors timidly characterised these claims as ''borderline offensive,'' knew they would anger staff and readers, and worried that ''printing more ads with a similar message would change the nature of the magazine and undermine the broad cultural values our editorial policy seeks to advance,'' they concluded that the ad ''does not seem fraudulent to us . . . . Bad politics and wrong ideas are best challenged by good politics and ideas, not censorship.'' 254(5) *The Nation* 148 (February 10, 1992). But that is just the question. Sometimes it is better to expose homophobia, sometimes it is wiser to deny it further publicity. Calling the latter decision censorship does not advance the ethical inquiry.

[69] *New York Times* 47 (December 14, 1991). The Council of Islamic Education, founded to combat stereotypes, objected to the statement in a sixth-grade textbook that all Muslims are Bedouins who rub sand over their faces before kneeling to pray to Allah. A seventh-grade text attributes a white face to the angel Gabriel (respected as God's messenger by Muslims, Christians, and Jews). It uses a camel to symbolise Islam's ''moment in time,'' comparable to Spanish cartographers, Samurai war-

*Taking Sides*

riors, Austrian crusaders, and English printers. *Los Angeles Times* B4 (October 3, 1992).

[70] *Guardian* 21 (November 13, 1991).

[71] *New York Times* A1, C9 (March 2, 1992) (gay press); *New York Times Magazine* pt 2 p.14 (April 5, 1992) (description of a lesbian couple who collect and sell antiques). Ralph Lauren, which for years identified itself with upper-class Edwardian Enlgand, now is following Benneton in using women, minorities, and inner city youths as models. *New York Times* B1 (September 14, 1992). Even in South Africa, the growing purchasing power of the huge black majority is compelling producers to seek black advertising agencies, which can appeal to that market. Herdbuoys, the first such agency, had 12 million rand in billings within a year after its April 1991 launch. *New York Times* s.3 p.3 (May 24, 1992).

But fewer than 10 per cent of American journalists are Black, Hispanic, or Asian American. *New York Times* s.1 p.16 (June 28, 1992).

[72] *New York Times* 9 (February 22, 1992).

[73] *New York Times* s.1. p.44 (December 1, 1991).

[74] *New York Times* s.3 p.12 (December 15, 1991). On the ways in which material culture expresses racism, see Dubin (1987).

[75] Quoted from the *Washington Post* in the (Johannesburg) *Weekly Mail* 12 (August 16, 1991). But progress is fitful. The anti-feminist backlash is epitomised by Mattel's latest Barbie doll, whose recorded voice simpers: "Math is hard!"

[76] I am obviously seeing society as constructed of relationships among otherwise incomplete beings rather than rights between autonomous individuals. Cf. Gilligan (1982).

Los Angeles's Cardinal Roger M. Mahony issued a report on the mass media in which he asserted: "Artistic freedom is essential to the creative process. But a moment's reflection will convince [writers] that the freedom they cherish cannot be separated from the moral order, the demands of truth, a concern for the common good or the well-being of other people." If characters are "saying something with their bodies they do not mean with their minds, hearts, and souls," he asked, "is the picture honest about the inauthenticity, the inadequacy, the terrible emptiness, the shallowness and the self-deception of such a one-dimensional approach to human sexuality?" Is violence "demanded by the story" and "presented as a desirable way to solve problems and resolve conflict?" Are women portrayed as "possessing the same intrinsic dignity as their male counterparts . . . ?" He was applauded by the president of the Writers Guild of America West, the senior vice president of Atlantic Records (who was also chair of the Southern California ACLU), the vice president of the Directors Guild of America, and the president of the Motion Picture Association of America. *Los Angeles Times* A1 (October 1, 1992).

[77] In response to listener objections, NBC stopped using "darky" and other racially derogatory terms in the 1930s. As late as the 1950s, entertain-

ment programmes could not mention divorce. *New York Times* B4 (April 27, 1992). A month after his first acquittal on charges of beating Rodney King, Stacey C. Koon "wrote" a book about the LAPD, generously seasoned with racial slurs. He referred to King as "Madingo" and George Holliday (who shot the incriminating video) as "George of the Jungle". Once when Koon repeatedly shot a black man his fellow officers joked that the man would survive because blacks "are too dumb to go into shock." Koon claimed he had become a "legend" for viciously kicking a Latino drug suspect in the testicles. The new LAPD chief (an African American from Philadelphia) quickly denounced the comments. When the book appeared five months later all this material had been cut. Koon said "that was part of the editing process. Those were just raw notes." *Los Angeles Times* B1 (May 16, 1992), B3 (May 21, 1992), B3 (October 15, 1992). Daryl F. Gates, the police chief who had just been forced into retirement, made his debut on KFI's radio call-in show the same day that federal prosecutors indicted the four LAPD officers for civil rights violations. Gates exulted: "Just think, I don't have the restraints that I had before, when I was Chief of Police. Now I can say almost anything I want to say." He had not been noticeably reticent before. *New York Times* A8 (August 7, 1992).

78 Witness the extraordinary success of Deborah Tannen's books (1986; 1990).

79 Paley (1992).

80 Hall (1991), reviewed in *The Guardian* 25 (November 21, 1991).

81 *Observer* 3 (November 17, 1991).

82 *New York Times* s.1 p.26 (December 8, 1991).

83 *New York Times* A12 (January 29, 1992), A12 (January 30, 1992), A19 (March 26, 1992), A14 (April 1, 1992), A17 (April 2, 1992), s.1 p.14 (April 5, 1992). Jackson addressed the Jewish World Congress in Brussels in July, urging the two groups to work together against "scapegoating, racism, anti-Semitism, polarization and violence." He repudiated Louis Farrakhan, retracted his earlier statement that Israel was "occupying the birthplace of Jesus Christ," and apologised for "Hymietown." The WJC secretary general said: "He condemned anti-Semitism 42 times in his speech, 42 times. What more do you want?" *New York Times* A1 (July 8, 1992); *Los Angeles Times* A1 (July 8, 1992).

84 *Los Angeles Times* A20 (October 8, 1992).

85 Delgado (1982); Volokh (1992).

86 *New York Times* s.1 p.17 (March 8, 1992).

87 *Los Angeles Times* B1 (March 6, 1992).

88 *New York Times* B3 (March 5, 1992).

89 *New York Times* A12 (August 29, 1991); *Chronicle of Higher Education* A1 (October 23, 1991); *Los Angeles Times* B1 (September 21, 1992) (AIDS march).

90 Richard West Jr., a Stanford law graduate and Cheyenne-Arapaho, the

first director of the Smithsonian's National Museum of the American Indian, declared: ''No other modern museum has so self-consciously sought focused input of special concerns from a user population.'' 12 of the 25 governing board members must be Indian. ''We're part of the 'we,' not the 'them.' '' A pre-opening show in New York, ''Pathways of Tradition,'' was shaped by the recommendations of 28 ''culturally based'' artists, religious leaders, educators, and museum administrators. *New York Times* s.2 p.53 (September 13, 1992).

[91] *New York Times* A1 (March 2, 1992).

Many African Americans have condemned *Huckleberry Finn* as racist, deploring Mark Twain's use of the word ''nigger'' (200 times) and urging its exclusion from schools and libraries. Now a white literature professor has found an 1874 article in which Twain identified a 10-year-old black boy as the inspiration for Huck's speech patterns. Henry Louis Gates Jr., an African American professor of literature at Harvard, commented: ''What we discover after all this time is that it is the black American linguistic voice which forms the structuring principle of the great American novel, and that ain't bad.'' *New York Times* A1 (July 7, 1992); Fishkin (1993).

[92] *New York Times* B9 (December 1, 1989), B2 (December 4, 1989).

Evanston, Illinois, planned a public service announcement on television, created free of charge by a Chicago advertising executive. It began with a neo-Nazi giving the Sieg Heil salute while a voice over said ''If they gave a medal for killing black people, this gang would win a bronze'' for 12 murders in the last decade. Then the hooded Ku Klux Klan appeared with a torch while the voice over said: ''This gang would win the silver'' for 20 murders in the last three decades. Finally a young tattooed black man wearing a baseball cap, cutoff shorts, heavy jewellery, and a tank top appeared with sounds of gunfire in the distance while the voice over said ''But this gang would win the gold. If you're in a gang, you're not a brother. You're a traitor.'' The screen showed 1300 murders in 1991 alone. A black city councillor condemned the ad, while the head of the Police Department gang unit endorsed it. *New York Times* s.1 p.10 (August 23, 1992).

[93] A judge has since held that the Alderman violated the student's constitutional rights and ordered the policemen to stand trial. *New York Times* A9 (August 12, 1992).

In *Negrophobia*, a black author wrote the story of a white teenager transported to a world where the most bigoted stereotypes prevail. A white artist designed the cover, showing a scantily clad white girl with the shadow of an oversize black caricature peering over her shoulder. A black woman employee of the publisher was enraged: ''it gives credence to the old stereotypes that too many people still believe.'' The publisher had anticipated that ''less hip'' readers might be ''turned off'' but concluded that ''this was an appropriate reflection of the parody in the book.'' The author explained:

black people should start taking back these images from our iconography that have been stolen and corrupted through the years by racists. . . . You see these rap and hip-hop artists wearing tiny little braids just like those stereotypical pickaninny pictures. But it's a statement of our power instead of self-loathing. . . . It is subverting the perversion. *New York Times* B3 (June 17, 1992); James (1992).

[94] Germans were naïvely surprised by British anger at the proposed commemoration of the 50th anniversary of the launching of the V-2 rocket. Organisers claimed they were only honouring the "outstanding scientific and technical achievement" of "the first step into space." The head of the German Aerospace Trade Association, which sponsored the event, complained that "the celebrations have unfortunately become the subject of political discussions, which do not do justice to the scientific facts." Winston Churchill (a Conservative MP and son of the wartime Prime Minister) pronounced: "civilised nations do not celebrate weapons systems." To which the *Münchner Merkur* replied: "Some of those now protesting stood by silently or applauded when the Queen Mother unveiled a monument to Sir Arthur Harris, who as head of the British Bomber Command in World War II was responsible for the reprehensible bombardment of German cities and the deaths of hundreds of thousands of civilians." *New York Times* A1 (September 29, 1992).

[95] *New York Times* A7 (February 19, 1991), s.3 p.1 (March 22, 1992).

[96] Bettelheim (1976). The South African Broadcasting Company thinks differently. A report urging a ban on the occult concluded: "Good children's stories try to help children to create an aversion to what is evil (and to everything and everyone associated with it) and to appreciate and strive after what is good." *Weekly Mail* 15 (September 18, 1992).

[97] Felstiner et al. (1980–81). When France passed a law against sexual harassment (the toughest in Europe), a public opinion poll revealed that 20 per cent of French women would not consider themselves harassed if asked to undress during a job interview, and 45 per cent would not if a male superior asked them to spend a weekend discussing a requested promotion. *New York Times* s.1 p.10 (May 3, 1992).

[98] Nader (1980); Harris et al. (1984); Abel (1985b); Hensler et al. (1991); Merry (1990); Yngvesson (1988); Mather & Yngvesson (1980–81); Baumgartner (1986); Engel (1987); Greenhouse (1986).

[99] Russell & Howard (1983); Bourque (1989). Extrapolating a study based on telephone interviews with 4008 women, the National Victim Center and the Medical University of South Carolina estimated that at least 12.1 million American women had been raped once, 61 per cent as minors; 683,000 adult women were raped in 1990; 70 per cent did not want their families to find out; two-thirds were afraid of being blamed themselves. This figure was *five* times the Justice Department estimate. *New York Times* A14 (April 24, 1992). A Senate Judiciary Committee study estimated that three out of four women who suffer spousal abuse do not report it. The Surgeon General lists violence as the leading health risk

among women 15–44 years old. *Los Angeles Times* A2 (October 3, 1992).

[1] *Independent on Sunday* 2 (October 20, 1991). In the U.S. Navy 56 per cent of women harassed did not report it. *Los Angeles Times* A1 (February 10, 1992). The Los Angeles Commission on the Status of Women found that 37 per cent of city employees had been sexually harassed, compared to the 25–30 per cent reported in national surveys. Only 9 per cent made informal complaints and 5 per cent formal complaints. Within that group, 16 per cent found that coworkers and supervisors became unfriendly, 11 per cent suffered health problems, 5 per cent were transferred, and 4 per cent said their job evaluations suffered. *Los Angeles Times* A1 (September 23, 1992).

[2] *New York Times* s.4 p.6 (November 24, 1991). Because these figures included physical assaults the proportion of insults reported is even lower.

[3] 2–5 per cent in Camden, Newham and Southwark. 193 *Searchlight* 6 (July 1991); *Daily Telegraph* (May 14, 1991); *Independent* (May 14, 1991). 5 per cent in Newham in 1987. Home Office (1989: para 15). A survey of a single housing estate in Tower Hamlets disclosed 111 incidents in an eight-month period of 1982, although the police recorded only 205 for the entire borough. 72 of those respondents had called the police, who recorded no incidents. When the Metropolitan Police required a report every time a complainant alleged a racial motivation for a crime, the monthly average increased almost tenfold, from 25 in 1981 to 219 in 1982. GLC (1984d: 4, 6, 33, 49). The Leeds Housing Department increased complaints of racial harassment nearly fivefold by responding promptly. Independent Commission (n.d.: 33–36).

[4] Best & Andreasen (1977). The clearest example is spousal abuse.

[5] Tyson also insinuated that Washington was after his money. In fact, an intermediary offered her a million dollars to drop the charges. *New York Times* B14 (January 31, 1992), A8 (March 16, 1992).

When the tabloid *New York Post* reported that a forthcoming book accused Bush of spending the night with a female aide in the cottage of the U.S. Ambassador to Switzerland in 1984, Clinton piously declared "I don't think it has any place in this campaign"—thereby ensuring the charge would be repeated. The *Los Angeles Times* ran a story about the fact that there was insufficient evidence to warrant covering the allegation! *Los Angeles Times* A20 (August 13, 1992).

[6] Hirschmann (1970).

[7] Heinz & Kerstetter (1979).

[8] Moriarty (1975).

[9] Bentley (1955); McFeely (1968); Crouch (1992).

[10] Genn (1982).

[11] *Guardian* 5 (November 20, 1991).

[12] *Observer* 7 (September 19, 1991); *Guardian* 2 (October 31, 1991).

[13] Mothers Against Drunk Driving, Sisters Against Drunk Driving. See, *e.g.*

*Notes*

Ball (1986) (above-ground nuclear testing); Brodeur (1985) (asbestos); Erikson (1976) (Buffalo Creek dam burst) Stern (1977) (Buffalo Creek); Whiteside (1979) (dioxin); Levine 1982 (Love Canal); Gibbs (1982) (Love Canal); Schuck (1987) (Agent Orange); Insight Team (1976) (thalidomide); Teff & Munro (1976) (thalidomide).

[14] In the United States, the NAACP, Maldef, GLAAD, NOW, etc. In England the Campaign Against Racism and Fascism and *Searchlight*. In France, the Mouvement Contre le Racisme, l'Antisémitisme et pour le Paix (MRAP) and the Ligue Internationale Contre Racisme et Antisémitisme (Lica). 14(1) *Patterns of Prejudice* (January 1980); 15(4) *Patterns of Prejudice* (October 1981); Gordon (1982: 34–36).

[15] Curran (1978); Marks et al. (1974).

[16] Felstiner et al. (1980–81: 643).

[17] See Phelps & Winternitz (1992); Morrison (1992). 2100 cheering women listened to Anita Hill speak six months later, chanting "We Believe Anita Hill" and wearing buttons "Graduate of Thelma and Louise Finishing School." The chair of the National Commission of Working Women said: "This is one of those awakenings. It's like before, and we feel powerful again, and she did it." *New York Times* s.1 p.31 (April 26, 1992).

[18] *Guardian* 29 (November 14, 1991); *Los Angeles Times* F4 (February 15, 1992). Complaints to the Equal Employment Opportunities Commission increased more than 50 per cent from the first half of the 1991 fiscal year to the first half of the 1992 fiscal year. *New York Times* A1 (July 13, 1992).

[19] On retaliatory actions against complainants, see Canan & Pring (1988); *New York Times* A17 (April 24, 1990) (consultant to campaign against housing discrimination sued for libel). On retaliation against whistle-blowers, see *New York Times* A1 (March 22, 1991) (Dr Margot O'Toole, who accused Dr Thereza Imanishi-Kari and Dr. David Baltimore of scientific fraud); *New York Times* C1 (March 17, 1992) (employee of arms company may lose job and pension for informing US government of illegal sales); *Guardian* 7 (November 12, 1991) (teacher who exposed sexual abuse himself accused of perversion).

[20] *Guardian* 2 (October 22, 1991), 2 (October 23, 1991), 1, 3 (October 26, 1991).

[21] The Court of Appeals freed the three victims. *Weekend Guardian* 12 (October 12–13, 1991).

[22] Teubner (1982; 1988).

[23] CRE (1988: 24) (Leeds schools); *Observer* 9 (September 22, 1991) (Gatehouse School, East London); *Los Angeles Times* B3 (March 19, 1992) (Occidental College, California); *Chronicle of Higher Education* A35 (February 12, 1992) (Brown University, Emory University, UCLA, Eastern Michigan University, University of Arizona, University of Oklahoma, Harvard Medical School); *Doe* v. *Univ. of Michigan*, 721 F.Supp 852 (E.D.Mich 1989); Fineman (1992); Rohde (1991); Gale (1990–91; 1991).

[24] Delgado (1982: 133); Leonard (1991); Volokh (1992). The Supreme Court

165

*Taking Sides*

will hear an appeal in *Robinson* v. *Jacksonville Shipyards*. *New York Times* A11 (January 23, 1991); *Los Angeles Times* A3 (September 24, 1991). England has no reservations about protecting workers from abuse.

*Guardian* 2 (November 14, 1991) (£20,000 to black Metropolitan police-man abused by other police); 193 *Searchlight* 6 (July 1991) (£2000 to construction worker whose boss called him "nigger," "black bastard" and "mongrel" merely to make him work harder).

[25] Bethnal Green (1978: 88).

[26] Tompson (1988: 125) (Newham Council); 194 *Searchlight* 6 (August 1991); 191 *Searchlight* 13 (May 1991) (Edinburgh); 194 *Searchlight* 6 (June 1991) CRE (1987: 27); FitzGerald (1989) (Hackney).

[27] 192 *Searchlight* 6 (June 1991).

[28] Abel (1982). Others remain sceptical about the possibility of informalism in western societies. Fitzpatrick (1992).

[29] Feeley (1979), paraphrasing Marshall McLuhan.

[30] Matsuda (1987). For a feminist critique of tort damages, see Bender (1990a; 1990b).

Punishment can nullify the status degradation of apology by evoking sympathy for the offender. After a New York Mets baseball player was found nude in a van with a joint and a woman not his wife he declared at a press conference: "I wish to apologize publicly to my wife and children, the Mets' ownership and management, my teammates, to all Met fans and to baseball in general for my behavior in St. Petersburg." But when the Mets chairman denounced the behaviour as "bad for baseball's image" and fined the player $2000, audience outrage turned to sympathy. The spokesman for the Japanese American Citizens League sought to prevent collective American guilt from turning into resentment of the $20,000 compensation paid by the United States to every surviving internee. Money showed that the apology was "sincere," although it "could not begin to compensate a person for his or her lost freedom, property, livelihood or the stigma of disloyalty." I have taken this and all other otherwise unattributed examples of apology from Tavuchis (1991).

[31] *Cf.* Habermas (1984).

[32] Scott & Lyman (1968); Blumstein (1974).

[33] Garfinkel (1956); Blum-Kulka et al. (1989); Schlenker & Darby (1981); Darby & Schlenker (1982); Coulmas (1981).

Rep. Patricia Schroeder (D-Colo) has been a harsh critic of sexual harassment in the military, most recently the Navy's 1991 Tailhook Association convention, where many women were manhandled. When a fighter-pilot party at the Miramar Naval Air Station unfurled a lewd sign imputing that she engaged in oral sex, Admiral Frank B. Kelso 2d, Chief of Naval Operations, visited Schroeder's office to apologise even before she heard of the incident. Vice Admiral Edwin Kohn Jr (Commander of Naval Air Force in the Pacific) echoed the apology, saying he was "humiliated, disgusted, frustrated." "We are going to change . . . a decaying culture that has proven more and more unproductive and unworthy." *Los*

*Angeles Times* A32 (July 3, 1992); *New York Times* A7 (July 3, 1992). The Tailhook chairman subsequently wrote the Acting Navy Secretary: "We apologize to the women involved, the Navy and the nation for our part in what has become a source of embarrassment." *Los Angeles Times* A26 (August 8, 1992).

When Treasury Secretary Nicholas F. Brady said to an informal breakfast meeting of reporters "We have been told our workers . . . can't compete with the Japs . . ." Reps. Robert T. Matsui (D-Calif) and Norman Y. Mineta (D-Calif), both of whom had been interned during World War II, called for his resignation. Matsui said: "It really demonstrates the kind of insularity of this Administration . . . " The Japanese Embassy also complained. Brady responded: "At no time did I intend to offend anyone. If I did, I apologize." *New York Times* s.1 p.16 (August 2, 1992).

[34] *New York Times* s.1 p.24 (November 24, 1991).

[35] *New York Times* A9 (February 24, 1992).

[36] Examples include the "Truth Commission" established in El Salvador as part of the peace negotiations endings its civil war, and Argentina's investigation into the disappeared. Amnesty International (1987).

[37] 14(1) *Patterns of Prejudice* (January 1980); 15(4) *Patterns of Prejudice* (October 1981); Gordon (1982: 34–36). This extends the more common practice of retraction and apology for defamation.

[38] *New York Times* B16 (November 28, 1991), 12 (December 28, 1991). South African President F.W. de Klerk's recent statement was similarly qualified and unsatisfactory:

> For too long we clung to a dream of separated nation-states, when it was already clear that it could not succeed sufficiently. For that we are sorry. . . . Yes, we have made mistakes. Yes, we have often sinned and we don't deny this. But that we were evil, malignant and mean—to that we say "no."

*Los Angeles Times* A10 (October 10, 1992).

[39] The man who pleaded guilty to kidnapping the president of Exxon International, shooting him "accidentally," and locking him in a box, where he died from a combination of blood loss, asphyxiation, dehydration, and starvation, said he never intended to harm his victim, was extremely remorseful, and wished to apologise to the widow. *New York Times* A16 (September 16, 1992).

Japan refused to allow a visit by the American pilot who dropped one of the atom bombs and sought absolution through an apology. It was not required to respond to the following full-page advertisement by the Peninsula Peace and Justice Center (California).

> To the People of Japan, On the Forty-Seventh Anniversary of the First Use of Atomic Weapons.
> We citizens of the United States of America express our sorrow for the suffering caused by the cruel and unnecessary bombings of Hiroshima and Nagasaki. We pledge to work for the elimination of nuclear

weapons. We further pledge our efforts to end the continuing misuse of technology for the destruction of life.
*New York Times* A11 (August 6, 1992).
The Soviet Union refused to acknowledge that Jews were the dominant victims of the Babi Yar massacre. On the 50th anniversary in October 1991, Ukrainian President Kravchuk apologised to Ukrainian Jews and said other Ukrainians must accept "part of the blame." Aleksandr A. Shlayen, director of the Babi Yar Center, was surprised and gratified. "He repented. He came to me personally and apologized. I was at a loss, frankly speaking. We aren't used to apologies." Shalyen made Kravchuk an honourary member of the Center. *New York Times* A3 (August 27, 1992).

[40] *Los Angeles Times* B3 (March 19, 1992).

[41] *Chronicle of Higher Education* A35 (February 12, 1992). Senator Larry E. Craig (R-Id.) introduced an amendment to the Higher Education Bill barring any college or university receiving federal funds (except religious and military institutions) from punishing a student for constitutionally protected speech. *Chronicle of Higher Education* A24 (February 19, 1992). The University of Wisconsin repealed its regulations concerning hate speech in the wake of the Supreme Court's invalidation of the St. Paul ordinance. *New York Times* A10 (September 14, 1992).

[42] Shapiro (1976); Hine (1966); Houriet (1971); Carden (1971); Zablocki (1971).

[43] When the Slovak Prime Minister cracked down on media opposition, his supporters quit the journalists union and formed Journalists for a Correct Picture of Slovakia. *New York Times* s.1 p.7 (October 11, 1992).
For balanced collections on the debate, see Berman (1992); Aufderheide (1992); *Partisan Review* (1991). For the conservative case, see Bloom (1987); Bennett (1984; 1988); Cheney (1988); d'Souza (1991a; 1991b); Kimball (1990); Presser (1991); Schlesinger (1992); *Heterodoxy* (a foul-mouthed journal launched in 1992). For replies, see Diamond (1991); Beers (1991); Tushnet (1992); Carby (1992); Denning (1992); Garcia (1992); Scott (1992); Gates & Smith (1992). The antagonists are now organised into the National Association of Scholars, on the right, and Teachers for a Democratic Culture, on the left.

[44] *Los Angeles Times* A3 (January 24, 1992); *New York Times* A8 (February 13, 1992). The owner of a downtown Santa Cruz restaurant commented: "If someone has 14 earrings in their ears and their nose—and who knows where else—and spiky green hair and smells like a skunk, I don't know why I have to hire them." The executive director of the Chamber of Commerce warned that at least three businesses were considering leaving because of publicity about the law. *Los Angeles Times* A3 (May 25, 1992).

[45] *Guardian* 22 (September 17, 1991).

[46] *Los Angeles Times* A3 (April 23, 1992).

[47] The University of Massachusetts *Daily Colleagian* allocated an editor and

two pages a month to numerous constituencies: blacks, women, third world, multicultural, Jewish, and lesbian-bisexual-gay. But when it failed to publish an editorial condemning the Rodney King verdict, angry students attacked the building, threatened a staff photographer, removed the paper from newsstands, and called for a boycott of advertisers. The demonstrators demanded a minority co-editor, an editorship for women of colour, separate elections for minority editors, and seats on the executive board. The editor-in-chief accepted all this, saying he had been threatened with violence and mass resignations. *New York Times* B8 (May 27, 1992).

[48] Styron (1967); Clarke (1968) (black criticism of Styron); Gates (1991).

[49] *Los Angeles Times* F6 (April 23, 1992). A Canadian male critic reviewing five exhibits of photographs of women by men questioned "why men are suddenly so fascinated with these issues" and proceeded to attack each:

Chagnon's "positive images" imply that all is well, that women are now being accepted as equals and that no further struggle is required.

it is unfortunate that Mitchell seems to have passed up an opportunity to deal with how he felt about not seeing his kids during the day . . .

*The Birth Report* appears to be a celebration of white, middle-class, heterosexual couples, a project that essentially maintains the status quo.

Replacing out-dated and counter-productive cliches with new positive ones still ultimately leaves you with prescriptions.

he is *still* using the porn images and perhaps to gain a certain degree of attention and notoriety, still using the porn controversy.

The reviewer concluded disarmingly: "I don't want to imply that 'women's problems' should not be addressed by men." Samuels (1985). Indians on the Pine Ridge Lakota Reservation staged a four-month protest against the white manager of radio station KILI, established by the American Indian Movement in 1989 to preserve the Oglala Sioux language and culture. He had lived on the reservation since 1975, was married to a Lakota, and taught social science at the tribal college. *Los Angeles Times* A5 (August 31, 1992).

[50] Santiago (1983). Nineteenth-century abolitionists wrote novels in the form of "slave memoirs" in order to enhance their propaganda value. Gates (1991). Such ventriloquism continues. The screenwriter for a 1971 film on ecology produced by the Southern Baptist Radio and Television Commission had Chief Seattle tell his people in 1854: "I have seen a thousand rotting buffaloes on the prairies left by the white man who shot them from a passing train." Susan Jeffers repeated the phrase in her children's book *Brother Eagle, Sister Sky: A Message from Chief Seattle*, which reached fifth place on the *New York Times* Best Seller list and sold 250,000 copies in its first year. Told there were no bison within 600 miles of Puget Sound and the railroad only reached it 15 years after Chief

Seattle's death, she replied: "Basically, I don't know what he said—but I do know that the Native American people lived this philosophy, and that's what is important." Knowing that the speech was apocryphal, organisers of the 1992 Earth Day celebration nevertheless performed it after checking with some Indians. *New York Times* A1 (April 21, 1992).

[51] Carter (1990); Gates (1991). Rennard Strickland, a distinguished American Indian law professor, wrote the foreword to the 1990 reissue of the 1976 book.

[52] Leon Higginbotham (1992), the most senior black judge on the U.S. Court of Appeals, wrote a scathing open letter to Thomas after his confirmation, which elicited thousands of requests for reprints, as well as support from other prominent black legal academics like Lani Guinier of the University of Pennsylvania and Derrick Bell of New York University. *Los Angeles Times* A1 (February 14, 1992).

[53] Katt Shea's "Poison Ivy" infuriated most of the audience at the Seattle International Festival of Women Directors. At New York's Museum of Modern Art two months later "half the audience thought it should be seen and talked about . . . the rest found it beneath consideration." Shea commented:

I've been called a male-basher and a female-basher. At a screening, one woman said to me, "How could you, as a woman, write a character like Ivy?" At that point I was really into saying, "You can't censor art to be the way you want it depicted. Because pretty soon no one can be bad. There can't be bad men. There can't be bad black people.

*New York Times* s.2 p.13 (May 3, 1992).

[54] Research on the possible biological basis of homosexuality, for instance. The prestigious *Proceedings of the National Academy of Science* reported that the structure connecting the left and right brain hemispheres, which is larger in women then men, is larger still among homosexuals. A spokesperson for the Gay and Lesbian Task Force in Washington welcomed the finding: "This study supports our belief that nature created us just the way we are and that there is no reason to fix anything because nothing is broken." Gorski & Allen (1992); *Los Angeles Times* B1 (August 1, 1992). A t-shirt declaring "It's a brain thing" quickly became popular in the West Hollywood gay community. But some gay activists are reluctant to stress such scientific findings, fearing they may be disproved. And they do little to influence the religious right. *Los Angeles Times* B1 (August 12, 1992).

The National Institutes of Health withdrew support for a conference on "Genetic Factors in Crime: Findings, Uses and Implications" under attack from black scholars and the Congressional Black Caucus. The deputy director for extramural funding criticised the conference brochure for touting "genetic research as offering the prospect of identifying individuals who may be predisposed to certain kinds of conduct." "The N.I.H. cannot condone the unjustified leap to the conclusion that there is a

genetic predisposition to crime." He added disingenuously: "the suggestion that this is political is offensive to the N.I.H. and personally offensive
to me as an African-American." The Secretary of the Department of
Health and Human Services, also African American, denied that the
National Institutes finance studies of the relationship between race and
crime or violence. "I have full confidence in the scientific and ethical
merit of the Public Health Service's research activities on the problem of
violence and pledge that these programs and their leadership are free of
any racial bias." The president of the Association of Black Psychologists
denounced the conference as "a blatant form of stereotyping and
racism." A spokesman for the University of Maryland, which had organised the conference, called this "political correctness in motion. The
University of Maryland has had conferences on racism and sexism, and
just having such a conference doesn't mean the university endorses
racism or sexism." In fact, the conference was to begin by critically
examining a 1970s fad—the extra Y chromosome—which was shown to
have nothing to do with criminality. And the conference prospectus stated
that any genetic markers probably would "have little specificity, sensiti-
vity or explanatory power: most people with the markers will not be
criminals" and "most criminals will not have the markers." *New York
Times* 1 (September 5, 1992), B5 (September 15, 1992), A18 (October 2,
1992) (letter to The Editor, September 24).

Consider the furor over Oscar Lewis (1961) on the culture of poverty,
Daniel Patrick Moynihan on dysfunctional families (Rainwater & Yancey,
1967), Hannah Arendt (1964) on Jewish passivity in the Holocaust, Fogel
and Engerman (1974) on living conditions under slavery, or Lawrence
Harrison (1992) on culture and inequality.

[55] A black woman's criticism of black men for relationships with white
women (Campbell, 1992) provoked angry replies:

I happen to be a black woman who is tired of hearing other black
people's complaints about things like "racial mixing," which would be
construed as racist and offensive if uttered by white people.
I'm an African-American man who happened to fall in love with a
white woman. . . . I will not let the color of my skin limit my life's
possibilities.
The pain of being made to feel unattractive or "not good enough" as a
black woman because of our cultural definition of beauty . . . is not
justification enough for the dissemination of prejudicial stereotypes
. . . As one of those blond white women who was involved with a
black man for five years, I was neither "docile" nor "obedient."
My wife and I find that maintaining an "interracial" marriage in a
society as obsessed with race as the United States is hard enough. The
last thing we need is more divisive rhetoric.
*New York Times Magazine* 12–13 (September 13, 1992) (letters to The
Editor).

Israel's Law of the Return has raised awkward questions about who is a

Jew. Although the country celebrated the airlift of Ethiopian Jews, orthodox rabbis required Ethiopian men to undergo a ritual circumcision
before marrying and refused to recognise the religious authority of the
*kessim* (62 traditional elders). A spokesman for the Chief Rabbinate said:
"It is the same as with physicians from Russia who headed hospital
departments there but have to take tests here." Israel is more uncomfortable with the 50–100,000 Falash Mura, who converted to Christianity in
the nineteenth century; thus far it has admitted only a hundred, who have
a least one child in Israel. The 1300 members of the Black Hebrew
movement—African Americans claiming to be one of the biblical tribes,
who settled in the Negev—were not admitted under the Law of the
Return, although they have just been given temporary resident status.
*New York Times* A4 (September 29, 1992).
[56] Sarat (1977).

# Appendix

Lyrics from "The Buck". See page 36.


That's the only way to give her more than she wants,
Like a doggie-style, you get all that cunt.
Cause all men try real hard to do it,
To have her walking funny so we try to abuse it.
Bitches think a pussy can do it all,
So we try real hard just to bust the wall.
. . .
I'll break you down and dick you long.
Bust your pussy and break your backbone.
. . .
I'm gonna slay you, rough and painful,
You innocent bitch! Don't be shameful!
. . .
That dick will make a bitch act cute,
Suck my dick until you make it puke
. . .
Lick my ass up and down,
Lick it till your tongue turns doodoo brown.

# References

Abel, Richard L. 1973. "A Comparative Theory of Dispute Institutions in Society," 8 Law & Society Review 217.
———. 1982. "The Contradictions of Informal Justice," in Richard L. Abel, ed. The Politics of Informal Justice, vol. 1: The American Experience. New York: Academic Press.
———. 1985a. "Law Without Politics: Legal Aid Under Advanced Capitalism," 32 UCLA Law Review 474.
———. 1985b. "£'s of Cure, Ounces of Prevention," 73 California Law Review 1003.
———. 1989a. "The Contradictions of Legal Professionalism," in School of Justice Studies, Arizona State University, eds. New Directions in the Study of Justice, Law and Social Control. New York: Plenum.
———. 1989b. "Taking Professionalism Seriously," 1989(1) Annual Survey of American Law 41.
———. 1991. "The Costs of War," 7 Negotiation Journal 235.
Akhtar, Shabbir. 1989. Be Careful with Muhammad! The Salman Rushdie Affair. London: Bellew Publishing.
Alderfer, Hannah, et al., eds. 1982. Diary of a Conference on Sexuality. New York: Faculty Press.
Amnesty International. 1987. Argentina: The Military Juntas and Human Rights. London: Amnesty International Publications.
Appignanesi, Lisa and Sara Maitland, eds. 1989. The Rushdie File. London: Fourth Estate Ltd.
Arendt, Hannah. 1964. Eichmann in Jerusalem: A Report on the Banality of Evil. New York: Viking.
Arkes, Hadley. 1975. "Civility and the Restriction of Speech: Rediscovering the Defamation of Groups," in Philip Kurland, ed. Free Speech and Association. Chicago: University of Chicago Press.

## References

Arons, Stephen. 1983. Compelling Belief: The Culture of American Schooling. New York: McGraw Hill.

Assiter, Alison. 1989. Pornography, Feminism and the Individual. London: Pluto Press.

Aufderheide, Patricia, ed. 1992. Beyond P.C.: Toward a Politics of Understanding. St. Paul, Minn.: Graywolf Press.

Bagdikian, Ben H. 1987. The Media Monopoly (2nd ed.). Boston: Beacon Press.

Baker, C. Edwin. 1989. Human Liberty and Freedom of Speech. New York: Oxford University Press.

———. 1992. "Advertising and a Democratic Press," 140 University of Pennsylvania Law Review 2097.

———. n.d. "Harm, Liberty, and Free Speech."

Ball, Howard. 1986. Justice Downwind: America's Atomic Testing Program in the 1950's. New York: Oxford University Press.

Barbach, Lonnie, ed. 1984. Pleasures: Women Write Erotica. New York: Doubleday.

Barker, Martin, ed. 1984. The Video Nasties. London: Pluto Press.

Barnes, Julian. 1992. " 'The Proudest and Most Arrogant Man in France,' " 39(17) New York Review of Books 3 (October 22) (review of Petra ten-Doesschate Chu, ed., Letters of Gustave Courbet).

Barnum, David G. 1982. "Decision Making in a Constitutional Democracy: Policy Formation in the Skokie Free Speech Controversy," 44 Journal of Politics 480.

Barrett, Michèle. 1982. "Feminism and the Definition of Cultural Politics," in Rosalind Brunt and Caroline Rowan, eds. London: Lawrence and Wishart.

Barthes, Roland. 1976. Sade Fourier Loyola. New York: Hill and Wang.

Baumgartner, M.P. 1986. The Moral Order of a Suburb. New York: Oxford University Press.

Beers, David. 1991. "Behind the hysteria: how the Right invented victims of PC police," Mother Jones 34 (September/October).

Bell, Derrick. 1987. And We Are Not Saved. New York: Basic Books.

Bender, Leslie. 1990a. "Feminist (Re)torts: Thoughts on the Liability Crisis, Mass Torts, Power, and Responsibility," 1990 Duke Law Journal 848.

———. 1990b. "Changing the Values in Tort Law," 25 Tulsa Law Journal 759.

Bennett, William J. 1984. To Reclaim a Legacy: Report on the

Humanities in Higher Education. Washington, D.C.: National Endowment for the Humanities.

———. 1988. "Why the West?" National Review 37 (May 27).

Bentley, George R. 1955. History of the Freedmen's Bureau. Philadelphia: University of Pennsylvania Press.

Berman, Paul, ed. 1992. Debating P.C.: The Controversy Over Political Correctness on College Campuses. New York: Dell.

Best, Arthur and Alan R. Andreasen. 1977. "Consumer Response to Unsatisfactory Purchases: A Survey of Perceiving Defects, Voicing Complaints, and Obtaining Redress," 11 Law & Society Review 701.

Bethnal Green and Stepney Trades Council. 1978. Blood on the Streets: A Report by Bethnal Green and Stepney Trades Council on Racial Attacks in East London. London: Bethnal Green and Stepney Trades Council.

Bettelheim, Bruno. 1976. The Uses of Enchantment: The Meaning and Importance of Fairy Tales. New York: Vintage.

Bharucha, Rustom. 1990. "The Rushdie Affair: Secular Bigotry and the Ambivalence of Faith," 11 Third Text 61.

Bloom, Allan. 1987. The Closing of the American Mind. New York: Simon & Schuster.

Blum-Kulka, Shoshana, Juliane House and Gabriele Kasper, eds. 1989. Cross-Cultural Pragmatics: Requests and Apologies. Norwood, N.J.: Ablex Publishing Corp (XXXI Advances in Discourse Processes).

Blumstein, Philip W., et al. 1974. "The Honoring of Accounts," 39 American Sociological Review 551.

Bogdan, Robert. 1988. Freak Show: Presenting Human Oddities for Amusement and Profit. Chicago: University of Chicago Press.

Bolton, Richard, ed. 1992. Culture Wars: Documents from the Recent Controversies in the Arts. New York: New Press.

Borovoy, Alan, Kathleen Mahoney, Barry Brown, Jamie Cameron, David Goldberger, and Mari Matsuda. 1988/89. "Language as Violence v. Freedom of Expression: Canadian and American Perspectives on Group Defamation," 37 Buffalo Law Review 337 (James McCormick Mitchell Lecture).

Bourdieu, Pierre. 1991. Language and Symbolic Power. Cambridge: Polity.

Bourque, Linda B. 1989. Defining Rape. Durham, N.C.: Duke University Press.

Bower, Marion. 1986. "Daring To Speak Its Name: The Relationship of Women to Pornography," 24 Feminist Review 40.

## References

Brennan, Timothy. 1989. Salman Rushdie and the Third World. New York: St. Martin's Press.

Brest, Paul and Ann Vandenberg. 1987. "Politics, Feminism, and the Constitution: The Anti-Pornography Movement in Minneapolis," 39 Stanford Law Review 607.

Brodeur, Paul. 1985. Outrageous Misconduct: The Asbestos Industry on Trial. New York: Pantheon.

Bromwich, David. 1992. Politics by Other Means: Higher Education and Group Thinking. New Haven: Yale University Press.

Brown, Colin. 1984. Black and White Britain: The Third PSI Survey. London: Heinemann.

Brown, Lyn Mikel and Carol Gilligan. 1992. Meeting at the Crossroads: Women's Psychology and Girl's Development. Cambridge, Mass.: Harvard University Press.

Buford, Bill. 1992b. "The Lads of the National Front," New York Times Magazine 32 (April 26).

———. 1992b. Among the Thugs. New York: W.W. Norton.

Burrough, Bryan. 1992. Vendetta: American Express and the Smearing of Edmond Safra. New York: HarperCollins.

Burstyn, Varda, ed. 1985a. Women Against Censorship. Vancouver: Douglas & McIntyre.

———. 1985b. "Beyond Despair: Positive Strategies," in Burstyn (1985a).

Callwood, June. 1985. "Feminist Debates and Civil Liberties," in Burstyn (1985a).

Campbell, Bebe Moore. 1992. "Brothers and Sisters," New York Times Magazine (August 23).

Canan, Penelope and George W. Pring. 1988. "Studying Strategic Lawsuits Against Public Participation: Mixing Quantitative and Qualitative Approaches," 22 Law & Society Review 385.

Carby, Hazel V. 1992. "The Multicultural Wars," Radical History Review.

Carden, Maren Lockwood. 1971. Oneida: Utopian Community to Modern Corporation. New York: Harper & Row.

Carter, Forrest. 1990. The Education of Little Tree. Albuquerque: University of New Mexico Press.

Carter, Stephen L. 1991. Reflections of an Affirmative Action Baby. New York: Basic Books.

Centerall, Brandon S. 1992. "Television and Violence: The Scale of the Problem and Where to Go From Here," 267 JAMA 3059.

Cheney, Lynne. 1988. Humanities in America: A Report to the

President, the Congress, and the American People. Washington, D.C.: National Endowment for the Humanities.

Chester, Gail and Julienne Dickey, eds. 1988. Feminism and Censorship: The Current Debate. London: Prism Press.

Chester, Laura, ed. 1988. Deep Down: The New Sensual Writing by Women. Boston: Faber & Faber.

Childress, Steven Alan. 1991. "Reel 'Rape Speech': Violent Pornography and the Politics of Harm," 25 Law & Society Review 177.

Clarke, John Hendrik, ed. 1968. William Styron's Nat Turner: ten black writers respond. Boston: Beacon.

Coliver, Sandra, ed. 1992. Striking a Balance: Hate Speech, Freedom of Expression and Non-discrimination. London: Article 19 and Colchester: Human Rights Centre, University of Essex.

Commission for Racial Equality. 1984. Racial Harassment on Local Authority Housing Estates. London: CRE.

——. 1987. Living in Terror: A report on racial violence and harassment in housing. London: CRE.

——. 1988a. Learning in Terror: A survey of racial harassment in schools and colleges in England, Scotland and Wales, 1985–1987. London: CRE.

——. 1988b. Racism and Freedom of Speech on the Campus. London: CRE.

Coon, Carleton S. 1962. The Origin of Races. New York: Knopf.

Coulmas, Florian. 1981. " 'Poison to Your Soul': Thanks and Apologies Contrastively Viewed," in Florian Coulmas, ed. Conversational Routine: Explorations in Standardized Communications Situations and Prepatterned Speech. The Hague: Mouton.

Crenshaw, Kimberlé. 1991. "Beyond Racism and Misogyny: Black Feminism and 2 Live Crew," 16(6) Boston Review 6 (December).

Crouch, Barry C. 1992. The Freedmen's Bureau and Black Texans. Austin: University of Texas Press.

Csathy, Peter D. 1992. "Taking the Rap: Should artists be held accountable for their violent recorded speech?" Los Angeles Lawyer 34 (April).

Curran, Barbara. 1977. The Legal Needs of the Public. Chicago: American Bar Foundation.

Curran, James, Jake Ecclestone, Giles Oakley and Alan Richardson, eds. 1986. Bending Reality: The state of the media. London: Pluto Press and Campaign for Press and Broadcasting Freedom.

Darby, Bruce W. and Barry R. Schlenker. 1982. "Children's Reactions to Apologies," 43 Journal of Personality and Social Psychology 742.

## References

Davies, Christie. 1982. "Ethnic jokes, moral values and social boundaries," 33 British Journal of Sociology 383.

Dean, Joseph. 1953. Hatred, Ridicule, or Contempt: A Book of Libel Cases. London: Constable.

de Grazia, Edward. 1992. Girls Lean Back Everywhere: The Law of Obscenity and the Assault on Genius. New York: Random House.

Delacoste, Fréderique and Priscilla Alexander, eds. 1987. Sex Work: Writings by Women in the Sex Industry. Pittsburgh: Cleis Press.

DelFattore, Joan. 1992. What Johnny Shouldn't Read: Textbook Censorship in America. New Haven: Yale University Press.

Delgado, Richard. 1982. "Words That Wound: A Tort Action for Racial Insults, Epithets, and Name Calling," 17 Harvard Civil Rights-Civil Liberties Law Review 133.

Denning, Michael. 1992. "Cultural Studies and the Thought Police," Radical History Review.

Diamond, Sara. 1991. "Readin', Writin', and Repressin'," Z Magazine 45 (February).

Diamond, Sigmund. 1992. Compromised Campus: The Collaboration of Universities with the Intelligence Community, 1945–1955. New York: Oxford University Press.

Dickey, Anthony. 1968. "Prosecutions Under The Race Relations Act 1965, s.6 (Incitement to Racial Hatred)," 1968 Criminal Law Review 489.

Dickey, Julienne and Campaign for Press and Broadcasting Freedom (CPBF). 1985. Women in Focus: Guidelines for eliminating media sexism. London: CPBF.

Dienes, C. Thomas. 1972. Law, Politics and Birth Control. Urbana: University of Illinois Press.

Downs, Donald Alexander. 1985. Nazis in Skokie: Freedom, Community and the First Amendment. Notre Dame:, Ind.: University of Notre Dame Press.

———. 1989. The New Politics of Pornography. Chicago: University of Chicago Press.

D'Souza, Dinesh. 1991a. "Illiberal Education," Atlantic Monthly 51 (March).

———. 1991b. Illiberal Education: The Politics of Race and Sex on Campus. New York: Maxwell Macmillan International.

Dubin, Steven C. 1987. "Symbolic Slavery: Black Representations in Popular Culture," 34 Social Problems 122.

Duggan, Lisa, Nan Hunter and Carole S. Vance. 1985. "False

Promises: Feminist Antipornography Legislation in the United States," in Burstyn (1985a).

Dworkin, Andrea. 1989. Pornography: Men Possessing Women. New York: Dutton.

Edelman, Murray. 1964. The Symbolic Uses of Politics. Urbana: University of Illinois Press.

———. 1971. Politics as Symbolic Action. New York: Academic Press.

Edwards, Susan. 1991. "A plea for censorship," New Law Journal 1478 (November 1).

Ehrenreich, Barbara. 1989. Fear of Falling: The Inner Life of the Middle Class. New York: Pantheon.

Emerson, Thomas I. 1970. The System of Free Expression. New York: Random House.

Engel, David M. 1987. "The Ovenbird's Song: Insiders, Outsiders, and Personal Injuries in an American Community," 18 Law & Society Review 551.

English, Deirdre. 1980. "The Politics of Porn: Can Feminists Walk the Line?" Mother Jones 20 (April).

Entman, Robert M. 1989. Democracy without Citizens: Media and the Decay of American Politics. New York: Oxford University Press.

Erickson, Kai T. 1976. Everything in Its Path: Destruction of Community in the Buffalo Creek Flood. New York: Simon & Schuster.

Ernst, Morris L. and Alexander Lindey. 1936. Hold Your Tongue! Adventures in Libel and Slander. London: Methuen.

Essed, Philomena. 1991. Understanding Everyday Racism: an interdisciplinary theory. Newbury Park, Calif.: Sage Publications.

European Parliament, Committee of Inquiry into the Rise of Facism and Racism in Europe. 1985. Report of the Findings of the Inquiry (Dimitrios Evrigenis, draftsman). Brussels: European Parliament.

Eysenck, H.J. 1971. The I.Q. Argument: Race, Intelligence and Education. New York: Library Press.

Faludi, Susan. 1991. Backlash. New York: Crown.

Feeley, Malcolm. 1979. The Process is the Punishment: processing cases in a lower criminal court. New York: Russell Sage.

Felstiner, William. L.F., Richard L. Abel and Austin Sarat. 1980–81. "The Emergence and Transformation of Disputes: Naming, Blaming, Claiming . . . .," 15 Law & Society Review 631.

Ferguson, Ann, et al. 1983. "Forum: The Feminist Sexuality Debates," 10 Signs 107 (Autumn).

## References

Fineman, Martha Albertson. 1992. "Who Pays for Free Speech?" 9(5) Women's Review of Books 17 (February).

Fishkin, Shelley Fisher. 1993. Was Huck Black? Mark Twain and African-American Voices. New York: Oxford University Press.

Fiske, John. 1989. Understanding Popular Culture. Boston: Unwin Hyman.

FitzGerald, Marian. 1989. "Legal approaches to racial harassment in council housing: the case for reassessment," 16 New Community 93.

Fitzpatrick, Peter. 1992. "The Impossibility of Popular Justice," 1 Social & Legal Studies 199.

Flam, Jack. 1992. "The Alchemist," 39(4) New York Review of Books 31 (February 13).

Fogel, Robert W. and Stanley L. Engermann, eds. 1974. Time on the Cross: The Economics of American Negro Slavery. New York: W.W. Norton.

Fox, Robin Lane. 1992. The Unauthorized Version: Truth and Fiction in the Bible. New York: Alfred A. Knopf.

France, Anatole. 1927. The Red Lily (first published 1894). New York: Wm. H. Wise & Co.

Freed, Leonard. 1991. Photographs 1954–1990. Manchester: Cornerhouse Publs.

Friedberg, David. 1992. "The Play of the Unmentionable": An Installation by Joseph Kosuth at The Brooklyn Museum. New York: New Press.

Friedrich, Otto. 1992. "Olympia": Paris in the Age of Manet. New York: HarperCollins.

Galanter, Marc. 1974. "Why the 'Haves' Come Out Ahead: Speculations on the Limits of Legal Change," 9 Law & Society Review 95.

———. 1983. "Mega-Law and Mega-Lawyering in the Contemporary United States," in Robert Dingwall and Philip Lewis, eds. The Sociology of the Professions: Lawyers, Doctors and Others. London: Macmillan.

———. 1984. Competing Equalities: Law and the Backward Classes in India. Berkeley: University of California Press.

Gale, Mary Ellen. 1990–91. "On Curbing Racial Speech," 1 The Responsive Community 47.

———. 1991. "Reimagining the First Amendment: Racist Speech and Equal Liberty," 65 St. John's Law Review 119.

Gambrell, James. 1992. "Moscow: The Front Page," 39(16) New York Review of Books 56 (October 8).

## References

Garcia, Mario T. 1992. "Multiculturalism and American Studies," Radical History Review.

Gardner, John. 1978. On Moral Fiction. New York: Basic Books.

Garfinkel, Harold. 1956. "Conditions of Successful Degradation Ceremonies," 61 American Journal of Sociology 420.

Garry, Patrick M. 1990. The American Vision of a Free Press. New York: Garland.

Gates, Darryl J. and Barbara Herrnstein Smith, eds. 1992. The Politics of Liberal Education. Durham, N.C.: Duke University Press.

Gates, Henry Louis, Jr. 1991. " 'Authenticity', or the Lesson of Little Tree," New York Times Book Review 1 (November 24).

———. 1992. Loose Canons: Notes on the Culture Wars. New York: Oxford University Press.

Genn, Hazel. 1982. Meeting Legal Needs? An evaluation of a scheme for personal injury victims. Oxford: Centre for Socio-Legal Studies and Manchester: Greater Manchester Legal Services Committee.

Gibbs, Lois. 1982. Love Canal: My Story. Albany: SUNY Press.

Gifford, Lord, Wally Brown and Ruth Bundy. 1989. Loosen the Shackles: First Report of the Liverpool 8 Inquiry into Race Relations in Liverpool. London: Karia Press.

Gilligan, Carol. 1982. In a Different Voice: Psychological Theory and Women's Development. Cambridge, Mass.: Harvard University Press.

Gillmor, Donald M. 1992. Power, Publicity, and the Abuse of Libel Laws. New York: Oxford University Press.

Gilroy, Paul. 1987. 'There Ain't No Black in the Union Jack': The cultural politics of race and nation. London: Hutchinson.

Gitlin, Todd. 1986. Watching Television: A Pantheon Guide to Popular Culture. New York: Pantheon.

Glassner, Barry. 1993. Bodies: Overcoming the Tyranny of Perfection. New York: Simon & Schuster.

GLC. 1984a. Challenging Racism in London: Report of the conference held on March 12, 1983. London: GLC.

———. 1984b. Ethnic Minorities and the Abolition of the GLC. London: GLC.

———. 1984c. Rastafarianism in Greater London. London: GLC.

———. 1984d. Racial Harassment in London: Report of a panel of inquiry set up by the Greater London Council Police Committee. London: GLC.

*References*

——. 1984e. Racial Harassment on GLC Estates in Tower Hamlets—
Emerging Patterns (Nov 1983-Aug 1984). London: GLC.

GLC Gay Working Party. 1985. Changing the World: A London
Charter for Gay and Lesbian Rights. London: GLC.

GLC Women's Committee. n.d. Women on the Move: GLC Survey
on Women and Transport, vol. 6: Ideas for Action. London: GLC.

Goffman, Erving. 1976. "Gender Advertisements," 3(2) Studies in
the Anthropology of Visual Communication (Fall) (reprinted New
York: Harper & Row, 1979).

Goldman, Robert. 1992. Reading Ads Socially. New York:
Routledge.

Goode, J. William. 1978. The Celebration of Heroes: Prestige as a
Control System. Berkeley: University of California Press.

Gordon, Bette. 1984. "*Variety*: The Pleasure in Looking," in Vance
(1984).

Gordon, Paul. 1982. Incitement to Racial Hatred: A Brief Paper.
London: Runnymede Trust.

——. 1990a. Racial Violence and Harassment (rev. 2d ed.). London: Runnymede Trust.

Gordon, Suzanne. 1983. Off Balance: The Real World of Ballet.
New York: McGraw-Hill.

Gorski, Roger A. and Laura S. Allen. 1992. "Sexual Orientation and
the Size of the Anterior Commissaure in the Human Brain," 15
Proceedings of the National Academy of Sciences 7199.

Gould, Stephen Jay. 1981. The Mismeasure of Man. New York:
W.W. Norton.

Grace, Della. 1991. Love Bites: Photographs. London: GMP
Publications.

Green Paper on Public Order. 1980. London: HMSO (Cmnd 7891).

Greenhouse, Carol. 1986. Praying for Justice: faith, order and
community in an American town. Ithaca, N.Y.: Cornell University
Press.

Gubar, Susan and Joan Hoff, eds. 1989. For Adult Users Only: The
Dilemma of Violent Pornography. Bloomington: Indiana University Press.

Gusfield, Joseph R. 1963. Symbolic Crusade: Status Politics and the
American Temperance Movement. Urbana: University of Illinois
Press.

Habermas, Jürgen. 1984. The Theory of Communicative Action,
vol. 1: Reason and the Rationalization of Society. Boston: Beacon
Press.

Hacker, Andrew. 1992. Two Nations: Black and White, Separate, Hostile, Unequal. New York: Charles Scribner's Sons.

Hall, N. John. 1991. Trollope: A Biography. New York: Oxford University Press.

Hall, Ruth. 1985. Ask Any Woman: A London inquiry into rape and sexual assault. London: Falling Wall Press.

Harris, Donald, Mavis Maclean, Hazel Genn, Sally Lloyd-Bostock, Paul Fenn, Peter Corfield, and Yvonne Brittan. 1984. Compensation for Illness and Injury. Oxford: Clarendon Press.

Harrison, Lawrence F. 1992. Who Prospers? How Cultural Values Shape Economic and Political Success. New York: Basic Books.

Harvey, Brett. 1984. "No More Nice Girls," in Vance (1984).

Heinz, Anne M. and Wayne A. Kerstetter. 1979. "Pretrial Settlement Conference: Evaluation of a Reform in Plea Bargaining," 13 Law & Society Review 349.

Hensler, Deborah R., M. Susan Marquis, Allan F. Abrahamse, Sandra H. Berry, Patricia A. Ebener, Elizabeth G. Lewis, E. Allan Lind, Robert J. MacCoun, Willard G. Manning, Jeannette A. Rogowski, and Mary E. Vaiana. 1991. Compensation for Accidental Injuries in the United States. Santa Monica, Calif.: Rand Institute for Civil Justice.

Herrnstein, Richard. 1971. "IQ," Atlantic Monthly 43.

Heyn, Dalma. 1992. The Erotic Silence of the American Wife. New York: Turtle Bay Books.

Higginbotham, A. Leon, Jr. 1992. "An Open Letter to Justice Clarence Thomas from a Federal Colleague," 140 University of Pennsylvania Law Review 1005.

Hine, Robert V. 1973. California's Utopian Colonies. New York: W.W. Norton & Co.

Hiro, Dilip. 1971. Black British, White British. London: Eyre and Spottiswoode.

Hirsch, Fred. 1976. Social Limits to Growth. Cambridge, Mass.: Harvard University Press.

Hirschman, Albert. 1970. Exit, Voice, and Loyalty: responses to decline in firms, organizations and state. Cambridge, Mass.: Harvard University Press.

Holmes, Oliver Wendell, Jr. 1897. "The Path of the Law," 10 Harvard Law Review 457.

———. 1918. "Natural Law," 32 Harvard Law Review 40.

Home Affairs Committee. 1980. London: HMSO (HC 756).

Home Office. 1975. Racial Discrimination. London: HMSO (Cmnd 6234).

# References

Home Office, Inter-Departmental Racial Attacks Group. 1989. The Response to Racial Attacks and Harassment: guidance for statutory authorities. London: Home Office.
Houriet, Robert. 1971. Getting Back Together. New York: Avon.
Hughes, Robert. 1980. The Shock of the New. New York: Random House.
Hunter, James Davison. 1991. Culture Wars: The Struggle to Define America. New York: Basic Books.
Hunter, Nan D. and Sylvia A. Law. 1987/88. "Brief Amici Curiae of Feminist Anti-Censorship Taskforce, et al., in *American Booksellers Association* v. *Hudnut,*" 21 Journal of Law Reform 69.
Hytner Report. 1981. Report of the Moss Side Enquiry Panel to the Leader of the Greater Manchester Council.
ILEA Inspectorate Working Party on the Provision of Equal Opportunities for Girls and Boys. 1982. Equal Opportunities. London: ILEA.
Independent Commission of Enquiry into Racial Harassment. n.d. Racial Harassment in Leeds, 1985–1986. Leeds: Leeds Community Relations Council.
Ingber, Stanley. 1984. "The Marketplace of Ideas: A Legitimizing Myth," 1984 Duke Law Journal 1.
Insight Team of the Sunday Times. 1979. Suffer the Children: The Story of Thalidomide. New York: Viking.
James, Darius. 1992. Negrophobia. New York: Citadel Press.
Jansen, Sue Curry. 1991. Censorship: The knot that binds power and knowledge. New York: Oxford University Press.
Jenkins, Peter. 1989. "Is Rushdie just the tool of Allah's Will?" Independent 21 (March 1).
Jensen, A.R. 1969. "How Much Can We Boost IQ and Scholastic Achievement?" 33 Harvard Education Review 1.
Jones, Peter. 1980. "Blasphemy, Offensiveness and Law," 10 British Journal of Political Science 129.
Jussawalla, Feroza. 1989. "Resurrecting the Prophet: The Case of Salman, the Otherwise," 2 Public Culture 106.
Kappeler, Susanne. 1986. The Pornography of Representation. Cambridge: Polity Press.
Kaufmann, Tara and Paul Lincoln, eds. 1991. High Risk Lives: Lesbian and gay politics after the clause. London: Prism Press.
Kennedy, Florynce. 1971. "The Whorehouse Theory of Law," in Robert Lefcourt, ed. Law Against the People: Essays to Demystify Law, Order and the Courts. New York: Vintage.

References

Kensington Ladies' Erotica Society. 1984. Ladies Own Erotica. New York: Pocket Books.
Kimball, Roger. 1990. Tenured Radicals: How Politics Has Corrupted Higher Education. New York: Harper & Row.
King, Lynn. 1985. "Censorship and Law Reform: Will Changing the Laws Mean a Change for the Better?" in Burstyn (1985a).
Kinzer, Stephen. 1992. "East Germans Face Their Accusers," New York Times Magazine 24 (April 12).
Kirp, David L. 1991. "Textbooks and tribalism in California," 104 The Public Interest 20.
Kiss & Tell. 1991. Drawing the Line: Lesbian Sexual Politics on the Wall. Vancouver: Press Gang Publications.
Klug, Francesca. 1982. Racist Attacks (Runnymede Trust Submission to the GLC Police Commission). London: Runnymede Trust.
Lacombe, Dany. 1988. Ideology and Public Policy: The Case Against Pornography. Toronto: Garamond Press.
Lawrence, Charles. 1990. "If He Hollers Let Him Go: Regulating Racist Speech on Campus," 1990 Duke Law Journal 431.
Lawrence, David. 1987. "Racial Violence in Britain: trends and a perspective," 14 New Community 161 (Autumn).
Layton-Henry, Zig. 1984. The Politics of Race in Britain. London: George Allen & Unwin.
Lederer, Laura, ed. 1980a. Take Back the Night: Women on Pornography. New York: William Morrow & Co.
———. 1980b. "Introduction," in Lederer (1980a).
———. 1980c. "Then and Now: An Interview with a Former Pornography Model," in Lederer (1980a).
———. 1980d. " 'Playboy Isn't Playing,' An Interview with Judith Bat-Ada," in Lederer (1980a).
Lee, Simon, 1990. The Cost of Free Speech. London: Faber & Faber.
Leonard, Alice. 1991. "Remedies for sexual harassment," New Law Journal 1514 (November 8).
Lessing, Doris. 1984. The Diaries of Jane Somers. New York: Random House.
Lester, Anthony. 1987. "Antidiscrimination legislation in Great Britain," 14 New Community 21.
Lewis, Anthony. 1992. Make No Law: The Sullivan Case and the First Amendment. New York: Random House.
Lewis, Oscar. 1961. The Children of Sanchez. New York: Random House.
Linden, Robin Ruth, Darlene Pagano, Diana Russelll and Susan Star,

eds. 1982. Against Sado-Masochism. San Francisco: Frog in the Wall Press.

Lippard, Lucy R. 1990. "Andres Serrano: The Spirit and The Letter," Art in America 238 (April).

Longino, Helen E. 1980. "Pornography, Oppression, and Freedom: A Closer Look," in Lederer (1980a).

Luban, David, ed. 1983. The Good Lawyer. Totowa, N.J.: Rowan & Allanheld.

———. 1988. Lawyers and Justice: An Ethical Study. Princeton, N.J.: Princeton University Press.

MacArthur, John R. 1992. Second Front: Censorship and Propaganda in the Gulf War. New York: Hill & Wang.

Macdonald, Ian, Lily Khan, Gus John and Reena Bhavnani. 1989. Murder in the Playground: The Burnage Inquiry. London: Longsight Press.

MacKinnon, Catherine A. 1987. Feminism Unmodified: Discourses on Life and Law. Cambridge, Mass.: Harvard University Press.

Mann, Sally. 1992. Immediate Family. New York: Aperture.

Marchand, Shoshana. 1992. "Hooked: Mind and body games among the modern primitives," The Bay Guardian 23 (May 27).

Marks, F. Raymond, Robert Paul Hallauer and R. R. Clifton. 1974. The Shreveport Plan: An Experiment in the Delivery of Legal Services. Chicago: American Bar Foundation.

Mather, Lynn and Barbara Yngvesson. 1980–81. "Language, Audience, and the Transformation of Disputes," 15 Law & Society Review 775.

Matsuda, Mari J. 1987. "Looking to the Bottom: Critical Legal Studies and Reparations," 22 Harvard Civil Rights-Civil Liberties Law Review 323.

———. 1989. "Public Response to Racist Speech: Considering the Victim's Story," 87 Michigan Law Review 2320.

Matthiessen, Peter. 1983. In the Spirit of Crazy Horse. New York: Viking.

———. 1991. In the Spirit of Crazy Horse. New York: Viking.

Mazrui, Ali. 1990. "Witness for the Prosecution: A Cross-Examination on The Satanic Verses," 11 Third Text 31.

McFeely, William S. 1968. Yankee Stepfather: O.O. Howard and the Freedmen. New Haven: Yale University Press.

Medved, Michael. 1992. Hollywood vs. America: Popular Culture and the War on Traditional Values. New York: HarperCollins.

Meiklejohn, Alexander. 1948. Free Speech and Its Relation to Self-Government. New York: Harper.

———. 1960. Political Freedom: The Constitutional Powers of the People. New York: Harper.

Mercer, Kobena. 1990. "Welcome to the Jungle: Identity and Diversity in Postmodern Politics," in Rutherford (1990b).

Merry, Sally Engle. 1990. Getting Justice and Getting Even: legal consciousness among working class Americans. Chicago: University of Chicago Press.

Miller, Mark Crispin. 1992. Spectacle: Operation Desert Storm and the Triumph of Illusion.

Mindes, Marvin W. and Alan C. Acock. 1082. "Trickster, Hero, Helper: A Report on the Lawyer Image," 1982 American Bar Foundation Research Journal 17.

Mitchell, Greg. 1992. The Campaign of the Century: Upton Sinclair's Race for Governor of California and the Birth of Media Politics. New York: Random House.

Modood, Tariq. 1990. "British Asian Muslims and the Rushdie Affair," 61 Political Quarterly 143.

Morgan, Robin. 1977. "Theory and Practice: Pornography and Rape," in Going Too Far. New York: Random House.

Moriarty, Thomas. 1965. "A Nation of Willing Victims," Psychology Today 44 (April).

Morrison, Toni, ed. 1992. Race-ing Justice, En-gendering Power. New York: Pantheon.

Mulcahy, Kevin V. and C. Richard Swaim, eds. 1982. Public Policy and the Arts. Boulder, Colo.: Westview Press.

Nader, Laura, ed. 1980. No Access to Law: Alternatives to the American Judicial System. New York: Academic Press.

Nair, Rukmini B. and Rimli Battacharya. 1990. "Salman Rushdie: Migrant in the Metropolis," 11 Third Text 17.

Osborne, John. 1991. Almost a Gentleman: An autobiography. Vol. 2: 1955–66. London: Faber.

Oshima, Nagisa. 1992. Cinema, Censorship and the State: The Writings of Nagisa Oshima, 1956–1978. Cambridge, Mass.: MIT Press.

Paglia, Camille. 1990. Sexual Personae: Art and Decadence from Nefertiti to Emily Dickinson. New York: Oxford University Press.

———. 1992. Sex, Art and American Culture: Essays. New York: Vintage.

Paley, Vivian Gussin. 1992. You Can't Say You Can't Play. Cambridge, Mass.: Harvard University Press.

Partisan Review. 1991. "The Changing Culture of the University," 58(2) Partisan Review (special issue).

References

Perry, Ruth. 1992. "Historically Correct," 9(5) Women's Review of Books 15 (February).
Phelps, Timothy M. and Helen Winternitz. 1992. Capitol Games: Clarence Thomas, Anita Hill and the Story of a Supreme Court. New York: Hyperion.
Pileggi, Nicholas. 1986. Wiseguy. New York: Simon & Schuster.
Pindell, Howardena. 1990. "Covenant of Silence: De Facto Censorship in the Visual Arts," 11 Third Text 71.
Popper, Karl R. 1969. Conjectures and Refutations (3rd ed.). London: Routledge & Kegan Paul.
Presser, ArLynn Leiber. 1991. "The Politically Correct Law School," 71 ABA Journal 52 (September).
Pulle, Stanislaus. 1973. Police-Immigrant Relations in Ealing. London: Runnymede Trust.
Qureshi, Shoaib and Javed Khan. 1989. The Politics of the Satanic Verses: Unmasking Western Attitudes (2nd ed). Leicester: Muslim Community Studies Institute.
Rainwater, Lee and William Yancey, eds. 1967. The Moynihan Report and the Politics of Controversy. Cambridge, Mass.: MIT Press.
Ravitch, Diane. 1974. The Great School Wars: New York City, 1805–1973. New York: Basic Books.
Reinhold, Robert. 1991. "Class Struggle," New York Times Magazine 26 (September 29).
Remnick, David. 1992. "Defending the Faith," 39(9) New York Review of Books 44 (May 14).
Riesman, David. 1942. "Democracy and Defamation: Control of Group Libel," 42 Columbia Law Review 727.
Robbins, Natalie. 1992. Alien Ink: The F.B.I.'s War on Freedom of Expression. New York: William Morrow & Co.
Rohde, Stephen F. 1991. "Campus Speech Codes: Politically Correct, Constitutionally Wrong," Los Angeles Lawyer 23 (December).
Rubin, Gayle. 1984. "Thinking Sex: Notes for a Radical Theory of the Politics of Sexuality," in Vance (1984).
Rushdie, Salman. 1988. The Satanic Verses. New York: Viking.
———. 1991. "1,000 Days in a Balloon," New York Times B8 (December 12).
———. 1992. Imaginary Homelands: Essays and Criticism 1981-1991. London: Granta Books.
Russell, Diana E.H. with Laura Lederer. 1980. "Questions We Get Asked Most Often," in Lederer (1980a).

Russell, Diana E.H. and Nancy Howell. 1983. "The Prevalence of Rape in the United States Revisited," 8 Signs 688.

Rutherford, Jonathan. 1990a. "A Place Called Home: Identity and the Cultural Politics of Difference," in Rutherford (1990b).

——, ed. 1990b. Identity: Community, Culture, Difference. London: Lawrence & Wishart.

Ruthven, Malise. 1990. A Satanic Affair. Salman Rushdie and the Rage of Islam. London: Chatto & Windus.

Samuels, Chuck. 1985. "Supportive, Exploitive, Appropriative? Five Male Photographers Approach 'Women's Issues,' " 8(6) Fuse 29 (Spring).

Santiago, Danny. 1983. Famous All Over Town. New York: Simon & Schuster.

Sarat, Austin. 1977. "Studying American Legal Culture: An Assessment of Survey Evidence," 11 Law & Society Review 427.

Schauer, Frederick. 1982. Free Speech: A Philosophical Enquiry. New York: Cambridge University Press.

Schlenker, Barry R. and Bruce W. Darby. 1981. "The Use of Apologies in Social Predicaments," 44 Social Psychological Quarterly 271.

Schlesinger, Arthur M., Jr. 1992. The Disuniting of America. New York: W.W. Norton.

Scholder, Amy and Ira Silverberg, eds. 1991. High Risk: An Anthology of Forbidden Writings. New York: Dutton.

Schuck, Peter H. 1987. Agent Orange on Trial: Mass Toxic Disasters in the Courts. Cambridge, Mass.: Harvard University Press.

Scott, Joan Wallach. 1992. "The Campaign Against Political Correctness: What's Really At Stake," Radical History Review.

Scott, Marvin B. and Stanford M. Lyman. 1968. "Accounts," 33 American Sociological Review 46.

Sennett, Richard and Jonathan Cobb. 1972. The Hidden Injuries of Class. New York: Random House.

Shapiro, Allan E. 1976. "Law in the Kibbutz: A Reappraisal," 10 Law & Society Review 587.

Shepherd, Gail. 1992. "Positive images," 9(5) Women's Review of Books 11 (February).

Simon, William. 1978. "The Ideology of Advocacy," 1978 Wisconsin Law Review 29.

Singer, Mark. 1992. "The Prisoner and the Politician," The New Yorker 108 (October 5).

References

Smolla, Rodney A. 1992. Free Speech in an Open Society. New York: Knopf.
Sontag, Susan. 1982. "The Pornographic Imagination," in A Susan Sontag Reader. New York: Farrar Straus Giroux.
Spivak, Gayatri Chakravorty. 1989. "Reading *The Satanic Verses*," 2 Public Culture 79.
———. 1990. "Reading *The Satanic Verses*," 11 Third Text 41.
Steele, Lisa. 1985. "A Capital Idea: Gendering in the Mass Media," in Burstyn (1985a).
Steinem, Gloria. 1980. "Erotica and Pornography: A Clear and Present Difference," in Lederer (1980a).
Stern, Gerald M. 1977. The Buffalo Creek Disaster. New York: Vintage.
Stober, Paul. 1992. "Evening of desire . . . and no dirty raincoats," 8(5) Weekly Mail 6 (January 31-February 6).
Stoller, Robert J. 1991. Porn: Myths for the Twentieth Century. New Haven: Yale University Press.
Styron, William. 1967. The Confessions of Nat Turner. New York: Random House.
Tannen, Deborah. 1986. That's Not What I Meant! How conversational styles make or break your relations with others. New York: William Morrow.
———. 1990. You Just Don't Understand! Women and Men in Conversation. New York: William Morrow.
Teff, Harvey and Colin Munro. 1976. Thalidomide: The Legal Aftermath. Westmead: Saxon House.
Teish, Luisah. 1980. "A Quiet Subversion," in Lederer (1980a).
Teubner, Gunther. 1982. "Substantive and Reflexive Elements in Modern Law," 17 Law & Society Review 239.
———. 1989. Autopoetic Law: a new approach to law and society. New York: W. de Gruyter.
Tompson, Keith. 1988. Under Siege: Racism and Violence in Britain Today. Harmondsworth: Penguin.
Tushnet, Mark. 1992. "Political Correctness, the Law, and the Legal Academy," 4 Yale Journal of Law & the Humanities 127.
Tybor, J.R. 1978. "Ouster in Chicago: It Ain't Cheap," National Law Journal 18 (August 7).
Unger, Roberto Mangabeira. 1975. Knowledge and Politics. New York: Free Press.
Upham, Frank K. 1987. Law and Social Change in Postwar Japan. Cambridge, Mass.: Harvard University Press.
U.S. News & World Report. 1965. "Is quality of U.S. population

declining? interview with a Nobel prize-winning scientist [William B. Shockley]," 59 U.S. News & World Report 68 (November 22).

van Dijk, Teun A. 1987. Communicating Racism: Ethnic Prejudice in Thought and Talk. Newbury Park, Calif.: Sage Publications.

Vance, Carole S., ed. 1984. Pleasure and Danger: Exploring Female Sexuality [Proceedings of the Scholar and Feminist IX Conference: "Toward a Politics of Sexuality," Barnard College April 1982]. Boston: Routledge & Kegan Paul.

Volokh, Eugene. 1992. "Freedom of Speech and Workplace Harassment," 39 UCLA Law Review 1791.

Walker, Alice. 1980. "Coming Apart," in Lederer (1980a).

Waller, P. J. 1981/82. "The riots in Toxteth, Liverpool: a survey," 9 New Community 344.

Warner, Kenneth E., Linda M. Goldenhar and Catherine G. McLaughlin. 1992. "Cigarette Advertising and Magazine Coverage of the Hazards of Smoking: A Statistical Analysis," 326 New England Journal of Medicine 305.

Wasserstrom, Richard. 1975. "Lawyers as Professionals: Some Moral Issues," 5 Human Rights 1.

Webster, Richard. 1990. A Brief History of Blasphemy. Southwold: Orwell Press.

Weeks, Jeffrey. 1990. "The Value of Difference," in Rutherford (1990b).

Wellesley College Center for Research on Women. 1992. How Schools Shortchange Girls: The A.A.U.W. Report. Washington, D.C.: AAUW Education Foundation and National Education Association.

Whiteside, Thomas. 1979. The Pendulum and the Toxic Cloud. New Haven: Yale University Press.

Wilkes, Michael S., Bruce Doblin and Martin Shapiro. 1992. "Pharmaceutical Advertisements in Leading Medical Journals: Experts' Assessments," 116 Annals of Internal Medicine 912.

Williams, Linda. 1989. Hard Core. Berkeley: University of California Press.

Williams, Patricia J. 1991. The Alchemy of Race and Rights. Cambridge, Mass.: Harvard University Press.

Wilson, A.N. 1992. Jesus. New York: W.W. Norton.

Winn, Marie. 1985. The Plug-In Drug: Television, Children and the Family. Baltimore: Penguin.

Wolf, Naomi. 1991. The Beauty Myth. New York: Morrow.

References

Wolff, Robert Paul. 1968. The Poverty of Liberalism. Boston: Beacon Press.

Yngvesson, Barbara. 1988. "Making Law at the Doorway: The Clerk, the Court, and the Construction of Community in a New England Town," 22 Law & Society Review 409.

Zablocki, Benjamin. 1971. The Joyful Community. Baltimore: Penguin.

Zurcher, Louis A., Jr. and R. George Kirkpatrick. 1976. Citizens for Decency: Antipornography Crusades as Status Defense. Austin: University of Texas Press.

# Index

# Index

Cuban-American interests, 58, 79

**"Deep Throat"**, 6
**Divorce**
secrecy agreement, 44
**Doctors**
referrals, payments for, 72
**Drugs**
penalties for, 156

**Education**
segregation, voluntary, 133–134,
158
**Election campaigns**, 50–51, 53, 54, 63,
65, 77, 80, 119, 150
distortion of free speech, 102
**Endowments**
universities, control of, 75
**Erotica**
pornography, differences in, 87

**FBI**
censorship, 41
**Feminism**
actresses, exploitation of, 37
pornography, reaction to, 4–5
**Films**
African American, reaction to, 95–96
restrictions on, 54–55
reviewers, censorship of, 73
**First Amendment**, 6, 25, 28, 29, 102,
128, 146
**Flag burning**, 39
**Freedom**
private, illusion of, 47–58
**Freedom of speech**
American flag, use of, 39
black popular music, effect of, 36
censorship, government departments
by, 40
communism, demise, effect of,
49–50
contractual prevention of, 43
costs of, 34–38
film industry, 42
government, neutrality of, 44–47
law, failure to regulate, 86–93
military censorship, 39–40
penalties, legal, 97–105
political donations, 50–51

**Freedom of speech**—*cont.*
private agreements to waive, 43–44
private freedom, 47–58
publications, government regulation
of, 41–42
regulation of, 38–44
schools, regulation of, 43
state regulation, 38–44
university activities, 35–36
**French law**
racial hatred, penalty for, 147

**Hamlyn lectures**
author, aims of, 1–3
history, 1
**Holocaust revisionists**, 101
**Homosexuality**
behavioural study, banning of, 46
biological basis for, 170
denial of, 126, 159
employment discrimination, 112
ethnic reaction, 126
*Local Government Act 1988, clause
28*, 45
military reaction to, 64
schools, reaction to 66–67
**Huckleberry Finn**, 162

**ICE-T**, 59
"Cop Killer", banning of, 105, 115
**In the Spirit of Crazy Horse**, 38
**"Informercials"**, 61
**Intellectual property rights**, 48
lawsuits, 70
**Interracial relationships**, 171
**Islamic Front**, 127

**Jackson, Michael**, 137
**Jones case**, 34–35
**Judicial system**
censorship, 66

**King, Rodney**, 161
**Ku Klux Klan**, 103, 104, 109, 111

**Law**
failure to regulate freedom of speech,
86–93
regulate, inability to, 94
violence, causality, link, 96
**Lawsuits**
media influence against, 116

198

# Index

**Schools**
  advertising in, 71
  censorship of books, 45
**Science**
  donations towards, 51
  publications, censorship of, 53, 65
  state regulation over, 45–46
**Sex education**
  censorship of, 41, 45–46
**Sexism**
  employment, 153, 163
**Sex objects**
  men, 153
**Sexual harassment**
  reporting of, 164
**Skokie**
  Nazi march, 9–11
**Smith, Kennedy William**, 8, 23
**Smoking**
  advertising campaigns, 37
**"Son of Sam" law**, 49
**South Africa**
  media, ANC reaction to, 79–80, 118
  President F W de Klerk, 167
**Speech** *see also* **Freedom of Speech**
  apologies for, 146–148, 166–167, 168
  communication through, 136–137
  communities, regulation by, 145
  complaints, encouraging, 141–144
  dissemination, 141
  effect on status, 137–141
  freedom of, problems caused, 28–29
  motive, 138–139
  speaker identity, 137–138
  speaker & target, relationship between, 139–140
  status competition, effect on, 25–29
  style, 141
  target, 139
  utilitarianism, effect on, 93
  victims of, 142–144
    consciousness of, 142
    crime, reporting of, 142

**Speech**—*cont.*
  Victims of—*cont.*
    state intervention, 143
**State regulation**
  art, attempt to, 88–89
  excesses of, 90–93
  freedom of speech, effect on, 38–47
  history of, 82–86
  information, withholding of, 63–64
  legal penalties, ineffectiveness of, 97–105
  political campaigns, 63
  property rights, 48–58
  science over, 45–46
  threats against the state, 127–128
**Status competition**
  role of, 22–29
  speech, effect on, 25–26
**Status victims**, 144–149
**Strippers**, 118

**Television**
  censorship, 68–69
  real life events, 70
**Thomas, Clarence**, 8, 23, 42, 75, 126, 155
**Tobacco**
  advertising of, 37, 99, 101–102, 119
  censorship, 40
**Trump, Ivana**, 44

**Utilitarianism**
  speech, effect on, 93

**V-2 Rocket**
  commemoration of, 163
**Victimisation**, 141–144
**Voting**, 100

**Women's magazines**
  influence of, 94

**Yakuza**, 80